Bud Fowler

Bud Fowler

Baseball's First Black Professional

Jeffrey Michael Laing

McFarland & Company, Inc., Publishers
Jefferson, North Carolina, and London

LIBRARY OF CONGRESS CATALOGUING-IN-PUBLICATION DATA

Laing, Jeffrey Michael.
 Bud Fowler : baseball's first Black professional / Jeffrey Michael Laing.
   p.   cm.
 Includes bibliographical references and index.

 ISBN 978-0-7864-7264-2
 softcover : acid free paper ∞

 1. Fowler, Bud, 1858–1913 2. African American baseball players — Biography. 3. Baseball players — United States — Biography. 4. Baseball — United States — History. I. Title.
GV865.F645L35 2013
796.357092—dc23
[B]   2013009827

BRITISH LIBRARY CATALOGUING DATA ARE AVAILABLE

© 2013 Jeffrey Michael Laing. All rights reserved

No part of this book may be reproduced or transmitted in any form or by any means, electronic or mechanical, including photocopying or recording, or by any information storage and retrieval system, without permission in writing from the publisher.

On the cover: Bud Fowler, from an 1885 Keokuk, Iowa, baseball club team photograph (National Baseball Hall of Fame Library, Cooperstown, New York)

Manufactured in the United States of America

McFarland & Company, Inc., Publishers
 Box 611, Jefferson, North Carolina 28640
  www.mcfarlandpub.com

For Jacqueline

Preface

Bud Fowler: Baseball's First Black Professional began with an obscure fact about Bud Fowler that caught my eye. Long noted for its devotion to the arts and its natural beauty and favorable weather, Santa Fe, New Mexico, has never been known for successful sports teams, especially on the professional level. However, I discovered that in 1888 in the only year of the New Mexico Baseball League (and in the only year in its 400-year-old existence that Santa Fe had a baseball team in what was recognized as organized baseball) the City Different won the pennant. I soon discovered that African American baseball pioneer Bud Fowler was a key member of that club, integrating the NMBL and purchasing a barber shop with a white partner on the famed Santa Fe Plaza. With the aid of a SABR-Yoseloff grant and a few local historians, I soon found myself immersed in the life of an African American Renaissance man of the baseball diamond who lived in an exciting time in the history of America — the late 19th and early 20th centuries when the nation was on the cusp of becoming a modern industrialized nation and expanding from coast to coast.

This book certainly stands on the shoulders of previous authors of this period and their scholarship, beginning with Jerry Malloy, Harold and Dorothy Seymour, and Leonard Koppett and continuing with such baseball historians as Tom Melville, Robert Peterson, George Kirsch, William Ryczek, Jules Tygiel and Warren Goldstein. I found the work of Brian McKenna, John Thorn, and Peter Morris especially helpful in filling in the blanks of Bud Fowler's playing and management careers.

However, the newspaper archives provided by for-profit companies, universities, non-profit educational organizations, and devoted individuals might collectively have been the greatest resource at my disposal. The hours I spent poring over them reliably yielded fresh facts and insights into the period and about Bud Fowler himself. A relentless self-promoter and de facto press agent for his black touring teams, Fowler was one of the first baseball men to employ the media in creating local and national interest to broaden his potential fan base. Furthermore, the newspapers of the period provide a multi-sided picture of the major social and economic issues of the day that directly impacted the national pastime.

My fondest wish is that this consideration of Bud Fowler's life and times will encourage others to study the man and his achievements on and off the diamond, and lead eventually to a reconsideration of the Hall of Fame's decision to close the door on African American players who never played in the major leagues. Cooperstown was Bud Fowler's literal home; it should now become his final resting place with his induction into the same institution that his pioneering endeavors helped open for the very deserving African American stars of the 20th and 21st centuries.

Bud Fowler was baseball's first professional African American ballplayer — and much more. He was born in the last years of slavery and died on the brink of World War I. His life also spanned the birth and development of baseball from a leisure activity for middle-class urban Easterners into a major business enterprise encompassing two professional major leagues that could be legitimately classified as the national pastime. Fowler lived through Reconstruction, the Great Compromise, the establishment of Jim Crow laws, the "separate but equal" solution, which amounted to the political and social institutionalization of racial discrimination. In his chosen profession, he faced verbal and physical abuse, social ostracizing, and uneven and very tenuous team and ownership support.

In an age of financial depression, fears of European immigration, and westward expansion, people were asking themselves "What does it mean to be an American?" Bud Fowler was asking himself "What does skin color have to do with success on the baseball diamond and in the business world?"

Bud Fowler's search for a defining identity in a culture that was itself undergoing the anxieties of growth and development resulted in a three-and-a-half-decade journey from coast-to-coast employing the newly expanded railroad system and recently created outlet of sports journalism to promote both his career as a ballplayer and as a black baseball entrepreneur. Tireless in his pursuit of greatness and a livelihood,

Preface

Bud Fowler was a successful player, team captain, team manager, talent scout, and black baseball organizer, entertainer, executive, investor, and owner. With self-possession, perseverance, and integrity, he resisted the many cultural and legal obstacles his society created to thwart his ambition to make a career at the highest levels of the national pastime.

Bud Fowler's narrative is that of a late 19th century African American's attempt to become an accepted and full participant in the country's most popular sport.

Bud Fowler was a man of his age and for our age.

This is his story.

Prologue
Grand Island, Nebraska, May 1892 — Bud Fowler's Fight

By playing in the Nebraska State League in 1892, Bud Fowler was one of the very few African Americans playing minor league baseball. The sport's color line had begun to emerge in 1867 in the form of decisions that excluded African American teams and players from national and state baseball associations. In the decades that followed, a series of on-field conflicts and social developments that weakened the national economy slowly but surely shut the door on African American participation in organized baseball. The Nebraska State League (NSL) ignored the ban on signing black ballplayers primarily because the organization was in its initial campaign and wished to ease its entrance into the professional game by hiring talented players who might also be curiosities or gate attractions. Yet the signing of African American players was never accepted without some opposition, and within the first month of play, the Nebraska State League had its first racial incident.

Bud Fowler began the 1892 baseball campaign with high hopes for a successful season. After playing for independent teams in Missouri, Wisconsin, and Ohio in 1891, Bud was making his return to organized baseball in a state through which he had previously barnstormed. It was reported in April that Fowler had signed with Lincoln and "was assigned second base."[1] He was the first club member to arrive in Lincoln and a local reporter speculated that "Fowler will in all probability captain the team."[2] In an era when the captaincy included setting the lineup, establishing team strategy in the field and at bat, coaching, and establishing and maintaining club discipline, it was a singular honor for an African American to attain such a position on an integrated team.[3] In the same newspaper account, Fowler's likely influence on roster signings is demonstrated: Lincoln's manager Houseman signed Frank Fear of Burlingame (IA) to catch. Fowler would have had intimate knowledge of Fear's diamond abilities since they both played in the Illinois-Iowa League in 1890 and in the Wisconsin State League the following year.[4]

Equally important, Bud Fowler was among the most talented and experienced players in the NBL. Early in the season, his team relocated from Lincoln to Kearney. In a report from Kearney that detailed the home team's rise in the league standings, the captain received the following plaudits: "Fowler, on second needs no introduction as he has played ball all over America.... He covers more ground in his position, makes as many hits and runs and has more stolen bases and is probably worth more to a team than any man in the league."[5] The local Nebraska newspapers were equally sanguine about the addition of Fowler to the new league: "Bud Fowler will be put on second base so that he can play everywhere. Everyone knows who he is. His fame is not as obscure as his face. The latter is very obscure in the dark, but he can play ball. He ought to, for he has been in the arena now for twenty-four years."[6]

Early reports on the formation of the 1892 Nebraska State League were enthusiastic and focused on the creation of a first-class professional baseball league: Salaries were set at $550 a season; players were to be bound to the national reserve clause in contracts, thus reducing the roster instability that plagued late–19th-century organizations; franchises were to provide decent playing fields while receiving strong civic support from the local Nebraska communities; and umpires were to be paid $75 per month.[7] Yet, just one week later, the same publication saw fit to issue a warning about the folly of signing African Americans: "Good, steady, sober players will do well to correspond with the Hastings manager. It is reported that Plattsmouth has signed several colored players. I think that is a mistake. The colored men who played with visiting teams in this city last year gave exhibitions of dirty ball, and the base ball fans here will not attend games where colored players participate."[8]

The same fixation on race was evident even when the reports were positive. At the beginning of the season, the African Americans in the NSL had earned praise, with some of the most effusive comments being directed toward Fowler: "Bud Fowler, our colored second baseman, and captain is a whole team in himself. He is everywhere at all times and keeps the boys moving."[9] Prior to the season, Manager Houseman had been praised for signing a stellar African American hurler who had starred for a black touring team, the Lincoln Giants: "[...he] has secured a first class pitcher in [Will] Castone who will land his team pretty near the top. If it were not for his color he would be in faster company to-day."[10]

Furthermore, overt racism was an undeniable fact in the NBL. Before the first official pitch was thrown, reporter William Shellak noted a "curiosity" of the individual team rosters: "There is a curious feature connected with the clubs of this League — each club, with the exception of Hastings and Grand Island [Freemont also had no African Americans on its roster], have one or more colored players signed, and the fans here are making wagers that the clubs with the colored players do not take the rag [pennant] at the finish."[11] Early on in the season, racial relations among players also became strained. Within six weeks of the start of the schedule, team unrest was being reported: "The Nebraska league is the only league in the country which permits the employment of colored players. Quite a number of negroes [sic] are playing on the various teams, but their white fellows make their lives burdensome."[12]

In May Bud Fowler got into the only on-field fight of his more-than-three-decade involvement with the national pastime. After fielding a ground ball at second base, Fowler applied a hard tag to Grand Island captain W.A. Rourke, who responded by attacking the Kearney captain. While a local reporter unequivocally indicated that the African American was the instigator in this instance, he also stated that "both men are equally to blame," suggesting that Rourke had overreacted. Another Grand Island reporter was more sympathetic to Fowler, criticizing Rourke's "apparently ungovernable temper" and condemning "slugging" and "scrapping matches" as unacceptable in general and as detrimental to the popularity of the game.[13] Neither player was disciplined or reprimanded in any manner and the incident was not commented on by the NBL, leaving the general public to assume that the fight had a racial basis.[14]

Three years earlier, an unidentified white International League player had commented on how African Americans in general and Bud Fowler and Frank Grant in particular had to deal with racially motivated attempts to injure them:

> An International [League] player, talking to the writer the other day, said, "While I myself am prejudiced in playing in a team with a colored player, still I could not help pitying some of the poor black fellows that

played in the International league. Fowler used to play second base with the looser parts of his legs encased in wooden guards. He knew that about every other player that came down to second base on a steal had it in for him, and would, if possible, throw the spikes into him. He was a good player, but left the base every time there was a close play in order to get away from the spikes.

"I have seen him muff balls intentionally, so that he would not have to try to touch runners, fearing that they might injure him. [Frank] Grant was the same way. Why, the runners chased him off second base. They went down too often trying to break his legs or injure them, [so] that he gave up his infield position the latter part of last season and played right field. This is not all.

"About half the pitchers try their best to hit these colored players when at the bat. I know of a great many pitchers that tried to soak Grant.... One of the International League pitchers pitched for Grant's head all the time. He never put a ball over the plate but sent them straight and true right at Grant. Do what he could he could not hit the Buffalo man, and he [Grant] trotted down to first on called balls all the time."[15]

As a result of this treatment, Bud Fowler is credited by many baseball historians with inventing shin guards by placing slats of wood inside his uniform pants in order to counter the numerous spiking attempts he faced as a second baseman.[16] However, in all likelihood, race was not the only reason that Fowler was targeted by his white opponents in 1892. In spite of hitting a subpar .273 for Kearney, the African American led the league with 45 steals. The taunts and high spikes of his adversaries were probably attempts to slow the African American speedster's base-running abilities.[17]

It was into such a world of segregationist thinking and racial bias that Bud Fowler sought entry, first as a stellar ballplayer and then as an enterprising promoter and owner of late 19th-century black barnstorming baseball teams. Fowler's fight for recognition and acceptance within professional baseball spanned four decades and helped to define the term "success" for African American athletes in the late 19th century, both on the diamond and in the business world.

— ONE —

The Rise of Baseball in the Nineteenth Century

Bud Fowler's 19th century baseball odyssey paralleled and often reflected the monumental changes in the emerging nation in which he lived and the sport of baseball flourished.

Team sports have a dual — individualistic and communal — nature that makes them compelling: "By the end of the [nineteenth] century the urge towards team sports and spectator sport became powerful, the great Caribbean thinker C. L. R. James reminds us in his seminal study of cricket and national feeling, *Beyond a Boundary*, "People begin to pay to watch other people compete.... Now we take this so much for granted — sports 'r' us — that it is difficult for us to see how peculiar, how unusual, this new thing was." James explains that for almost 1500 years, since ancient times, sport as a national or civic adhesive had largely vanished. Then, very suddenly, in the last part of the 19th century it returns: "The Football Association was founded only in 1863. It was in 1866 that the first athletic championship was held in England ... in the United States the first all-professional baseball team was organized in 1869. And so on and on: team sport is an entirely and thoroughly *modern* phenomenon." James continues:

> Many social forces had come together to make the transformation of team sports happen. In one way it was a sign of increased "solidarity" among working people and of the birth of that other new thing, the weekend. People who labour together on Friday play together on Sunday. Department stores sponsored team sports. In other ways it was a mirror of new mass militarism. Even the move against professionalism and spectator sports — the cult of Olympic amateurism sponsored by Baron Coubertin — involved an appeal not to pleasure but morality. There was a whole rhetoric of purification and renewal attached to team sports, specifically anti-sexual. The Winter Olympics, which

began in its current form in the 1920s but was foreshadowed by "Nordic Games" at the turn of the twentieth century, with its cult of amateurism, with its insistent national regimentation, also involved a cult of implicit militarism. Organized team sport was a way of escaping this dangerous flirtation with freelancing that you could find in the middle of the century. You lost yourself not in your inner self but in a common cause.

... for the most part team sports involved finding a complex balance between solidarity, bringing people together in a common culture, and rivalry, dividing people through a common cult of competition. Above all it was moved by that curious and fragile but utterly real thing we call identity. We play and watch sports above all to connect — with our friends, our neighbors, our city, and even our country. In a modern time, when those things are uncertain, up for definition — Who are our neighbours? What's the nature of our city? What is our country all about? — a game is the easiest way to say what our identity is, who we really are. Team sports are always a form of mock warfare, clan against clan, city against city and nation against nation. But we play them because, well, they're play. They're also a parody of warfare. They mock the passions they exemplify. Their intensities and energies stop just short of murder, just this safe side of rage. The whistle blows and we shake hands and plan to play again tomorrow. Where politics highlight social difference and try to end it, sports dramatize social difference and then perpetuate it.... Stylizing tribal passions, team sports help us transcend them, or at least treat them as a game, as in every sense a sport.[1]

Beyond the obvious vicarious identification of athlete and spectator, the value of sport is that it is both drama and history:

But sports also entertain us as forms of drama. We get engaged, even in the absence of a single great player or performance with the way the game tells a thrilling and unpredictable narrative woven by ten or twenty players at once. A great game is a great show, and it's also a great story. What makes those stories great is when they're unpredictable but not unjust — uncharted enough that there's no certainty of the result but organized enough that the result does not seem to be pure chance.[2]

The meaning of all modern sport, from the late nineteenth century on, is that it connects us; it is the easiest form of history we have, and

Opposite: Atchison, Topeka, and Santa Fe train at Lamy Junction, New Mexico. The railroads were a key component in the rapid expansion and development of baseball as the national pastime in the United States (photographer: J.R. Riddle [1884]; courtesy Palace of the Governors Photo Archives [NMHM/DCA], 076033).

the one place where the politics of identity play out as play. At their worst, sports encourage our violent and voyeuristic instincts — the players are acting out our anger. At their best they encourage our analytic and communal inclinations — see, even quick, bright things can happen in patterns and for a reason. So, with ourselves invested in our games, we have to save the game to save ourselves.[3]

This assessment of the centrality of team sports in our past is borne out by an examination of competitive sports in the late 19th century. In an age when sport was a popular if near-exclusive male enclave, that enclave was threatened by "seemingly uncontrollable trends in urbanization, industrialization, and immigration ... and many middle-class men struggled to adjust to the new realities."[4] Feeling powerless, men turned to an "updated, rigorous, and physical understanding of their manliness." They valued "valor, strength and prowess [more] than upright behavior.... Strength, endurance, and physicality" now trumped "diligence, independence, and self-control" in the 19th-century man's definition of his own identity.[5]

Competitive athletics were championed since they combined physical skill and gentlemanly behavior with the emphasis on the former. Theodore Roosevelt summed up the great value of physical culture in the Gilded Age as follows: "In life, as in a football game, the principle to follow is: 'Hit the line hard; don't foul and don't shirk and hit the line hard.'"[6]

The Railroads

Team sports, especially the national pastime of baseball, needed some means by which to extend across the continent from their roots in the east. The development of the railroads and the expansion of the United States military helped spread the game of baseball to the far reaches of the continent while providing a set of cultural reasons for embracing the sport.

The railway system radically changed Americans' experience of space and time. By the mid–1850s, the railroads had conquered the limitations of space, thereby accelerating the Industrial Revolution and expanding the world for Americans. The railroads not only made travel faster and cheaper, but also changed its nature from the rather solitary nature of the stagecoach to the more public and democratic train. Suddenly, anyone who could afford the price of what was the equivalent of a ticket in steerage could travel to the same destination and arrive at the same time as a first-class passenger.

The railway station itself became the hub of public life in both large urban centers and on the frontier. These edifices were of enormous importance in the history of architecture and urban development and planning. The rail companies decorated their stations to advertise their potential for adventure and travel and helped to generate business for the tour promoters and travel agents who worked with the rail companies to increase ridership. These businesses focused on the sensual (and even dangerous) nature of the passenger train experience.[7] The train became an optimistic symbol of modernity and adventure that altered the average American's pocketbook and outlook.

The initial rapid expansion of the railroads was primarily the result of economic reasons, including the exploitation and extraction of mineral resources, the transportation of cattle and beef from ranches to slaughterhouses, and the shipment of timber to urban areas.[8] However, the importance of the railroads was demonstrated even more in its movement of consumer goods and people. For example, before the coming of the railroads, two million dollars in sales and goods would travel overland annually into the New Mexico Territory; with the arrival of the railroads, the movement of the same number and value of goods could be achieved on a weekly basis! The geographical placement of a railroad line became a key element in the economic growth of an area, often determining if a town would survive or go bust. Furthermore, railroads also influenced national and local architecture, the developing highway system, and the growing national preoccupation with Native American culture.[9]

The railroads, in fact, did much to develop the tourist industry in the late 19th century. The western companies worked closely with the chain of Harvey Houses, whose promise of "good food, clean accommodations, and efficient and impeccable service" made them tourist magnets by emphasizing that travel could be both modern and comfortable.[10] The railroads would market the West's health benefits and its real estate opportunities as well as "exploiting the history and scenic attractions ... and 'true freedom' of the West and the Native American cultures."[11]

Railroads also heavily promoted real estate sales. Having been the beneficiary of millions of acres of government land grants, the railway companies used the income derived from such sales for maintenance and further rail line construction. The increased prosperity introduced by the railroads created a more stable society and an end to lawlessness that combined with the economic and work opportunities to make the west attractive to settlers. The newcomers included adventuresome entrepreneurs and investors, recent European immigrants looking for work and cheap land, and the young, the dispossessed and the down-on-their-luck looking for a first opportunity or a second chance.

Baseball flourished in this atmosphere in the west and throughout the country as the boomtown optimism increased competition among the newly connected communities for investment and prestige. These fast-rising towns needed a cultural identity and the local baseball club provided a social focus and a psychological release for the rapidly expanding populace. Rail companies supported this interest in baseball by significantly reducing round-trip fares to away games and by often promoting upcoming games in the local press.[12]

The extensiveness of the American railroad system also made possible the easy and relatively inexpensive movement of players across the continent. Such mobility aided the development of regionally and nationally recognizable players, which hastened the creation of a talented class of players whom enthusiastic spectators would pay to see play. The desire for successful teams was a further step in the creation of a professional class of players in 19th-century baseball.

The railroads moved more than people and goods in the late 19th century; they also transported (and influenced) an American culture that embodied a desire for communal security and for individual initiative. The arc of the history of railroads in the United States—"persistent struggle ... and corporate consolidation"[13]—paralleled both the economy of the Gilded Age and the development of professional baseball during its infancy.

The United States Military

The United States military had a major influence in the introduction and popularization of baseball throughout the United States and the Western Territories at the very time the country itself was expanding in the vast geographical area west of the Mississippi River. While baseball

Baseball among the Union troops during the Civil War. The Civil War had a negative impact on the growth of baseball in areas where it was already established, such as the north and midwest, but it aided in bringing the sport to other regions of the country (National Baseball Hall of Fame Library, Cooperstown, New York).

was being played in the 1850s in New Orleans and Galveston (TX), it was the Union troops who introduced what was an urban Eastern sport to the South during the Civil War. Baseball was played in prisoner-of-war camps and between Union regiments in the many hours of tense anticipation while preparing for battle. Baseball was employed to burn off excess energy, to relieve boredom, and to stay fit. When the war ended, the combatants returned home and brought the game of baseball into areas of the country that had had little experience of the game prior to 1860.

Furthermore, in the years immediately following the Civil War, baseball was a chief leisure activity in the military. For example, in Kansas by 1867, there were military installations in Fort Leavenworth, Lawrence, Fort Hays, Fort Dodge, and Camp Gibbs that were playing each other in spirited competitions. As in the civilian world during baseball's infancy, the United States military employed the national pastime to celebrate historical events and to invoke feelings of patriotism. In 1868, a game of baseball was played at the San Jacinto Battle Grounds on April 21, the anniversary of Sam Houston's defeat of Santa Anna.[14]

Devised to protect American citizens from Indian raids and general lawlessness, the United States Fort system had much to do with introducing baseball to the indigenous peoples of the West. Equally important, African Americans who had an early involvement with baseball during slavery did much to affect the growth of baseball after the Civil War as members of the military.

As was the case in Anglo-American culture, African Americans began playing ball as children. Among slaves, playing baseball and shooting marbles were the most popular adolescent activities. On holidays, especially between Christmas and New Year's Day, adult slaves engaged in baseball games as early as the 1830s.[15] Following the conclusion of the Civil War, many black economic migrants worked in the mines or on the railroad as chair car attendants, porters, dining car waiters, chefs, and roadhouse workers. In fact, Bud Fowler's ability to move with such speed across the continent to play baseball in the 1880s and beyond was aided by his knowledge and use of the railroads and, in all probability, was further aided by the many African American employees who manned

Buffalo soldiers from the 10th Cavalry in New Mexico camp. African American Buffalo soldiers had a major influence socially and culturally in the Western territories and were key agents in spreading the game of baseball west of the Mississippi River (photographer: Henry R. Schmidt [1891]; courtesy Palace of the Governors Photo Archives [NMHM/DCA], 058556).

the trains. Such newly available physical mobility for African Americans was also abetted by the U.S. military, which in 1867 allowed black regiments to enter the service.

Sent to the Western Territories on patrolling and policing duties, these African American troops also engaged in necessary civil work that hastened the settlement of the west. Such non-military labor included exploring, mapping, road building, and stringing telegraph lines. These Buffalo soldiers (given the name because African Americans' coarse hair reminded Native Americans of the noble beast of the plains), though relatively small in numbers, were a large presence in the local communities with whose local inhabitants they sought to establish positive relations. One such successful endeavor to engage with the civilian world was their organization of excellent bands and singing groups that performed at funerals, concerts, dances, grand openings and parades.[16] A second avenue taken by the Buffalo soldiers at creating a positive relationship between the military and civilian worlds was in the teaching of and participation in the national pastime. Participation in these larger community activities allowed African American soldiers an opportunity to develop a sense of personal pride that was frequently denied them in the civilian world.[17]

Within the army, baseball was praised for "improving discipline and reducing idleness." Ironically, baseball functioned in a similar fashion for those incarcerated in penitentiaries and reformatories of the same period by "diverting prisoners' attention from the undesirable to the acceptable." Though perhaps tending to the hyperbolic, some reformers praised baseball as a means of building character "by improving the mental and physical health of inmates by teaching them cooperation, teamwork, sportsmanship, and so-called constructive use of leisure [time]." Baseball also enforced institutional discipline "by making playing or watching the sport a privilege."[18] The U.S. military went even further in praising the virtues of baseball during the training sessions of the Spanish-American War: baseball became a regular form of discipline and recreation that helped develop soldiers who "were models of propriety and neatness."[19]

In the westward expansion across the American continent and in a few imperialist adventures in the 19th century, a lasting influence of black military men was their steadfastness in pursuit of their duty and their creation of a positive relationship with the general population during

Troop L Fort Wingate (New Mexico) baseball team (1888). African American and integrated teams of "coloreds" were playing in the United States military at the very moment the colored line was being established in organized baseball in the civilian world (courtesy Palace of the Governors Photo Archives [NMHM/DCA], 98374).

the Gilded Age. Baseball was a key element of that exchange.[20] It is ironic that African American soldiers who faced racial prejudice on a daily basis were sent to fight against red and brown men in order to protect white men. It is doubly ironic that some of these same influential governmental Anglo-Americans were the chief agents in limiting and, finally, denying African Americans' access to the country's national pastime in the 1890s.

1850s: "The Hurrah Game of America"[21]

Baseball had its roots in the urban spaces of the east in the 1840s and in the bat-and-ball games that stretched back to pre–Revolutionary War America and its earlier antecedents in Mother England. In the mid–19th century, the United States was ripe for expansion and development due to its natural cornucopia of natural resources and "an almost unlimited amount of unpopulated and undeveloped land ... [that] could absorb 300,000 to 400,000 immigrants per year without draining resources."[22]

The 1850s was a period of rapid change and experimentation in the United States. Baseball's development paralleled the social and cultural changes taking place in the country and was influenced by such national issues as the growing sectionalism, the stresses resulting from immigration, the rising cultural tensions in the aftermath of the Mexican-American War, and the addition of the Texas, Utah, New Mexico, and California territories.[23] During this period, New York City, as the largest city and financial center of the United States,[24] was at the forefront of the forces of industrialization that were altering the lifestyles of the populace. With more leisure time and less physical activity in the typical urban dweller's daily existence in the 1850s, young men in Brooklyn and Manhattan began seeking a recreational activity that was fraternal and fun and provided a way to meet young women. Equally important, in order to capture the spirit of the times, such an activity needed to be an exclusively American experience. Baseball, particularly the New York version of the game, seemed to meet that need.

Baseball claimed to have no direct ties to Europe — unlike the most widely contested game of the 1850s, cricket. Originally a participation sport, baseball was the first outdoor American team game that could accommodate a large number of players. An added attraction was that anyone could play the game: one need not possess specialized skills, or a particular physique, or an inordinate amount of leisure time to take part. This last fact was especially important to the urban professionals who first played the game. Since the early baseball players were clerks and bankers and lawyers, they did not have the time to spend an entire day (or an entire week) to complete a match. Cricket was also too slow and too foreign in comparison to the fast-paced, energetic self-image that Americans embraced.[25] Moreover, since baseball cost little in terms of time and money and provided opportunities for fun and recreation, it appealed to the waves of recent immigrants. The sport thus emphasized common social and cultural values and was a unifying force for a country that was seeking to define and promote the notion of patriotism.[26]

By 1855, cricket was still the leading ball game in the United States, but increasing nationalism on the part of Americans led to a general acceptance that baseball had "more constant motion" in its frequent switching from offense to defense and was a livelier game for both players and spectators. As the nation itself was searching for an identity, baseball provided a diverse population with a leisure activity that Americans could call their own.[27]

Baseball's very nature — "cyclical, repetitive, and generational" — captured the American imagination, further establishing the game as the national pastime. Yet, it is not baseball's metaphoric and mythic qualities that made it so immediately popular. The game is a series of tensions with every pitch being a potential source of excitement or disappointment, thus replicating the boom-and-bust cycle of the period and the discovery-disillusionment pattern of life itself.[28]

The rapid development of baseball in the 1850s was also fueled by the enthusiasm of the press, which lionized such individual stars as James Creighton and such successful teams as the Brooklyn Atlantics. The sporting reporters were instrumental in publicizing and promoting major contests, especially those between neighboring cities; they also praised the sport in general with encomiums about its physical, moral, and entertainment value.[29] The sporting press not only served as a conduit for promotion of the game but reflected the intense popularity of baseball. If newsmen sold the game of baseball, the national pastime sold newspapers. This symbiotic relationship held fast for most of the 19th century as baseball became the first American team sport that published player and team statistics. An official guidebook even appeared in 1860 — fans could follow the progress of their teams and players while comparing and debating the sport's rules, peruse last year's statistics, and read Henry Chadwick's assessment of the moral and physical benefits of baseball in *Beadle's Dime Base Ballplayer*.[30]

From the earliest days of baseball's arrival on the American sporting scene, the press collaborated with the players in creating a jargon that underscored the game's embrace of old-fashioned values. Note how in the following newspaper account of what was reportedly the first baseball contest between African American clubs the observer employs the racially charged language and condescending tone of the day: "The dusky contestants enjoyed the game hugely, and, to use a common phrase, they 'did the thing genteelly.' ... All appeared to have a very jolly time, and the little pickaninnies laughed with the rest." The Unknowns of Weeksville (a freedmen's village near Bedford [NY]) defeated the Monitor team (another club from Brooklyn), 41–15.[31]

However, not all sections of the country embraced baseball equally enthusiastically in the 1850s. The Southern aristocracy did not succumb to the early seductions of baseball, finding it rather too physical, unrestrained, and chaotic. Baseball was too democratic and "offended honor" with its many "role reversals" and did not make significant in-roads in the region until much later in the century.[32]

In the 1850s, baseball was still a sport rather than a commercial endeavor. The early baseball clubs were organized like fraternal and service organizations; they hosted visiting teams with dinners and post-game music and entertainment and socialized among themselves throughout the year. The famed Knickerbocker Club was one of about a dozen clubs in the Manhattan-Brooklyn area in the early 1850s. Baseball was then perceived to be a participatory outdoor activity for upper-middle-class sportsmen that fostered "health, recreation and social enjoyment" with very little competition outside the club.

Baseball of the 1850s was also praised for its democratic nature—class and cultural differences were not divisive factors, while family and societal mores were fostered and extended. Without a major competitive challenger for sporting supremacy, baseball became the first sport to fill the desires of a nation for a shared physical and cultural activity.[33]

Simultaneously, the game of baseball itself was changing by becoming more "scientific": greater skill was needed to play the game as rundown plays, breaking pitches, and other timepoints were added to the game. Baseball was moving away from putting a premium on batting by improving fielding and balancing the scales between offense and defense. All of these changes also further separated baseball from its "foreign" competitor: cricket. Thus, though beginning as a local sport, the explosion of baseball led almost immediately to the development of a talented national pool of players that "had only a contractual connection" to a particular community. In turn, this could destroy the level of competitiveness among teams in a given geographical area. The fraternal nature of the game was threatened by the spectators' desire to view the best ballplayers and the most accomplished teams. This trend was heightened by the popularity and press coverage of the Brooklyn Excelsiors' 1860 tours of Western New York and Baltimore that demonstrated the interest in inter-sectional baseball matches.[34]

However, in the decade of the fifties, reformers still pushed for improved skills and an emphasis on victory to the displeasure of the recreational-focused traditionalists. The game was moving in the direction of becoming a professional business enterprise. Such a shift did not come without serious consequences that are encapsulated in the following image: "...hired hands of trained players, scouring the country, followed by crowds of gamblers and pickpockets."[35]

A number of social developments in the 1850s served as the death knell for the fraternal club model from which the national pastime sprung and led to its transformation into a capitalist endeavor based on competition and success:

> In the 1850s, Boss Tweed began creating the prototype of big-city machine politics. Public transportation was expanding rapidly, with horse-drawn "trolleys" along rails and the less limited "omnibus," a high coach drawn by two horses. Steam ferries moved rapidly to Brooklyn, Staten Island, and New Jersey. Newspapers proliferated: the *Tribune*, the *Sun*, the *Herald*, a dozen others (including, in 1851, one called the *Times*). City politics, transportation patterns, newspapers, the recently invented telegraph, and the constantly improving railroads — all these would soon make possible the transformation of club baseball into serious business.[36]

In 1857, the traditionalists were the driving force in the creation of the National Association of Base Ball Players (NABBP), whose goal was to stem the tide toward the increasing professionalism of baseball. The NABBP defined the rules, resolved disputes, and attempted to control baseball's development. Within two years, gambling and revolving (team-jumping) were banned in a futile attempt to slow the game's national development and retain its local, non-competitive aspects. Such regulations were clear attempts to keep baseball "a recreation rather than a vocation."[37] By 1860, with many essential organizational and philosophical battles still to be fought and decided, baseball was primed to become the national game.

1860s

Baseball spread throughout the United States in the 1860s as social and cultural factors coalesced to aid in the spread and popularity of the sport. The country was undergoing increased social mobility that was enhanced by transportation (railroads) and communication (telegraph) services. Equally important, there was no specific bat-and-ball game in competition with baseball that was vying for the desired position of national pastime.[38]

The New York version of baseball that became ascendant in the 1860s had particular advantages that stressed the adult nature of the game. Two rules changes were central to overcoming the objection to baseball as a childish endeavor. First, a foul ball became a non-event with the elimination of the bound rule in 1865 that declared a batter out if a ball was caught on one bounce. This rule allowed baseball fields to be created in areas with a limited amount of land and further differentiated the game from cricket. Second, soaking (hitting a runner with the ball when off a base to achieve an out) was prohibited in the New York game. This cut down on injuries[39] and eliminated much of the "childish" running around and chasing that had been a key element of the earliest variations of the sport. Youthful speed thus was replaced by adult strength and hand-eye coordination as the desired physical qualities for a ballplayer. With the calling of balls and strikes in 1864, the transition of baseball from a batter-fielder confrontation to a contest between the pitcher and batter was complete.[40]

The Civil War first retarded baseball's development during the 1860s and then was a primary source of the rapid spread of the game throughout the midwest, the west, the United States territories, and the defeated Confederacy. The war itself served as a classroom in which to learn that the game was both a morale booster and a form of excitement that could be shared by players and spectators alike. The Civil War had shattered traditional relationships and institutions: "The National Emergency [Civil War] revealed and altered community, regional, and national identities in both politics and baseball."[41]

Baseball filled an essential need for a truly national activity to replace the pervasive regionalism and sectionalism of the pre-war years. In fact, baseball provided a means for possible reunification between the warring parties after the Civil War. As Reconstruction was being abandoned, the United States was searching for a means to unite the fragmented populace. Baseball became a cultural unifier. With the development of a national system of inexpensive train travel and the invention of the telegraph and the typewriter to aid press coverage of the sport,[42] ball games became large civic occasions with town pride a key element. Major baseball tours in the 1860s — including those by the Brooklyn Excelsiors, Philadelphia Athletics, Washington Nationals, and Washington Olympics — introduced the game to the country west of the Alleghenies.[43]

As the national game took hold of the American populace's consciousness, local baseball associations continued to focus on the building of camaraderie by means of uniforms, club houses, songs, multiple teams based on ability (second, third, and muffin [inexperienced or untalented players] teams), and outside social activities, including parades, formal balls and suppers, singing and debating competitions. There was even winter baseball on ice skates.[44]

On the home front in the 1860s, baseball was continuing to gain in popularity. Key events were the spread of the "New York" game to Boston and Philadelphia and the heightened nationalism connected to the sport. The African American Philadelphia Pythians with their "enthusiasm for the game, their successful organization and operation of their own amateur clubs, the white-collar status and considerable education of their membership, their adoption of strict codes of behavior, their enterprise in taking trips to distant cities to play games and enjoy civilized social intercourse afterward" were a noble but failed attempt in 1867 to overcome the barriers preventing integrated ballplaying.[45] Even as women baseball club members began presenting the American flag to visiting teams, and the associations themselves began employing patriotic names such as "Nationals" and "Eagles,"[46] the truth with regard to equality among the races was starkly different from the reassuring public rhetoric. Within eighteen months of the end of the Civil War, the social and cultural principle of the separation of the races had begun to take hold and would influence and encourage the establishment of the color line in the national pastime two decades later.

However, the major development of the 1860s was the increased commercialization of the game, which led to a series of steps resulting in the establishment of professional baseball teams. Newspapers began to raise disputes about the level of play and the civic pride of competing municipalities. This led to town teams hiring talented outsiders to represent their clubs. Equally important, the typical post–Civil War baseball player was not a war veteran but a member of a younger generation who did not have direct ties to the earliest days of gentlemanly baseball. As camaraderie gave way to competition on the 1860s baseball diamond, professionalism replaced the amateur game and commercialism flourished with team sponsorships, enclosed playing grounds, paid admissions, and money over and under the table.[47]

Baseball between the lines emphasized those virtues and values that hastened competitiveness. The armed forces' support of baseball gave the sport the necessary credibility as a "manly" activity. An added benefit of baseball contests was the development of "healthy rivalries as in their [soldiers'] schoolboy days" as a deterrent to homesickness.[48] Furthermore, the very recruitment methods of the Union Army aided in the development of baseball associations throughout the country. Regiments and companies were formed locally with men who were neighbors and shared similar values, cultural and social institutions, and life experiences. Serving in the army, therefore, was similar to the voluntary organizations men had joined in their communities and served in the growth of baseball associations on the local level.[49]

The sporting press eagerly embraced war metaphors during and after the Civil War, employing military terms such as "weapons of war," "winter quarters," "next season's campaign," "make a score," and "grand matches."[50] The baseball magnate and former star player Albert Spalding praised both the Army and the Navy for helping to spread the sport throughout the world. Spalding also noted President Abraham Lincoln's love of baseball and his participation in pickup games as the nation's "first" fan.[51] At the end of the 19th century, future president Teddy Roosevelt invoked the character-building and physical conditioning benefits of baseball and football in underscoring his imperialist ambitions, which were based on an innate and culturally developed American superiority.

Politicians were not the only group that embraced the national pastime to create an air of respectability and belonging. Women were enthusiastically recruited to become members of baseball associations in order to stress that the sport was a respectable endeavor. The clubs employed a series of promotional strategies in the "courtship of ladies," including comfortable reserved seating, special (often free) ladies' day ticket prices, and, most important, the elimination (or curtailing) of bothersome, morally suspect crowd behaviors, such as "profanity, drunkenness, gambling, and hooliganism."[52] However, as the game in the 1860s loosened the grip of baseball-as-recreation thinking to the skill-oriented professional game, the presence of women spectators, while always desired, became secondary to fielding teams that provided the male fan with opportunities for emotional attachment and release while watching the game.

In the 1860s, as baseballplayers became more skilled and disciplined on the field and saw opportunities to make money via the win-at-all-

Bisbee (Arizona) Baseball Association at Cloudcroft (New Mexico). Women were a target audience from the earliest days of baseball both to establish that the sport was an adult pastime and not merely a boys' game and to increase the stature (and financial stability) of the professional teams (courtesy Palace of the Governors Photo Archives [NMHM/DCA], 077564).

costs mentality of the day, the typical ballpark experience underwent major changes from the early club days. Clubs built fences and gates to keep out the undesirable elements and to facilitate the collection of paid attendance fees, a practice that became standard practice during the decade. Spectators grumbled about the quarter or half-dollar ticket fees with the exception of benefit games, which were held to aid needy players or local causes.[53]

The growth of professional baseball went hand-in-hand with the development of the modern city culture in the decade. Urban dwellers found the game exciting as well as appropriate to their circumstances; the "everyday significance" of the game with its many "restraints and regulations" reflected their present environment. Furthermore, baseball fanned a spectator's elementary drive for competition and a socially acceptable release of emotions. The codifying of baseball rules further increased fan interest, shaped the game to appeal to spectators, and set up a framework for championship play. All of these elements aided betting, a less socially acceptable aspect of fan's competitive nature. With traditional values under attack, spectator sports provided workers with less extended but more frequent leisure opportunities that better fit their work weeks and the pace of city living. People were attracted to the "controlled energy of sports" and baseball's "commitment to standards of excellence."[54]

The way baseball was played was also in flux in the 1860s. The game was moving from its earliest inception as a hitting game with the pitcher serving a minor role to an era when pitching accuracy and skill became ascendant, while beginning to show signs of the future emphasis on teamwork with improved fielding, team strategy, and work ethic.[55] For example, fields in the 1860s were laid out so that in the afternoon — most games had a three o'clock starting time — the sun was in the eyes of the hitter, thus giving the pitcher an inherent advantage. Batting itself underwent a radical change from mere slugging to a more "scientific" approach to hitting in which players employing 45 to 50 ounce bats and a more controlled swing tried to place the ball just outside the reach of fielders. Furthermore, ballparks themselves were also undergoing major changes in size. Urban ball fields were becoming magnets for large-scale social interaction set near transportation and population centers. A representative ballpark of the era in the east would have fan capacities of upwards of 5,000.[56]

Besides watching the game in progress, fans in the 1860s filled their afternoons eating, drinking, and gambling. The food sold at the ballpark was traditional picnic fare, including peanuts, popcorn, candy, fruit, pies, and sandwiches. The "family-afternoon-at-the-ballpark" atmosphere so desired by team managements was in sharp contrast with the alcohol and gambling — both banned in the 1860s but winked at as paid attendance became standard — that also infiltrated the ballparks. Gambling was excoriated by the moral guardians of the game — "[Gambling is] a moral burlesque of the game" — and considered the leading detriment to universal acceptance of baseball as the national pastime.[57]

At the beginning of the 1860s, baseball formalized its rules to satisfy Americans' "rage for order" and to encourage competition among the highest level of teams and players. By the conclusion of the decade, baseball had become the national sport for three very concrete reasons: baseball created interest (gambling), importance (use of numerical statistics), and enthusiasm (regular press coverage).[58]

The ascension of baseball as a national obsession in the mid–1860s developed both quickly and nearly universally; however, it did not come without popular public debate and consideration of the game's potential dangers. In essence, these objections recapitulated the argument of the previous decade over the increasing movement of the baseball toward professionalism and the fears of an over-emphasis on the game that would corrupt its inherent virtues. The original argument against commercial baseball was that the wealthier clubs would corner the market on the most skilled players and the individual clubs would lose their influence. In turn, the very nature of baseball as healthful and entertaining would be replaced by competition which remained a double-edged concept for many mid–19th century Americans. However, the social tide was irreversible. As the press continued to promote baseball, a changing population base began to embrace competition as the essence of the American experience. Professional baseball, with its added appeal of providing a venue for the spectators' deep-seated desire to gamble on anything, overcame all arguments in favor of keeping the sport on an amateur basis. Yet the fight to keep baseball as an amateur endeavor continued throughout the decade at the very time that professional baseball was gaining an undeniable position as the national pastime.

Key elements in the argument for the popularity of baseball were its simplicity, its wholesomeness, and its appeal to all American social classes:

> Our national game seems to be baseball. We had an illustration of its popularity over the river on Thursday, when 20,000 men assembled in the heat of a midsummer's day to witness the contest between the champion Atlantic and the Mutual, the two best clubs, we believe, in America. Gentlemen who claim to be familiar with the mysteries of those games, give cricket much prominence over base-ball, like those adepts who regard chess as fashionable and checkers as vulgar. Chess is the more fascinating, but at the same time more tedious and time-exhausting. Beyond the mental exhilaration of the moment, chess is no better than an hour or two spent over books or ledgers. The clerk who goes from his desk to the chess-club and spends the evening over a table, moving small pieces of wood or ivory, may have a great deal [sic] enjoyment; but he will probably return to his desk next morning stupid and dull. The prominence of base-ball over cricket lies in its simplicity, just as the skipping rope and hoop hold their own against the pleasant game of croquet. When a game has intricacies and laws, and is so much progressive that to one class of men it will be a science as absolute as engi-

neering or navigation, while to another class it will be as mystery, it can never become popular. We are too busy in America to make chess or cricket a profession, and therefore some many give their leisure hours to checkers and their play hours during the day to base-ball.

The writer continues in the vein of "selling" baseball's superiority by admiring its democratic nature, which precludes any specialized set of skills except for basic physical conditioning and a desire to play the game.

> Base ball comes home to the American, as its characteristics are eminently American. The main requisites are strength and precision in *batting*, activity in *fielding, quickness and energy in throwing and catching*. In cricket, the requisites are skill and swiftness in *bowling*, and watchfulness in *batting*. A good game of base ball has few *runs*, while a good game of cricket has many. [Emphasis added.] While cricket is full of interest and has many points of admiration, the professional ability of a few expert cricketers is apt to centralize and narrow the interest of the game. In base ball no such danger exists. The difference between good players is not much more than that between a school girl expert with the skipping rope and the Miss [sic] who steps daintily over it for fear of tripping. Any clerk may go into the field with his ball and bat, and, if his muscles are strong enough for him to run and jump, and his fingers are nimble enough to keep the ball from striking them, he may in a little time become a player as good as the members of our champion Atlantic, or the Mutual or Athletic. The easy method of learning base ball makes it popular, and in results it is as good as cricket.

(Finally, the author calls on educational institutions to establish physical training programs and to encourage outdoor team and individual sports clubs to ensure a healthier and more moral populace.)

> In this as in other things, our universitys [sic] should do the work. We like gymnasiums, but they are only partly efficient. A gymnasium in a back street and up three pairs of stairs will do when nothing else can be obtained; but we want fresh air, and sunshine, and the green grass growing under the feet. Let us, therefore, encourage cricket-clubs and ball-clubs, yacht-clubs and boat-clubs and let the best "bowler" in cricket and the best "batter" in base ball or the best oarsman in the boat, stand up among his fellows on Commencement-day [sic] and receive as nice a medal or diploma as his pale-faced classmate, who studied Horace until he was sent to the hospital with strange symptoms in his head. We shall have better preaching and better pleading at the bar, and more careful diagnosis in medicine, and clearer and more earnest editorials in the journals, if the men who preach and speak and physic and write come from the universities with hard hands and ruddy faces, and clear, glis-

tening eyes, full of the lusty beauty of manhood. Leave prize-fighting to the rowdies, horse-racing to the gamblers and jockeys, and bird and beast-slaying to the butchers — let our field sports be more innocent and useful. In the end we shall be a better people, and our children will bless us that the blood coursing in their veins is free from typhus and scrofula, and the wasting taint of consumption.[59]

In the 1860s, such enthusiasm for baseball was not limited to the large metropolitan areas of the East. In southeast Ohio, baseball was being championed for its healthful, exciting, and competitive nature(s): "Balls and bats have been sent for to Cincinnati. Ground has been laid out on the public square, and several games played already. This is a healthful game, good exercise and full of excitement. Every town and village in the country can boast of their Base Ball Club, and we are surprised that this has never been thought of here [Gallipolis] before. We trust that another club of the same kind will be soon organized. 'Competition is the life of trade.'"[60]

This "sound body, sound mind argument" when added to the civic nature of the sport and its relatively lively action made it a form of American self-definition that was enticing (and achievable) for a young polyglot people emerging from a civil war into a brave new world of westward expansion and social and cultural re-alignment. Baseball was seen as reflective of the national character, with one of its strongest attractions being that it was (supposedly) home-grown:

> Hence, our national game chimes exactly with our national characteristics. The phlegmatic element of the Anglo-Saxon family may be fairly represented in the English game of cricket, during which the original Anglo-Saxon can dawdle-off to smoke his democratic pipe or aristocratic cigar at intervals; but the new branch of the family in America, with young vigorous blood swelling the veins; wants constant life and motion in its sports. Hence the English game has almost fallen into decay among us, while the American game is every day attracting the interest which but a short time ago attached almost exclusively to the race course, or, among certain classes, to the prize ring.
>
> We might regard the match played in Brooklyn on Monday [between the Atlantics and the Philadelphia Athletics] as the culmination of success for our national game. In the first place it was a test of the quality of two of the best clubs in the country. In the next it was the most respectable and orderly gathering that ever assembled in the same numbers to witness where the diverse interests — each, of course, supported by their mutual friends — were represented. Twenty thousand people

were present and there was not the slightest breech of decorum observed in the four hours in which the issue of the game was being decided. The large force of police on the ground, finding their occupation as conservator of the peace altogether gone, sat on the greensward, and watched the game with as much pleasure as the rest.

Ladies waved their handkerchiefs and gentlemen shouted lustily now and then; but the Philadelphia Club received as much congratulation as the Brooklyn boys when they made a good run and a successful inning. The utmost courtesy was extended to the strangers, who were probably struck with the contrast between the confusion, crowding, and interruption which prevented the completion of the match a short time since when the Atlantics visited Philadelphia [on October 1, 1866] to try their mettle with the Athletics.

All the manly sports which serve to develop the muscle of our young men should be encouraged. They help to make better material for the future of our young country; material for "sound minds in sound bodies," upon the principle of the ancient philosophers, and we know of no game more calculated to effect this end than our national game of base ball.[61]

The national pastime was frequently mentioned in the 1860s in hyperbolic terms as a powerful force that needed to be controlled, especially since it was so fully embraced by American youth. In an Ohio youth game won by the visiting Gallia club over the home Academia of Gallipolis, 85–62, the post-game analysis added the observation that "This game of base ball has become 'the rage' throughout the country."[62] In Philadelphia, baseball had replaced cricket and shinty as the most popular summer sport: "The weather, indeed, was so warm as to awaken apprehension in the minds of Cassandras who see misfortune in everything which is uncommon. The thermometer measured within two degrees of summer heat."

In the suburbs the younger part of the population amused themselves and celebrated thanksgiving in the old orthodox style of playing ball though in this case it was base ball instead of the old time "shindy" [sic] and "cricket."[63]

After a local newspaper's report of Philadelphia's crushing home defeat of the Brooklyn Atlantics in a rematch of teams playing for the season's championship, the reporter commented on the good behavior of the fans as a possible antidote to that season's "epidemic" of baseball: "No one had any cause to complain of any mismanagement yesterday. Everything worked like machinery. There was no crush, no breaking of ropes, no fights, and no open betting. Too much credit cannot be given to the Athletic Club for its arrangements."[64]

The decade of the 1860s oversaw the rapid growth of baseball but the one nagging question that had plagued the sport since its earliest days continued to be raised: "Would baseball continue to move in the direction of professionalism and develop into a viable capitalist business opportunity for investors, players, and spectators or would the sport continue to remain an amateur leisure activity?" Paying ballplayers had been officially outlawed from the game's earliest inception in the 1850s, though star players were provided with financial and material incentives from the beginning of contested competitions. There were many in the world of baseball who wished to see no changes in this rule in the 1860s:

> There is a great deal of talk just now in base ball circles as to whether base ball first nine players should be paid. Section 39 says "No player who should at any time receive compensation for his services as a player shall be competent to play in any match." This would appear to settle the question; but we are assured that one or two, perhaps more, of the prominent clubs of the country, are in the habit of paying, directly and indirectly, some of their players. Of course, all who break the law will not too curiously interrogate rival clubs; but all others, before beginning a match, should put the President or Vice-President on the witness stand to answer, on honor, whether there are any players on the nine who receive pay for their services. This, we hear, will be the rule thereafter, and it will be found to work advantageously for the best interests of our noble national game. Let the hired men take notice — *New York Tribune*.[65]

Following the cancellation of the championship match in Philadelphia between the Brooklyn Atlantics and the Philadelphia Athletics due to fears of unruly crowd control, the local newspapers discussed the dangers of an over-emphasis on the sport:

> We admire the game of base ball. We admire the results, if indulged in moderately, and it is because we want to see young Americans have such a game as a recreation, that we oppose the present excess. Unless it is remedied and the over-indulgence abated, we see that it will disappear, as cricket did. Our business men will lack patience, and refuse continual absence from duty. At present it is positively losing money to both the employees and the employers. This state of affairs cannot continue, and as lovers of the sport, we call upon those who actively engage in it, "to draw it a little mild," as the meek philosopher says, and "not run the thing into the ground."[66]

In a fuller treatment of the cancelled game, a local reporter crystallized the game-sport, recreation-sophisticated play, amateur-professionalism dualities that were the essence of the debate about the future of baseball in the 1860s. Many adherents of the national pastime believed the sport in moderation was physically and socially beneficial, especially for the country's youth, but the devotion to the game of wild-eyed fans brought with it a Pandora's box of social ills that could lead to the eventual disappearance of baseball from the national scene.

> Yesterday the base-ball fever culminated in a scene disgraceful to Philadelphia. The much-talked of game between the Athletics and Atlantics was prevented by the ignorant conduct of the vast crowd assembled to witness the sport. We do not overestimate when we say there were 30,000 people present, and of those 30,000 a large proportion lacked common sense. In their eager desire to secure advantageous positions, they sacrificed all propriety, and overreaching themselves, prevented the game which they all had come miles to see. It is a matter of extremely slight importance whether the game in question occurs or not, but an instructive lesson can be drawn from the conduct of those present on the occasion. We stated yesterday that the admiration felt for baseball as for all physical sports, was a natural one; that it should be popular is proper. But at the same time we warned all lovers of the game that the excess to which it was being carried would prove its ruin.
>
> Yesterday was a fair example of the ultimate result. The rush to see the contest was so great that the contest itself was prevented. So it will be with the whole system, unless something like moderation is instilled into its devotees. The business men of our city are getting disgusted; and although they may like to see the young men indulge in the game once or twice a week, the present dissipation will not be tolerated much longer. But even if they were willing, the excitement now is at such a fever pitch that it will degrade the sport to a level with horse-races and prize-rings. We know that there are hundreds of respectable people who attend these matches, but there are hundreds of gamblers, pickpockets, and other scoundrels, who are present also; and the latter class will soon drive the former from the field.
>
> Yesterday we witnessed gambling freely and openly performed inside the field, and in the presence of a crowd of witnesses, notwithstanding the rules of the Athletics. Such infringements of the law and exhibitions of immorality are calculated to drive all honorable admirers of the game to their homes in disgust. It is a duty which the clubs owe to themselves, to save their amusement from becoming disreputable.
>
> This great congregation of people drew together a vast number of liquor booths, rum shops, and lager beer dealers. They surrounded the outskirts of the crowd, and made the game tend to promote intemper-

ance. The whole thing is "being run into the ground." The rowdyism exhibited was enough to drive all respectable people forever off the field. The betting engaged in resembled more the scenes of the old Suffolk Park Races than a respectable game of base-ball. The drinking done was calculated to alarm all lovers of morality, and unless a total revolution is effected, the game of base-ball will be ranked with the vices, and all little boys who engage in it will, like those of the novel, who watched horse races, be considered the synonym of fast young men, and parents will frown down that which will only degenerate.

We like the game of base-ball. We think it calculated to strengthen the muscles, invigorate the system, and counteract the evils of the sedentary life lead [sic] by some many of our young men. But at the same time it would be better to have no game than what we fear it will become. Let the nuisance be abated, for nuisance it has become. Let us have it in moderation; for as long as the fever does not cool, the whole sport will be ruined, and base-ball and cricket rank among the things that were.[67]

The decade of the 1860s ended with the game of baseball unchallenged. Though cricket remained popular, it was clearly relegated to "immigrant" status. Baseball's rapid expansion into all corners of the continent underscored the sport's appeal as a pursuit that championed reunification and helped eliminate the worst excesses of sectionalism. The amateur game evolved into a "profession and entrepreneurial endeavor" that held the attention of the American public, thus becoming a "centerpiece of national and local reporting," which further aided baseball's development. The sport of baseball remained a "popular pastime" and became an attractive "spectator sport" that was, finally, a "source of national pride."[68] As for African Americans and other peoples of color, they, for the most part, were invisible on the baseball diamonds and in the newspapers of the 1860s. Baseball was a segregated activity in the decade.

1870s

Until 1869 with the establishment and subsequent national success of the fabled Cincinnati Red Stockings, professionalism held a constant if mostly officially unacknowledged presence in baseball. During the 1850s, star players were provided with perks within the baseball association structure that quickly led to direct payment of players and crowd collections for key individual play and team victories. With the artistic success of Harry Wright's Cincinnati juggernaut still fresh in the minds of the fans and national sports media, the decade began with a new outlook: spectators would pay to see highly skilled, full-time professional players compete against equally talented rivals.

During the 1870s, baseball became a business that policed itself by its self-established centralized power to schedule, discipline, and arbitrate all contentious issues. This consolidation of authority put the game on a more secure financial footing and decreased spectator confusion over the constant turnover of team rosters. However, such a reorganization of the game also stripped individual players of their autonomy. By the end of the decade, the implementation of the reserve clause placed severe restrictions on player movement and signaled that the owners were in charge.[69]

In 1871, the split officially occurred between the traditionalists and reformers. On March 17, the 10-club National Association of Professional Base Ball Players (NAPBBP) and the 33-team National Association of Amateur Base Ball Players (NAABBP) were formed. Professional baseball was now a recognized and dominating force within organized baseball.

The sport itself was undergoing further changes with reduced scoring and improved fielding, though baseball gloves were still a novelty for all players except catchers. In 1876, during the first season of the National League, teams committed six to ten errors a game, a steep decline from the usual 20-plus errors of earlier years. Dramatic equipment changes also ensued. Never one to miss out on a good business opportunity, Albert Goodwill Spalding from his Chicago Sporting Goods Emporium signed a contract to produce the official baseball.[70]

The professional baseball player profile during the 1870s was a city-born (25 percent of all baseballplayers during the decade were from New York) young man (24 years of age) of average build (five feet nine inches and 150 pounds). With the Puritan notion of games as essentially childish now firmly rejected by the majority of Americans, professional baseball quickly became a successful industry that was highly attractive to young working-class men whose alternative careers were farm or urban blue-collar work in an age when the artisans and craftsmen of previous eras were becoming extinct. Ballplayers earned more than most other unskilled laborers while escaping the tediousness and physical demands of such work. The professional ballplayer led a relatively comfortable life with pleasant working conditions, short hours, travel opportunities and hotel stays, and an average eight-month salary of $1,000.[71]

However, the economic situation in baseball in the 1870s was not all rosy. Professional teams were highly unstable as the result of a weak economy and the under-funding of many teams. Teams frequently disbanded when unable to meet payroll and team expenses. Some wags considered bribery a more reliable form of payment for services rendered than signed contracts. Opposing teams also had major disputes, often ending in the courts, about the division of gate receipts.[72]

It was also in the 1870s that both middle and working-class Americans embraced baseball as the national pastime. The middle-class values of sobriety, fair play, and self-control, which were enforced by the rulebook, umpires, and the presence of women, stood side-by-side with the working-class desire for excitement and emotional release.[73] This dual nature of the sport created a constant tension in the game throughout the 19th century and served to make baseball a compelling experience for a wide spectrum of the American populace.

Team owners of the 1870s attempted to ensure club and financial security by creating a system that favored management. They eliminated opposition leagues and competition and restricted player movement by instituting the reserve clause, claiming that they were simply underscoring their commitment to their spectators who could afford the 50 cent admission fee. The 1870s thus ended with a business model that provided investors with a more secure opportunity for profits.[74] And it was financial success rather than the fairness and possible enhancement of revenues via integration that was the immediate concern of baseball executives.

While the 1870s ushered in professionalism with its "win at all costs" mentality and ballplayers themselves became "mercenaries rather than ambassadors" of the national pastime, muffin games with their parody of the new competitiveness remained popular through the early years of the decade as proof that baseball could still be played for fun.[75] Equally important, civic pride continued to play an important role in the popularity of baseball throughout the decade. In addition, the game was expanding to include women (Vassar had three teams by 1870) and both westward and internationally to Japan (1872) and to Cuba (winter tour of 1879).[76]

The man who had the most influence in moving "the enjoyment of the game from the playing fields to the parlor and beyond" in the 1870s was baseball pioneer Henry Chadwick, whom many in the game recognize as the "Father of Baseball." He developed a key element that led to the rapid spread and popularity of baseball — the clarifying and quantifying of the game — so that sports reporting was made possible. Chadwick's "game analyses, [creation of] uniform standards of play and a scoring system, and [the establishment of] statistics as the core of the game" became staples of baseball's widespread popularity. Chadwick's "moral fervor" combined with his creation of a vocabulary for baseball to make him an indispensable agent in the ascendancy of the sport from mid-century until his death in 1908.[77]

A final development in the 1870s that had a lasting impact on the professional progress of the game was the use of baseball statistics to help quantify those qualities of play that established player value. The use of player statistics by team owners to grade player performance was another step in moving baseball from a form of recreation into the corporate world. Such measures of player productivity as fielding and batting averages were employed to define an "efficient worker" and to define professional baseball as a business.[78]

It is into this rapidly changing world of 19th-century baseball that Bud Fowler makes his entry into organized baseball in the International Association (IA) in 1878. Founded one year earlier, the IA was a rival established one year after the founding of the National League. The next 35 years of the African American's life and career was a search for his place in the professional world of the national pastime.

Two

The Color Line
*Segregation and Racism in
Nineteenth Century Baseball*

While baseball could unequivocally claim to be the national pastime by the late 19th century, there was not equal opportunity for all Americans within the professional world of the sport. African Americans, especially, suffered from discrimination by white Americans, who themselves were undergoing a stressful period of social change and psychological dislocation.

The key reason for the outbursts of racial prejudice was less ideological than economic. In spite of the first flush of enthusiasm in an age of entrepreneurship and exploding economic opportunities, the late 1880s and 1890s were filled with economic busts and insecurities that resulted in a major bank panic (1893). The term "fear of sinking" was a catchphrase of the era; the desire to pull other people under was a basis for the virulent racism, the depths of which coincided with the floods of immigration in the last years of the 19th century. The "Grand Experiment" seemed to be failing. It was at this point that pro–American movements such as the Pledge of Allegiance were instituted. Robert Haven Schauffler's 1903 poem "Scum o' the Earth" captures the nation's insecurities and fears. The narrator, who is on Ellis Island, muses on the indignities heaped upon European immigrants and the apology they are owed:

> "Rabble and refuse," we name them
> And "scum o' the earth" to shame them.
> Mercy for us of the few, young years,
> Of the culture so callow and crude,
> Of the hands so grasping and rude,
> The lips so ready for sneers

At the sons of our ancient more-than-peers.
Mercy for us who dare despise
Men in whose loins our Homer lies;
Mothers of men who shall bring to us
The glory of Titian, the grandeur of Huss;
....
Forget and forgive, that we did you wrong.
Help us to father a nation, strong
In the comradeship of an equal birth,
In the wealth of the richest bloods of earth.[1]

Further, Ernest M. Crosby's 1899 poem "Real 'White Man's Burden'" satirizes the age's fervid expansionism overseas at a time of unresolved financial and social problems at home:

Take up the White Man's burden;
Send forth your sturdy sons,
And load them down with whisky
And Testaments and guns.
Throw in a few diseases
To spread in tropic climes
For there the healthy niggers
Are quite behind the times.

Take up the White Man's burden,
And teach the Philippines
What interest and taxes are
And what a mortgage means.
Give them electrocution chairs,
And persons, too, galore,
And if they seem inclined to kick
Then spill their heathen gore.

Take up the White man's burden;
To you who thus succeed
In civilizing savage hordes
They owe a debt, indeed;
Concessions, pensions, salaries,
And privilege and right,
With outstretched hands you raised to bless
Grab everything in sight.

Take up the White man's burden,
And if you write in verse,
Flatter your nation's vices

> And strive to make them worse.
> Then learn that if with pious words
> You ornament each phrase
> In a world of canting hypocrites
> This kind of business pays.[2]

The later part of the 19th century was a turbulent period of economic and social change. The popular, near-exclusive male province of sports was an enclave threatened by "seemingly uncontrollable trends in urbanization, industrialization, and immigration ... and many middle-class men struggled to adjust to the new realities."[3]

Men felt powerless to affect change in their lives in any meaningful fashion and turned from a Victorian notion of manliness to an "updated, rigorous, and physical understanding of their manliness." The working-class men who made up the bulk of the spectators at baseball games valued "valor, strength and prowess [more] than upright behavior.... Strength, endurance, and physicality" now trumped "diligence, independence, and self-control" in the 19th century males' definition of male identity.[4]

Competitive athletics were championed because they combined physical skill and gentlemanly behavior with the emphasis on the former. Theodore Roosevelt in his *The Strenuous Life* summed up the great value of physical culture in the Gilded Age.[5]

While baseball in the 1870s created a new vocation for young men looking for fame and fortune, the sport was not open to all Americans. Both African Americans and Native Americans suffered from the prevailing racial and cultural prejudices of the 19th century, though minority relationships with the dominant European white culture were somewhat fluid in the decade. Both minorities suffered from a cultural Catch-22 situation. As was said of African Americans in the late 19th century and which also applied to other minority groups, "In sum, the black was in a no-win situation: he was condemned as shiftless, stupid and generally of no-account, but if he tried to improve himself he was judged 'uppity.'"[6]

The 1880s witnessed an increasing embrace of what later came to be identified as "Jim Crow" laws. President Rutherford B. Hayes's contested election and the subsequent Congressional "compromise" led to a signature event in 1877 that allowed the South to enact highly restrictive racial laws.[7]

With Samuel Tilden winning the popular vote in the 1876 election, both major political parties met to resolve the contested votes in the electoral college that would determine the election of a new president. The Republicans cut a deal with the Democrats: if the Democrats would agree to allow the disputed electoral votes to be given to Hayes, the Republicans would agree to withdraw military rule from the South, effectively allowing the states to self-govern, which, in turn, led to laws that were even more racially restrictive than the pre–Civil War "Black Codes."[8] This shabby deal and three Supreme Court decisions put an effective end to Reconstruction and revealed just how racist much of America was and how undemocratic the electoral college was (and continues to be).

The development of black baseball traveled on the same social and cultural tracks as white baseball. Early black ball also had elite, middle-class roots and was an occasion for wider social activities such as picnics, dances, formal luncheons, and concerts. Entertainment was central to the black baseball experience and a carnival-like atmosphere became an essential part of black baseball until the demise of the Negro Leagues in the 1950s.

By the 1860s black teams began to leave the fraternal game behind and embraced the more competitive and skill-oriented game of the 1870s. While achieving a limited integration of white baseball, blacks faced resistance since the determination of "blackness" was not one's genealogy or culture but one's skin color alone. While African Americans suffered in the 1870s from "economic exploitation" and minor "social" problems such as patronizing comments in the sporting press and racial stereotyping, the decade welcomed a small number of extremely talented black ballplayers into organized baseball, including Bud Fowler, the first to integrate organized baseball.

The earliest days of limited baseball integration were also an age of economic instability and increased social stresses caused by immigration and the beginning of Reconstruction. Such financial and cultural dislocations, when combined with white paranoia about African American athletic prowess, created a toxic social mix. The fears were, ultimately, sexual in nature. African Americans were considered to be such a sexual threat that they were banned from municipal golf courses and public swimming pools because both places would bring blacks into close proximity with white women.[9]

The desire to control black sexuality was a first and vital step toward preventing desegregation on a larger social scale. In fact, there was a direct correlation between the number of inter-racial marriages in late

19th-century America and the brief acceptance and rapid disappearance of African American athletes during the same period. The establishment of the color line in the 1880s was based on the same canards as in earlier American race laws: white racial "purity" and superiority in contrast with black sub-human predatory "animal" inferiority.[10]

The segregationist white concept of African American sexuality was based on the notion of blacks as "primitive beasts":

> Many whites argued that many centuries of life in the "dark" continent of Africa had accelerated blacks' natural tendencies toward lust and passion. Black men were believed to be endowed with exceptionally large genitalia, gifted with extraordinary sexual prowess and an uninhibited, insatiable preoccupation with sex; though not only were black men considered to possess these sub-human traits, they were also seen as prone to violent aggression, especially towards white women.

Furthermore, the dominant white culture created absurd, unfounded pseudo-scientific tenets, such as the argument "that interracial procreation leads to mongrelization and abnormalities in the offspring, citing the biological differences between blacks and whites."[11] Along with the introduction of Christianity to the pagan hordes, slavery was justified by African Americans' supposedly "different" constitutions and a more general tendency to "numerous deteriorations such as frequent insanity, dementia, blindness, deafness, and overall physical degeneration."[12]

This image of the African American male as an out-of-control primitive with no intellectual, moral, or emotional restraints was often highlighted in the press, which often carried negative stories blacks in the sporting world:

> Bert Clay, alias Harry Johnson, a colored baseball player who claims to have been a member of the Cuban Giants team and whose home is in Syracuse was arrested here today for passing a worthless check. With his pocket full of bad paper on banks in Auburn and Syracuse he cashed one and attempted to pass several others before he was captured. The name of Gerald G. Metcalf, the former Yale half back, now engaged in business here, was forged as endorsement on one check for $24 that was cashed."[13]

When the confrontation was physical in nature and racially based, the reporting became more hyperbolic and the diction more over-heated, as in this Harlem incident, which resulted from a disputed gambling debt on a baseball game:

Two Badly Hurt in a Race Riot

A fight between a negro and a white man over the result of a baseball game played between white and negro teams, on Olympic Field, Fifth avenue, between 136th and 137th streets, yesterday afternoon, led to a riot in which scores were hurt and two persons injured so severely that they may die. It took the efforts of reserves from a dozen police stations to quell the disturbance.

As a result of more than an hour's bombardment from roofs and windows along 136th street in the vicinity of Fifth Avenue and hand to hand fighting with razors and brass knuckles along the side streets lined with negro tenements.... [What follows is a list of whites hurt in the fight and the comments of their doctors at Harlem Hospital.]

The Olympics, a white team, and the Harlem Colored Baseballplayers had a game early in the afternoon. At the end of the game a white man asked for the money on a wager that he said a negro lost on the result of the game. The negro, whose name was not learned by the police, ran into an apartment house on the southeast corner of 136th street and Fifth avenue, across the street from the ball grounds. Rousing the negro tenants with his story of the assault, he made his way to the roof. The rest of the negroes in the house, men and women alike, scrambled up and began to hurl bricks from the chimneys down on the whites below.

That was the signal for a fusillade from the windows of negro apartment houses across the street and from a stone pile on the corner. The whites made a rush on the apartment house at the corner, battered in the front door and went through the halls mauling every negro that could be found. They were repulsed when they tried to make their exit onto the roof by blacks who stood at the trapdoor with clubs and rods of iron.[14]

The prevailing racialist theory stated that, in compensation for their lack of intellect and their moral laxity, African Americans had innate physical advantages such as "a shorter trunk, more slender pelvis, longer arms, longer legs, denser bones and more muscles...." Even personal qualities of individual style were evaluated against the racist stereotype. For example, black athletes' "looseness"—the ability to let one's body act without tension—was seen as "animal and primitive."[15]

It is highly ironic that blacks were prized as athletes and entertainers in the late 19th century because of their physicality and sexuality but were openly discriminated against for these very same qualities. It is also highly understandable, then, that white society has had (and continues to have) an "ambivalence toward the black body" as evidenced in the simultaneous attraction and repulsion to African Americans and their demonstrated athletic prowess.[16]

From Reconstruction to the 1896 *Plessy v. Ferguson* Supreme Court decision on separate but equal treatment for blacks, there was a form of Social Darwinism taking root in the United States that led to unacknowledged categorizations of acceptable African American behavior. At one end of the spectrum was the conservative individual who was nonthreatening, while at the other end was the "bad nigger" who lived by his own set of rules and took the social and legal consequences. The middle range of behavior consisted of race-conscious individuals who were aware of their history and culture and activists who openly confronted racism and its proponents.[17]

During Bud Fowler's later years as a baseball owner and entrepreneur, heavyweight boxing champion Jack Johnson was the incarnation and embodiment of the "bad nigger." As undefeated champion from 1908 to 1913, Johnson flouted the standard behavior for African Americans in that period by "his arrogance, reckless behavior and love of white women." His behavior led to the lynching of other blacks, and Johnson served a jail sentence for violation of the Mann Act. His "self-centeredness" set back race relations in this period and his only "legacy [was that] he accepted no limitations" and "was not bound by custom, background, or race."[18] Bud Fowler's social behavior was the antithesis of Jack Johnson's. Proud and quite conscious of his unfair treatment within the national pastime, the race-conscious ballplayer strove for individual excellence and racial equity by the skill of his play and the force of his character.

During his barnstorming days, Fowler took a conventional approach that was devoid of political action or speech that black athletes have frequently embraced in subsequent eras. While the African American baseball pioneer was quite aware of his position as a symbol of racial pride, he was also conscious of his position as a black businessman who was "catering" primarily to white audiences and who realized that it was essential for his team to embrace and reflect the accepted "middle-class morality" of the majority of his white supporters. With pride, dignity, and restraint, Bud Fowler confronted the prevalent paternalism and virulent racism of the late 19th century every time he stepped on the baseball diamond.[19]

Segregationists soon discovered that the most effective manner in which to define and control African Americans within a sport is to have the athlete be the agent of his own marginalization:

> When you control a man's thinking you do not have to worry about his actions. You do not have to tell him not to stand here or go yonder. He will find his "proper place" and will stay in it. You do not need to send him to the back of the back door. He will go without being told. In fact, if there is no back door, he will cut one for his own special benefit. His education makes it necessary.[20]

This led to the creation of the myth that black ballplayers were incapable of playing such an adult sport as baseball because they lacked the right stuff intellectually and emotionally. While African Americans were acknowledged to possess the strength and speed to become effective ballplayers, they were perceived as being too undisciplined and too immature to practice and hone those skills sufficiently to play the game at the highest level.[21] Furthermore, the black showmanship that was an essential part of the development of a large fan base in black baseball was depicted by segregationists as a lack of necessary intensity and was a major stated reason for refusing to play with or against black individuals and teams. African Americans were too frivolous and unfocused to be taken seriously.[22]

African Americans were a convenient and hard-to-miss target in the segregationist fervor of the day. They were frequently portrayed in shameless stereotypical fashion either as violent thugs or as ignorant children:

> [Selma, Ala., June 23rd] Lawrence Jones and Ben Stevens, both colored, became involved in a quarrel in Murray Walter's barber shop tonight when Jones pulled a pistol and fired five at his intended victim, only one ball taking effect, which may prove fatal. The quarrel was over base ball teams of which both were managers.[23]

> [Charlottesville, Va.] An old negro man was engaged at thirty cents a day in the last term of court in Martinsville to place his head at an opening as a target for parties who pay five cents for three throws of a baseball at it. The old fellow was struck at least 100 times on the top of the head by a hard baseball thrown from a short distance, and didn't even wink, until a man who could throw the ball with the force of a shot from a gun struck him in the head. When the ball hit him, he scratched his head, and asked his employer how many hours he had put in. The man told him he earned twenty cents. "Well, give me dat," said he; "my head is getting soft. I felt dat last ball."[24]

The African American as an object of ridicule and derision and subject to gross physical abuse extended to even the youngest of the race:

"Four proprietors of Coney Island establishments — not four hundred — were notified last night by the police that their appearance in the Coney Island police court this morning would be desirable.... [the final owner summoned was] a man who conducts a place where baseballs are thrown at colored babies."[25]

These everyday incidents revealed an abiding racism that tolerated such Stepin Fetchit and Lightnin' stereotypes and that resulted in unacceptably callous treatment of African Americans in local newspapers. In a like manner, another reporter related how many people who attended the local minstrel shows thoroughly enjoyed the burlesque of baseball that was a mainstay of such productions: "[It was] one of the richest things ever shown here [Cedar Rapids Opera House]."[26]

Even in straight sports reporting articles, racial stereotypes were used consciously and with impunity. After a much anticipated 1895 exhibition game between the National League's Cincinnati Red Stockings and the Page Fence Colored Giants, the reporter of record employed pidgin black dialogue — "dem hot gentlemen up in the pavilion" — and patronizing racial images to underscore the rabid support the African American fans demonstrated for the Page Fence team:

> Along about the third inning, when the score stood 2–0 in favor of the Giants, you could have tossed a ripe Georgia watermelon or a fat possum, done to the last turn, down among that gang of colored rooters in the pavilion and they would have kicked it aside and gone on looking at the game. About this time you couldn't get close to the players to hand them a ripe peach.[27]

Though he was most often accorded respect for his play and demeanor on the field, even Bud Fowler had to deal with racist language and stereotypes in the press and from the grandstands. Such language was so ubiquitous in the nation's lexicon that it apparently never occurred to speakers that it was hurtful and demeaning.

African American responses to such racial stereotypes and blatant discrimination ran the gamut from outraged political commentary to simple pride in the play of African American clubs and individual black athletes:

> "Colored Folks Day" (yesterday, August 25) at the [Chicago] world's fair was a farce. Hardly one of the prominent persons advertised to participate — to speak, sing and play — was present. Even the promised watermelons were conspicuously absent. Joseph Banneker Adger of Philadelphia, Will Cook and Charles Morris, of Washington, D.C.,

ought to be ashamed of their connection with the alleged affair. It looks very much as if they would sacrifice the dignity and manhood of the entire race if only they could make a few paltry dollars as a result of it. Prominent world's fair authorities, who have studiously avoided recognizing the Afro-American in any but a menial capacity, and who intended to realize from such a "day" thousands of dollars for the needy treasury of the exposition, played upon the credulity of these and other Afro-Americans with the result stated in our opening sentence. The self-respecting, manly and womanly Afro-Americans all over the country have denounced the effort and the "day" and their good work has been crowned with the success it surely merited.[28]

Sports reporters for African American newspapers usually expressed restrained praise for the victory of black teams in inter-racial baseball contests and hinted at the distress of the white team's supporters in such cases:

Chillicothe — Chicago's Colored Base Ball Club in This City

The Logan Base Ball Club (white) played the Gordons (colored) of Chicago on the Logan's beautiful grounds last Friday and Saturday. Friday's game stood eight to seven in favor of the Logans, but Saturday the game was a close one and the best ever played in the city. The nine innings were played but not a tally made. The tenth was played and resulted in one tally being secured by the Gordons. It has left sad feelings among our white brethren, but they can't help themselves. They leave Monday for Tiffin to play the white club of that city. The captain says he has challenged the Cleveland nine (colored) but cannot get an answer from them.[29]

The African American press also took great pride in the physical talents of blacks and their contributions to the national good, as in this arduous task set forth by the U.S. Army:

Lieut. James A. Moss (white) of the Twenty-Fifth infantry, U.S.A, (Afro-Americans), is about to undertake a special mission by order of Gen. Miles. About June 1, in command of 20 Afro-American soldiers, he will start from Fort Missoula to ride on bicycles to St. Louis, nearly 2,000 miles across the roughest, rockiest country in the United States, for the trip means crossing the Rocky mountains. Careful preparations are now being made for the trip. Lieut. Moss' report to the war department will be used as a basis for deciding whether it would be advisable to form a bicycle corps as a feature of the army.[30]

In fact, African American support of the U.S. military and pride in the race's participation in the Civil War was a frequent topic of discussion in black newspapers as in this account published 20 years after the war:

The colored soldiers in the late war were as follows: From New England States, 7,916; Middle States, 13,922; Western States and Territories, 12,711; Border States, 45,184; Southern States, 63,571, making a total of 143,330. There were 5,083 not accounted for and 7,122 officers. There were about 92,570 who fought bravely, but were never registered as members of the army. Kentucky sent 23,703, the greatest number from any one State. Tennessee stands second. The first colored regiment was enlisted at Port Royal in the spring of 1862 by General Hunter. The first troops to enter Richmond and Petersburg were colored. The last shot fired at Lee's army was by colored soldiers.[31]

However, the disparagement of African Americans on the baseball diamond continued unabated throughout the era. Such behavior was not just due to ignorance or callousness but was employed consciously by white players to cover a multitude of their crimes. For example, white ballplayers who wished to break contracts by playing "ragged" ball would often claim non-existent racial turmoil on a team for their poor play or for having skipped town without paying their debts. As one critic aptly put it, "...the rhetoric of race provided political cover for their questionable actions."[32]

In a manner similar to the support rendered to white baseball, the 1870s African American press and business community were vital supporters of black baseball. With segregation providing for the legal and philosophical separation of the races, African Americans accepted the challenge to provide their growing population with their own cultural and religious institutions and businesses to fund their own schools, media, and leisure pursuits. The ethic of self-help and personal responsibility led to flourishing black communities.[33] Late–19th-century African Americans saw baseball as a viable business enterprise and a means of achieving respectability not only in their localities but in a much larger sphere. As with the players themselves, African American supporters saw baseball as "a symbol of pride and achievement," as is evidenced in their unrestrained support of solid play and black team victories against white professional teams.[34]

In spite of the decade's institution of Jim Crow laws and poll taxes and the ultimate failure of Reconstruction, African American ballplayers were able to participate in certain white leagues beginning in the late 1870s. King Solomon ("Sol") White, who was an African American star ballplayer and black baseball's first historian, noted that frequently African American ballplayers would be accepted in small towns where blacks were few in number (and therefore posed no "threat" to the community) and in cities with large African American populations. The seemingly sudden emergence of the black ballplayer in this era belied the fact that African Americans were "present at every stage of the creation of baseball" on both the national and local scene.[35]

African Americans were not the only minority group to play a significant role in baseball in the 1870s. Native Americans also began to embrace the game in earnest and the early history of their involvement with the national game directly parallels the experience of African Americans with a few notable exceptions.

Native Americans were accepted on white teams because of their talent and as drawing cards. However, as with African Americans, they were never fully integrated into the team or the community. The myth of the ballpark as a melting pot has always been fictitious. In fact, Native Americans were subject to cultural and racial prejudice and were literally the enemy in the New Mexico and Arizona territories, since the Indian Wars ended only in the 1890s. This prevalent Anglo-American belief in the "blood" and "culture" differences made "coexistence between primitive natives and civilized Europeans impossible." It is deeply ironic, then, that after a systematic attempt at total subjugation of native peoples, many railroad companies looking to increase ridership advertised the western Indian peoples as "gentle, peaceful, picturesque people" who were "saviors of a lost civilization" as tourism became a major industry in the late 19th century.

The most frequent term of derision was to call all Native Americans "Chief," thus highlighting a ballplayer's major identification as an Indian while indirectly denigrating the actual tribal structure. Also, as with African Americans, "humor" involving Native Americans was built on crass and demeaning stereotypes. This brief note in an 1887 midwestern publication is representative: "Athens, Mich., has an Indian baseball team. They generally take the field full of fire-water and do all their curved work reaching bases." Moreover, skin color was the central element in designating a player as an Indian. Light-skinned Native Americans were praised, as were those who lacked the physical appearance of "blanket or Western Indians."[36]

The history of baseball among Native Americans began with missionaries introducing the sport on reservations, followed by Indian interaction with neighboring baseball clubs. In a manner similar to its role

Indian School at Santa Fe, New Mexico. Baseball was a significant part of the physical education curriculum and Americanization goal of the United States government-run schools for Native Americans in the late 19th century (photographer: J.R. Riddle [1886]; courtesy Palace of the Governors Photo Archives [NMHM/DCA], 076039).

in the Civil War, the United States military also helped in bringing the game to the native peoples. However, Native American baseball truly blossomed in the 1870s in the government-sponsored Indian schools that were seen as a means of assimilating Native Americans into the dominant white culture.

Indian schools combined military discipline, academics (English, composition, mathematics, and some sciences), and vocational training. During the summers, the students were hired out to local businesses as cheap labor. The school administration rationalized this blandly named "outing" system as part of the overall assimilation plan, but it was essentially a form of economic exploitation. Native American students also had access to such extracurricular activities as brass band and drama. However, athletics, especially the American team sports of baseball and football, were at the heart of the entire government education program because they were the best pathway to achieving national recognition for Indian schools by playing and being competitive with off-reservation teams.[37]

As with African Americans, Native Americans adapted baseball to their culture. An example of this behavior involved legendary football coach Pop Warner when he served as the baseball coach of the Carlisle (PA) Industrial Indian School (the school of superstar athlete Jim Thorpe). After a severe dressing down by Warner, the Indian players met and requested that the coach change his off-color vocabulary to respect the culture of his players. It is said that Warner never repeated his original mistake of swearing and engaging in verbal abuse. In a like manner, baseball quickly became a cultural given in passing the game from father to son and from tribe to tribe. The game also complemented the Native American love of physical ball sports such as lacrosse and shinny, which they saw as "little brothers to war."[38]

The experience of Native Americans in early baseball also shared with African Americans a large measure of cultural resistance by the white world. Baseball was a mark of personal advancement and a proving ground while also being a means of beating "whites" at their own game. The game provided "cultural memory and pride" and allowed Native Americans "to show what an Indian could do."[39]

Latin peoples of the Caribbean experienced the introduction and development of the sport of baseball in a manner parallel to the development of minority baseball in the United States. The sport was introduced in Cuba by US-trained pioneers Nemesio Guillot, who brought the game home in 1866, and the first Latin baseball star, Esteban Bellan, who learned the game while attending Fordham University and who played professional baseball in America's National Association for the Troy (NY) Haymakers and New York Mutual (1871–1873) before returning to Cuba and organizing the first professional game in 1874. During the 20-year period prior to its own wars of independence from Spain, Cuba was searching for a pastime to replace the motherland's blood sports — cock fighting and bull fighting.

After their revolution, Cuban ex-patriots brought the sport directly to other Latin nations in the region, including Mexico, the Dominican Republic, Puerto Rico, and Venezuela. In the same era, adventure- and gold-seeking North Americans brought baseball to Nicaragua and Panama.[40] In some of these countries, there was such a serendipitous marriage of economic, political, geographical, and cultural events that *beisbol*'s popularity and success seemed inevitable. A case in point is the sport's rapid growth in Cuba:

> Baseball and sugar production fit perfectly. During the six months it took the cane to grow, baseball was a cheap and easy diversion for the

laborers. The slow pace of the game suited the hot Caribbean days, allowing plenty of rest in the shade, and only infrequent bursts of exertions. Bodies made strong by slashing the tough, wiry cane in the harvest were perfectly suited to action at home plate. In addition, the sugar mill owners wanted to field winning teams, so baseball skills brought a premium to workers who possessed them. The Cubans eventually sold out to U.S. investors, who continued the support of these "sugar leagues" for the next twenty years.[41]

In the 1890s, with more than 75 percent of Cuban natives being a mixture of "African black, Spanish white, and native Indian blood," there was never any statutory discrimination or segregation in the Latin countries. For African American ballplayers, winter league play in Cuba seemed to offer an attractive alternative to their segregated daily existence in the United States, but, in actuality, the pay and the life experience was less than promised.

Since the darkness of a player's skin was the only criterion by which one was judged to be fit or not to play in United States professional organized baseball, a few light-skinned African Americans would adopt Spanish-sounding names and try to "pass" as a Latin player. One such Cuban superstar who was encouraged to sign with a U.S. professional team because of his light skin was pitcher Jose Mendez, who was a member of the Cuban Stars barnstorming team that toured America from 1905 to 1911. Though he was 44–2 during the Stars' 1909 tour, Mendez refused to cash in on his talents by taking the "passing" route. Even all-black teams in the United States, including the famed Cuban Giants, included the name of the island in their team name to lessen the knee-jerk racism and the potential virulent animosity of Anglo-American players and their fans to the prospect of facing "negro" or "colored" opponents.[42]

It was into this racist and divided America that Bud Fowler attempted to carve out a career in professional organized baseball in the late 19th century. That African Americans embraced the same physical culture ideals only further exacerbated this stressful period of change for white males. It was an era when the integrationists and segregationists engaged in a pitched battle of words over the minds and hearts of their fellow Americans. In the world of baseball, sympathetic supporters of African Americans stressed their gentlemanly and manly behavior while opponents stressed their trickery, drunkenness, and dirty play. In this battle, the segregationists chose their racial slurs carefully to cause the most damage, most frequently referring to African Americans as "coons." This was a well-understood reference to a stock character of the minstrel shows — "Zip Coon" was a slick, overdressed con man who revealed his buffoonish nature and ultimate stupidity in his attempts to mock his (white) betters.[43]

However, by far the most typical treatment of African American stereotypical racist "character" was the portrayal of blacks as naïve, stupid, and violence-prone. Newspapers played an integral part in perpetuating stereotypes about African American athletes. The following extended anecdote is representative of this brand of patronizing insult "humor":

Jose Mendez. Mendez was a legendary Cuban pitcher who in the early 20th century toured the United States, once posting a 44–2 record against American teams in 1909. He turned down serious offers to play in the United States to stay in his native country (National Baseball Hall of Fame Library, Cooperstown, New York).

> Manchester, in Adams County, has a colored base ball nine that has been beating everything in southern Ohio. Not long since they sent word to West Union, the county seat of that county, that they wished to arrange for a game with the colored boys at that place. Although West Union had no regularly organized nine, the challenge was accepted. A team was got together and put to practice.
> The day for the game arrived and the two teams met on the fair grounds. The West Union boys had several players in their team who had never been in a match game and knew as little about the rules as they did about playing. One of them was Pete Johnson, a tall, rawboned darky, who was assigned to hold down first base. Pete's hands were as big as a barn door, and when he opened them out it looked as if it were impossible for a ball to pass him.
> The game was called and the visitors took the bat. The first man up hit any easy little pop up to first base. Pete got under it. It fell plumb

into his open hands, but bounced out and rolled to one side. The batter reached his base. Pete picked up the ball, and stepping up to the base, hit the runner in the back with the hand containing the ball and almost knocked the breath out of him.

He stood holding the ball, apparently waiting for the runner to vacate the base. Presently he said:

"You're out, niggah."

"Naw, I isn't out nuther," replied the runner.

"Mistah niggah, I sez you'se out," replied the burly first base man.

"Naw, I isn't out," protested the runner. "I wuz on my base when you touched me."

"An you sez you isn't out?"

"Course I isn't out, man. You tro' de ball to de pitcher."

The umpire called out that the man was safe, but Pete took no heed. He ran his hand down into his pants and drew out an ugly looking razor. Striking a menacing attitude, he again directed his attention to the runner and said:

"Mistah niggah, I sez once mo' you'se out. Now, isn't you'se out!" and he opened the blade of the razor.

"Yessir, yessir!" replied the now thoroughly frightened runner. "I'ze out — I'ze out!" and he hurried off the base.

That ended the game. The visitors saw that they had no possible show of getting past first base [*Ohio State Journal*].[44]

One result of such disparaging verbal treatment of African Americans was the creation of a dominant cultural bias against all perceived "foreign" elements based on race and language. These "others" were then denied full access to the economic and political opportunities of the "true Americans." A pseudo-"science" even was crafted to justify the age's "exclusionary social practices and discriminatory public practices" and to rationalize African Americans excellence in sports. The "physicality of blacks" was portrayed as a form of "compensation" for the absence of "discipline, courage, and sacrifice" and blacks' lack of "intelligence and advanced culture." Thus, the "reasoning" went, African Americans had certain "natural" and "innate" advantages which, in fact, disparaged African Americans' athletic success and character while simultaneously underscoring the superiority of the "more manly" Anglo-American sportsman. Acutely aware of the opportunity to improve their financial and social lot, African American ballplayers were most often highly disciplined and hard-working professionals who sought to move from their marginalized position into the mainstream of American society.[45]

Both the African American community and the U.S. Congress

seemed to bow to the inevitability of segregation as an acceptable compromise. In 1895 at the Cotton Exposition, Booker T. Washington gave his "Atlanta Compromise Speech" in which he argued the following: "The races could be as separate as the fingers on the hand in all but economic matters." A year later the Supreme Court decision *Plessy v. Ferguson* codified post-emancipation segregation into law.[46] It is little wonder that black leaders were ready to embrace a "separate but equal" society. From 1885 to 1900, 2,500 African Americans were lynched "by rope or faggot," including in the annus horribilis of 1892 when there were an average of four lynchings a week.[47] Only after 1900 with the Great Migration did African Americans leave their Southern rural roots. They spread throughout the country and began to lay the basis for the civil rights movement of the 1960s.

The 1904 *Statistical Abstract* provided African Americans with the statistics that belied the "inferior race" argument of the segregationists and the folly of the color line in mainstream American culture:

> The time is past when the only careers in life open to the Negro were to pick cotton, to make up berths in a Pullman car, or wait on a table. The study of the Negro population of the United States recently published by the census bureau discusses some facts that show very clearly that the colored race is steadily developing a complete social and industrial system of its own....
>
> A large city could be formed without a single white man in it and yet lack for no trade or profession. There are 21,258 Negro teachers and college professors in the United States, and 16,530 clergymen. The Negroes could finance a railroad through their eighty-two bankers and brokers, lay it out with their 120 civil engineers and surveyors, condemn the right-of-way by their 729 lawyers, make their rails with their 12,327 iron and steel workers, build the road with their 545,980 laborers, construct its telegraph system with their 195 electricians and their 529 linemen, and operate it with their 55,327 railway employees....
>
> [A comprehensive catalogue of occupations follows, with the fact that Negroes own one-eighth of the farms and over half of the cotton plantations in the United States. The report notes that "the colored population bears a marked resemblance to a European peasantry" with the example of nearly 600,000 women and girls engaged in farming....]
>
> In fact, there were a higher percentage of blacks gainfully employed than whites: "84.1 per cent of the colored males and 30.7 per cent of the colored females are engaged in gainful occupations, against 79.3 percent of the white males and 16 per cent of the white females similarly occupied. These are figures to which the Negro can "point with pride" when

he is accused of preferring the midnight chicken and the surreptitious watermelon to the joys of labor.[48]

However, the color line remained etched in granite in the national pastime. Two decades earlier, there had been African American integration success stories on the baseball diamond. As late as 1886–87, there were 20 African American ballplayers performing in integrated baseball leagues, including the International Association which was recognized as only a step below the major leagues in caliber of play. In the transitional years of 1887–88, several International Association African Americans had all-star years, including Bud Fowler (.350), Sol White (.381), Frank Grant (.366), and pitchers George Stovey (33–14) and Robert Higgins (20–7).[49] Yet by 1889, all African Americans were effectively out of the higher echelon of organized baseball. Complete separation of the races began in earnest and continued throughout the 1890s. By 1890, Cuba, with its minimal emphasis on race, offered "lucrative and viable alternatives" to independent and black touring baseball that were, effectively, the only alternatives to pursue a professional career in baseball for African Americans.[50]

In 1887, events both on and off the field underscored the rising tide in favor of separation of the races. These events included Cap Anson's relatively quiet refusal to take the field in an exhibition game against the Newark Eagles with African American Stovey on the mound and the more explosive threat to boycott games against the period's most storied all-black club by key members of the St. Louis Browns' major league club. In the latter instance, the bitterness of the event was evident from this article:

The "Wah" Still On
St. Louis Ball-Whackers Don't Want "Niggers" to Beat Them.

New York, September 12th — For the first time in the history of baseball the color line has been drawn, and the world's champions, of St. Louis, who have established the precedent that white players must not play with colored men. The Browns were in open revolt last night. Some time ago President Von Der Ahe arranged for his club to play exhibition games at West Farm, near New York, with the Cuban Giants, the noted colored club. He was promised a big guarantee, and it was expected that fully 15,000 persons would be present. The game was to be played today, and President Von Der Ahe yesterday purchased railroad tickets for all of his players and made all arrangements for the trip. Yesterday, while at supper, the following was placed in Von Der Ahe's hands:

"Dear Sir: We, the undersigned of the Sr. Louis Baseball Club, do not agree to play against the negroes to-morrow. We will cheerfully play against white people at any time, and think by refusing to play we are only doing what is right, taking everything into consideration and the shape the team is in at present."

The letter is signed by the following-named members of the club: W. A. Latham, J. E. O'Neill, W. E. Gleason, Charles King, John Boyle, R. L. Caruthers, W. H. Robinson, Curt Welch.

Considerable feeling has been created by this episode.[51]

With the darkness of one's skin color the sole determinant of the ability to participate in organized baseball, light-skinned African Americans were better served in the run-up to the color line of the 1880s. Existing photos and the occupations engaged in by the individuals (e.g., barbers, headwaiters, and domestic servants) reveal that the majority of the professional ballplayers in the late 19th century were mulattoes who developed an entire assimilationist culture separate from the mainstream black one. However, with the hardening of the color line in the late 1880s this "semi-acceptance" of mulatto culture disappeared. One final problematic avenue for light-skinned blacks to participate in organized baseball was available — "passing."[52]

Passing "meant crossing the racial line and winning acceptance as white in the white world." One example occurred in 1901 when John McGraw tried to pass off Charlie Grant as Chief Tokohoma, a full-blooded Cherokee; however,

Charlie Grant. The color of a ballplayer's skin was the only determination in the 19th century that prevented him from participating in the national pastime. Light-skinned African Americans were often encouraged to "pass" themselves off as Native Americans, Hispanics, or, especially, Cubans to escape the proscriptions of the "defenders" of baseball. New York Giants manager John McGraw almost signed Grant to a major league contract under the ruse that he was Chief Tokohama (National Baseball Hall of Fame Library, Cooperstown, New York).

the young infielder was so well-known for his skills on the diamond that the ruse was detected. The newspapers kept the spotlight and the pressure on any player even remotely suspected of being African American. What further hindered passing was the "one drop rule," which designated one as "colored" if any ancestor was identified as non-white. Yet in spite of such obstacles, a few African Americans were able to penetrate the color line.

Denying that he was African American, Dick Johnson changed his name to Dick Male and caught a few games for the 1886 International Association Syracuse Stars. The following year Male resurfaced as Dick Johnson, a black catcher for Zanesville in the Ohio State League. By 1889, the light-skinned Johnson was having a banner year for the Springfield Senators in the Central Inter-State League, where he was constantly under observation until *The Sporting News* revealed at the end of the season that Johnson was black.[53] Dick Johnson's partial passing was the exception to the rule in crossing the color line.

African Americans themselves were divided on how to deal with the racialist thinking that pervaded late 19th-century society. Two of the greatest African American players of the early game — Sol White and Moses Fleetwood Walker — became influential writers who opted for differing responses to racism in organized baseball. In his *History of Colored Baseball* (1907), White posited a measured approach that would eventually lead to assimilation into white society. On the other hand, in his pamphlet "Our Home Colony," Walker took the position of the black nationalists and urged American blacks to emigrate to Africa and opt out of America's racist society.[54]

Emboldened by an indifferent public that was facing major economic stresses and radical cultural change, the proponents of segregation attempted to codify the color line into law in areas that were vastly more significant than the cancellation of exhibition baseball games:

The Color Line
Georgia Exercised Over the Pending Anti-Negro School Bill

Atlanta (G). July 26th — The excitement caused by the introduction of the Glen bill in the Legislature is unabated and grows every day. The bill provides for the punishment of any teacher who instructs white and colored children in the same institution. Glen says the sentiment of the people of Georgia is strongly in favor of the bill, but he fears opposition from some politicians who still oppose the bill so as to avoid censure or criticism from the North. The negroes are loud in their protests against the bill, and indignation meetings have been largely attended and resolutions drafted showing the sense of the meeting. At one a memorial to the Legislature was started and signed by over 800 colored citizens. The memorial asked the Legislature not to allow the passage of the bill, asserting that it is oppressive, unjust, and unconstitutional.[55]

Grover Cleveland was a towering political figure in the last two decades of the 19th century. He was the only Democrat elected president between James Buchanan in 1856 and Woodrow Wilson in 1912. Running on a platform of political reform and fiscal austerity, Cleveland's direct and plain style made him a formidable force on the national scene. In a somewhat disingenuous argument, Republicans made this appeal to southern blacks:

Moses Fleetwood Walker. Walker was the second African American major league ballplayer. He caught for Toledo of the American Association in 1884 (while his brother Welday joined the same team later in the year). Later in life, Walker became a strong proponent of Black Nationalism and deemed integration to be a failure in the United States (National Baseball Hall of Fame Library, Cooperstown, New York).

> The white men of the south are, more than any other class, interested in this great question. They are the owners of the soil from which primarily comes all wealth. Labor, skilled and unskilled, capital which is nothing but labor condensed, are chary of investment in any country whose progress is endangered by the presence of so dangerous a factor to peace and progress as race prejudice.
> The opportunity is offered them, the invitation from their own chosen party leader, that they should divide upon the great economic questions which to-day divide the political and each for himself follow that party whose ideas best represent hat he believes to be the best interests of his country.

We say this invitation comes from President Cleveland, because it is the logical conclusion of his invitation to the colored men to do the same thing. President Cleveland is too wise a man not to understand this, and we believe he is too patriotic not to desire it.

And what should the colored men do? THE NATIONAL REPUBLICAN is a Republican newspaper because it believes in the principles of the Republican party. It understands fully the relations of that party to the colored men of the country. It knows the grand work the party has done for them, and what of good it has attempted and failed to accomplish. It knows that under our peculiar dual system of state and national governments, each holding a portion of the sovereignty, that the Republican party, even with the full control of the national government, could not remedy some of the evils under which the colored men of the south are now suffering, and it believes that it will be the part of wisdom for them to cease any longer to be united as a mass in the Republican party....

No fair minded, honest man will deny that in many states and sections of the south the Negroes are by fair means or foul deprived of that great privilege of American freemen, the right to vote for whomsoever they may choose to fill all official positions. This, as we have said previously, is because they are solidly Republican and race prejudice is aroused against them....

If the colored men of the south should divide upon the questions which divide the political

Sol White. Sol White played for 25 years on some of the best African American baseball teams in the late 19th and early 20th centuries. He is perhaps best known today for having written and compiled the first history of black baseball in 1907, *Sol White's History of Colored Baseball* (National Baseball Hall of Fame Library, Cooperstown, New York).

parties of to-day as they did in Atlanta upon the question in that local election, they will find that the white men will divide in the same manner, and each party will endeavor as earnestly, and in the usual way of recognition and support, to secure colored voters. The white Democrats will select colored men of prominence to strengthen their ticket and the Republicans will pursue a similar course, and thus each man will have the privilege of casting an honest ballot and having it fairly counted....

Should all or any part of the south be so blindly besotted as to refuse, on these conditions, all the rights of citizenship to the colored men, then there would be but one course left for them to pursue. *They should migrate* and seek some section of the great republic where, in the language of the fathers of the country, "all men are free and equal."

The colored men of the south, by their labor, add every year five hundred million dollars to the wealth of that section, and they expend what they earn, not hoarding, but using it, thus keeping all the product of their labor to active use. The south cannot afford to lose this vast army of producers, who are now restless because of the deprivation of their rights, and the owners of the soil will be glad to accept the method proposed as the most feasible one offered to settle questions which threaten the future prosperity of their section.

THE NATIONAL REPUBLICAN desires to reiterate its previous assertion a desire to benefit the colored men of the south especially, as well as the whole country generally. It has been and will continue to be a bold defender of every right and privilege of the colored men, and it is because of this that it points the way by which it honestly believes all these rights and privileges can best be secured.[56]

However, President Cleveland's desire for reform did not reach much beyond the political. He believed that African Americans needed to "prove" themselves along with white help in a formulation that approached the "white man's burden" doctrine:

[The colored man is] the equal of the white man in respect to his civil and political rights. He must make his own contest for position and power. By his own conduct and success he will be judged. It will be unfortunate for him if he shall rely upon political sympathy for position rather than upon duties well and intelligently discharged. Everywhere the white man should help him, but his main reliance should be upon himself. In that way, and given a reasonable time, the colored race will be able to blot out the race forever. Until then we must educate him and have patience.[57]

Even in discussions of the colored line that occurred in publications sympathetic to African American causes, blacks were frequently presented in the stereotypical manner of a race still striving to attain maturity. The

Colored Knights of Labor were a blacks-only organization whose core premise was that there was no distinction between white and black workingmen. Yet, those white investigators who supported the Knights found it necessary to report that "whites were better suited to trades unions" while the Knights would appeal more to African Americans because of the organization's secrecy, mystic names, ceremonies, vows, and required obedience.[58]

In the late 1880s, misconceptions about African Americans extended to the baseball diamond and resulted in a series of "fears" that aided the hardening of the color line in American society and eventually led to the total elimination of blacks from organized baseball. First, it was feared that southern players would refuse to play with African Americans or provide only half-hearted efforts to ensure that club management would not (re)sign black players no matter their talent level. This fear did have a basis in fact; however, the major reason for such player behavior was often not racial but the added competition blacks provided for limited roster positions. In fact, as early as the 1870s, players who would object to playing with an African American on one team would have no response to the same situation on another roster if he was not in competition with a black player for playing time. Club owners would cave in to such unreasonable demands by players because of the precarious financial nature of baseball in the late 19th century. Running a financially successful baseball operation was overly dependent on local gate receipts and any negative publicity or controversy had to be avoided at nearly all costs.

Another "fear" that had some basis in fact was the potential for violence on the field and in the stands if African Americans were allowed to participate on integrated teams. Baseball began its professional life as a rowdy affair with unrestrained drinking, betting, swearing, and fighting both inside and outside the lines. Yet, there are remarkably few instances of racial incidents on the field during the 19th century; in fact, an African American player on a roster would often increase fan interest and certainly raised the talent level of the team(s) who signed blacks.

Then there was the myth that African Americans did not have the combination of physical talent, desire, and intelligence that was needed to succeed in the national pastime. They were viewed as humorous entertainers lacking the grit of the true professional athlete. This falsehood was disproven at every level of organized baseball in the 19th century. A final fear raised by some whites in the sport was that the indignities suffered in travel, hotels, and restaurants in certain venues would be too much for African Americans on integrated teams. This concern was disingenuous at best. It should have been clear that racial segregation was both unnecessary and prejudicial. However, economic worries, immigration fears, and Jim Crow laws trumped fairness and decency when it came to the treatment of blacks in the Gilded Age.[59]

This racially divided country was Bud Fowler's playing field in 1887. It comes as no surprise that his separation that year from the Binghamton (NY) nine in the International Association was spurred by a threatened strike by some of his white teammates. His public statement that he was leaving Binghamton for a better opportunity with the all-black Gorhams touring club was an attempt, perhaps greased with monetary payments from team ownership, not to burn any bridges with organized baseball with regard to future employment on integrated teams.

The fall of 1887 saw Fowler located in upstate New York and planning to barnstorm with the Gorhams if no opportunities in organized baseball presented themselves.[60] The African American player-manager may have also begun to investigate the possibility of taking a barnstorming club to the Rocky Mountains and the West Coast, a life-long dream that he never realized. A Los Angeles newspaper lists in December of 1887 a "Bud Fowler" on a "List of Letters Remaining Uncalled for at the Los Angeles Post Office."[61]

Bud Fowler's 35-year career in baseball spanned the era of uneasy acceptance of African American players in the 1870s and 1880s on the playing field to their complete elimination from organized baseball in the last decade of the 19th century. Throughout his involvement with the national pastime, Bud Fowler fought against overwhelming odds, first to play the sport at its highest level and then, when denied all avenues of participation in organized baseball, to promote black baseball as a means of showcasing African American athletic talent, providing affordable social entertainment, and creating economic opportunities for a culturally disenfranchised segment of the American population.

— Three —

An African American in Organized Baseball (1878–1886)

Bud Fowler was born John W. Jackson in Fort Plain (NY) on March 16, 1858, to a father who was a hop-picker and a barber. In a truth-stranger-than-fiction circumstance for the first African American ballplayer in organized baseball, the first captain of an integrated team, and a major promoter, organizer and owner of black touring baseball clubs, Fowler was raised in Cooperstown the supposed cradle of baseball and the eventual home of the sport's Hall of Fame and Museum. Never one to shy away from any form of publicity, Fowler was proud of his roots in the New York village and a staunch proponent of A. G. Spalding and the National Commission's "immaculate conception" theory of baseball as a totally American pastime:

> [Fowler] learned to play ball on the old Cooperstown Seminary campus. On those same grounds was situated the old Military School from 1835 to 1851, where General Abner Doubleday received his military training. "Bud" insists that the general drew the first base ball diamond in the dust and named the first game played upon it baseball; and that the national game, therefore, originated at Cooperstown, Otsego county, N.Y., and, furthermore, that he [Fowler] is the only professional — white or colored — who ever played on that first diamond.[1]

The black baseball community embraced the myth that Cooperstown was the cradle of baseball, in part because of Bud Fowler's connection to the New York village. More than 15 years after Fowler's death, African American baseball historian Sol White reasserts Fowler's position as the first star of black baseball:

> The first scheme for playing baseball was devised by a gentleman in Cooperstown, N.Y., back in 1839. The first Negro ballplayer of promi-

nence was Bud Fowler. We heard of Bud when, as a little tot, we were watching a ball game on the public square of my home town. Fowler passed the home plate many years ago. We never learned the exact age of Bud, but it wouldn't take such a ridiculous range of imagination to place Fowler somewhere in the neighborhood of Cooperstown when the first diamond for playing the old game was devised. You see? Bud was playing ball when I was a kid.[2]

Ever the entertainer, Fowler even penned a song that would immortalize his adopted hometown for future baseball lovers: "He [Fowler] has just composed a baseball song which he had dedicated to the National Commission. It deals with Cooperstown, N.Y., where the game was first named and the first diamond was laid out by General Doubleday. This is also Fowler's birthplace."[3]

Much of Fowler's youth remains to be uncovered[4] but he did surface playing ball in Massachusetts in the late 1870s. He was already employing the sobriquet "Bud Fowler" at this early date. (While the matter of this name change remains in the area of speculation, the most plausible explanations are either Fowler's desire to retain his amateur status or to avoid family strife in an upwardly mobile African American household.)

1878 — Massachusetts

While apocryphal claims that would have had him playing competitive adult baseball at the ages of 9 and 14 continue to exist, Bud Fowler actually began his 21-year professional playing career at the age of 20 in Massachusetts. His rise within the ranks of organized baseball was meteoric and led to his integration of the International Association in 1878, just two years after the establishment of the National League.

In 1878, Bud Fowler was a member of a Chelsea (MA) amateur team when he received a rare opportunity to perform in an exhibition game in Boston on April 24, 1878, against the reigning professional champions, the Boston Red Caps. The young hurler was part of a "picked nine" that was composed of five of his teammates from the amateur Chelsea (MA) club, two Boston Beacons, and a former Highlands catcher. The day was cold and raw and Boston Manager Harry Wright's "boys were rather unwilling," as evidenced by their attire: star pitcher Tommy Bond[5] wore no uniform, most of the players wore no spikes, and all the team wore their jackets during the game.⁶ The game, lasting only 95 minutes, was played as if both teams had a train to catch. Bud Fowler had an unimpressive line in the box score with one notable exception. He went 0–3 at the bat; had 3 assists, 3 errors, 1 wild pitch, and 1 walk; and was booked for 17 called strikes and 15 called balls. The picked nine was equally unimpressive in the field with 10 errors to Boston's 6. However, Fowler was the winning pitcher in a 2–1 victory, hurling a complete game three-hitter and surrendering no earned runs. In fact, Boston scored no runs after the first inning when George Wright got to first base on an error, reached second on a passed ball, and scored on fellow future Hall-of-Famer Jim O'Rourke's single. At the beginning of the game, the picked nine appeared to be overmatched: "The amateurs went out in one two three order for five innings in succession."⁷ However, in the sixth inning, Lynch and Flint were left on base; then in the seventh, Woods and Gerish had hits and scored on catcher Pop Snyder's wild throw.

A local reporter pooh-poohed the result as a meaningless exhibition: "The game, if it could be called one...."⁸ Yet, for Bud Fowler the game was his ticket into the International Association (IA), a fledging league that was competing with the National League for baseball supremacy and attention.

On May 15, 1878, at the West Lynn Grounds, "The Live Oaks [of Lynn] were terribly whipped by the Buffalos" with starting pitcher Prince and reliever Phillips being lit up for 10 runs and 14 hits in a shutout loss.⁹ Two days later, Bud Fowler took the mound to replace the "lame" Prince who had been shelled in his previous two appearances. The Chelsea base ballist, thus, became the first African American to play in organized baseball.

Bud Fowler was again dominant. He held the London (Ontario) Tecumsehs, the defending league champions, to 2 hits and no runs with 3 strikeouts and only 1 wild pitch over seven innings. For the Live Oaks, Phillips had an RBI hit in the third inning while Lapham and Sullivan had RBI base knocks in the fourth. New acquisitions Fowler and Woods filled in admirably "to the satisfaction of everyone [among the Lynn supporters]."¹⁰ A rival Boston newspaper had this to say: "to retrieve their misfortunes of their past two games, they [Lynn] imported a pitcher and center fielder for the occasion, Fowler and [George] Wood of the Chelseas. Fowler's pitching was so effective, and the general play of the Live Oaks so sharp...."¹¹ The game ended in the seventh inning and "The result was a surprise to everyone."¹²

Leading 3–0, Lynn was awarded a 9–0 forfeit victory when London refused to continue play after a close call at the plate that went in the home team's favor. As early as the second inning, Tecumseh captain Ross Barnes was complaining loudly about the umpiring. After teammate Mike Burke walked in the second, he was thrown out stealing and Barnes demanded the replacement of Umpire Henry Murphy (who, a Boston reporter noted, had called 15 previous games that season without incident).[13] Though the London captain drew the ire of the home crowd — "Barnes was censured by all"—Murphy was "substituted for" by James Tuft. In the bottom of the seventh inning, Barnes hit a "caught fly" and Hornung "was put out at home" in a close play. At this point, "the Tecumsehs objected to this decision, as they had also done to others, and flatly refused to play."[14] Tuft then declared the Live Oaks forfeit winners.

The Lynn club clearly outplayed the defending league champions, outhitting their Canadian opponents 9–2 and fielding slightly better than the Tecumsehs. Fowler had a strong game with 18 called strikes and 13 called balls and only a single wild pitch: "Fowler's effective pitching and the handsome manner in which he was backed up fairly earned the game for the Oaks."[15]

On the following day at the West Lynn Grounds in front of a crowd of about 500 fans, Bud Fowler again occupied the pitcher's box and was the pitcher of record in a complete-game loss to the Worcester team in what was billed as the "first game of the New England Championship."[16] Lynn played an uninspired game: "The game was long [two hours and ten minutes] and uninteresting. The visitors out fielded the Oaks and their hits were brought in at a time when they did the most good."[17] Game statistics seem to bear out the reporter's assessment of the match. The Live Oaks committed 16 errors to their opponents' 7 and the Reds had only 6 hits in scoring 6 runs. Fowler had an unusually high number of called strikes (27) and called balls (16) with 3 wild pitches. However, it was his hits allowed that caught the eye of the Worcester reporter: "The batting of the Worcesters shows that the boys are improving in one respect, as they got more safe hits off Fowler than have been credited to any other nine this season."[18]

Before the Lynn team's next league match, it was reported that at a meeting of the Live Oak Base Ball Association the board had "voted to employ Fowler and Woods...."[19] The two former Chelsea players took the field as official members of the Live Oaks on May 29, 1878, before approximately 400 Lynn spectators. The Syracuse Stars thoroughly outclassed the home nine in a 9–3 victory. Fowler gave up 12 hits and 4 wild pitches in a complete-game effort that was marked by "loose fielding" on both sides: "The Oaks had a miserable fielding game" (19 errors) while "the Stars were a little off in that particular themselves" (13 miscues).[20] The regular Oaks hurler continued to be incapacitated for this game: "Price, the Oaks pitcher is sick in bed and was unable to play, his place being taken by Fowler of the Chelseas, whose pitching was very wild."[21]

On the next day, it was officially reported that the Live Oak Base Ball Association "will remove the organization to Worcester and keep their place in the championship."[22] The Worcester team was to be "disbanded" and certain key players such as the battery of Bobby Matthews and Ed McGlynn "will be retained." A few members of the active Lynn roster were put on notice that their positions on the new merged franchise may be in jeopardy: Oaks outfielders Mark Phillips and Michael Hayes "will be cancelled unless they reform in their habits."[23]

A newspaper account on the following day listed a new baseball nine that would "probably be named 'Bay State'" and would be located in Lynn: "Fowler will be the pitcher" with Hayes catching. The infield will include veterans King, Lynch and Flint; the outfield will be composed of Foye, Crossup and Welsh, a former member of the Guelph Maple Leafs.[24] Meanwhile, Manager Brackett of the recently disbanded Live Oaks arrived in Worcester on the same day, bringing with him seven members of his Lynn club and adding Matthews, McGlynn, Muldoon, Farwell, and Pitts of the now defunct Worcester franchise. A newspaper account reiterated that "the new team will take all the engagements of the Lynn club." The following "new" Live Oaks starting lineup and batting order was announced for the following day when the independent Westboros were to play at Worcester:

Sullivan cf	Say ss	McGlynn c
Giles 2b	Spence 3b	Muldoon rf
Wood lf	Lapham 1b	Matthews p[25]

Bud Fowler made one last appearance in the IA when he replaced Worcester starting pitcher Bobby Matthews, who was suspended for drunkenness. On July 11, 1878, he pitched in a 6–0 loss to New Bedford.[26] Fowler held his own that day: he gave up only two earned runs and five hits, including only one extra-base knock. Moreover, the replacement pitcher kept the ball in the infield for the most part; Worcester's first baseman Charlie Householder had 13 putouts on the day.[27]

Prior to Bud Fowler, joining Lynn, the African American's amateur Chelsea club played a game against the pre-merger Worcester franchise. On May 15, Bud Fowler took the loss while allowing only three hits: "Very little regard for the feelings of their visitors was shown by the Worcester (Mass.) Club on May 15, when the Chelseas couldn't secure a run, being completely mastered at all points. Their catcher [Walsh, who had seven errors in the game] played miserasbly."[28] Since both team rosters contained numerous players — for example, McGlynn, Muldoon, Lynch, Flint, and Wood among others — who played with and against him, it is abundantly clear that Fowler had in essence been "scouted" by local Massachusetts teams and was a known quantity by this point in his career. A final coincidence from that game in Worcester is that the winning pitcher who so dominated Fowler's team — his catcher had an unheard of 14 putouts in the game — was Bobby Matthews, the suspended pitcher whom Fowler replaced for a game in July on the reconstituted Worcester entry.

The New Bedford franchise that defeated Fowler in his last International Association appearance led a peripatetic existence in the few remaining months in the 1878 season, relocating first to New Haven and then to Hartford. Interestingly, manager Francis Bancroft reorganized the team in 1879 and established it in Worcester, where the team was so successful that it entered the National League in 1880.[29]

For the next five years, Bud Fowler was on the road from Ontario to New Orleans, playing for a series of independent and semi-professional teams while looking for a second chance to play on an integrated organized baseball team. He received just such an opportunity in 1884 by signing on with the Stillwater (MN) club in the Northwestern League, and he spent much of the following decade doing so until a racial color line was unequivocally established in the mid–1890s.

1879–1883 — In Search of a Team: Bud Fowler on the Road

After bursting on the baseball scene in rather sudden and successful fashion in 1878, Bud Fowler spent the next five years wandering in the wilderness of the amateur game, black baseball, and the lowest rungs of professional and semi-professional baseball. In 1879, Fowler continued to play baseball in Massachusetts, first with the semi-pro Malden club of the Eastern Massachusetts League. Little is known about this team, but the following note suggests that it was successful: "The General Worths and Maldens will play the first in a series of five games for $100 and the championship of Middlesex County, at Malden to-day."[30] Later in the season, Fowler surfaced with teams in South Adams and Pittsfield in the western section of the state, near the New York border. As for the following year, no record has yet been discovered of the young African American ballist's involvement, if any, with baseball.

In 1881, Bud Fowler headed north to Ontario to play baseball. The Guelph Maple Leafs had a long and storied history on the diamond prior to the African American's arrival. From 1869 to 1872, Guelph was the three-time "Silver Ball" winners as Canadian semi-pro champions; in 1874, the Maple Leafs became the first Canadian team to win the "non-professional" semi-pro championship in Watertown (NY), beating on the way to the championship a Ku Klux Klan entry from Oneida (NY). The local reporters had a field day employing hyperbolic language that was typical of the colorful, pun-filled, and overheated description and analysis of important baseball games in the 1870s:

> At an early hour crowds began leaving for the grounds [in Watertown, NY] in every class of vehicle available, except wheelbarrows and velocipedes, and the result was an immense crowd on the *qui vive* to witness the games to be played between the first-class clubs billed for the occasion. The lamps didn't shine, but the sun did over crowds of "fair women and brave men," bound to witness the contest between the Maple Leafs of Guelph and the Ku Klux of Oneida Castle, who, though unique as Ku Klux, yet are not Uniques [a quality baseball club of the era]. The Ku Klux won the toss, the Maple Leafs going to the bat at 10 o'clock precisely. The first inning started off in a business-like manner, giving some indication that a decent game was to be played, the whitewash being freely used on both sides, the score 0. The second inning again coated the Maple verdure with the whitening fluid, and also shed it copiously upon the Ku Klux. In the third inning the Leafs opened with a score of seven runs, the Ku Klux muffing badly. Our friends of the Dominion are a fine looking body of athletes, and play as though they meant it; the last half of the inning again totaling a cypher for the three K's, who worked hard, but without avail so far. The fourth inning [blanked] the Leafs and introduced the odiferous animal again to the

bearers of the Southern patronymic. Score 7 to 0, the Maple foliage still waving in the advance...."[31]

In the same column on this game, the author stretched for another synonym for whitewash —"kalsomining fluid"— and even employed alliteration in discussing the 13 to 4 Guelph victory: "Ku Klux Klan of the Kastle koming karefully...."[32]

During the same year, Guelph became the first Canadian team to import players from the United States. They were not paid a salary, but they did share in the team's revenues.[33]

By 1881, Guelph (and baseball in general in Canada) had fallen on hard economic times and suffered from a lack of a centralized organization. In July, Guelph owner George Sleeman pursued the young African American hurler Bud Fowler to pitch for Maple Leafs. However, his tenure was over before it began: "When he [Fowler] reached Guelph and the members of the club found he was a coloured youth, they snobbishly refused to play with him."[34] As for the racism Fowler experienced from his Guelph teammates, the consensus Canadian view is that the imported players from the United States evidenced their displeasure with having an African American on the club, perhaps fearing his talents might make them expendable. Bud Fowler was released to play a few games with another Ontario team, the Petrolia Imperials. However, the Petrolia club's response to the African American newcomer was unequivocally established after the first game Fowler pitched — his teammates committed 19 errors in his support. In addition, the Canadian press routinely employed racially offensive and demeaning diction to refer to visiting black players, such as "coloured mascot," "maroon," "sable" [skinned], and "coon."[35]

The local press and fans were not pleased with the turn of events and voiced their displeasure: "Fowler has forgotten more baseball than the present team [Guelph] ever knew."[36] At the end of the season, the influential *New York Clipper Annual* mentioned the historic importance of Fowler's play with Guelph and [Fleetwood] Walker's for the Cleveland Whites.[37]

The following year, Bud Fowler played for the all-black Pickwick club in New Orleans. Originally from Mobile (AL), the Pickwicks were a white, wealthy, exclusive, and secret social club that was founded to celebrate New Year's Day. It was quite typical in the 1860s and 1870s for black employees who organized baseball teams to take the name of their employers' elite club. As early as 1881, the team joined with Petna,

Dumont, and Dotson to form a New Orleans City Colored Amateur Baseball League.[38]

The New Orleans Pickwicks played a significant role in easing racial relations in integrated baseball. They played inter-racial baseball matches until 1888. The club even held a benefit game between two African American teams for white sportsman William B. Tracy, a founder of the Lone Star Baseball Club, which was one of the first clubs to schedule black competition.[39]

In 1882, Fowler was also the player-manager of the Richmond Black Swans, an all-black team founded the previous year.[40] At the pinnacle of baseball fever in the country in 1881, the Swans played the Douglas club, the self-proclaimed champions of Washington D.C., at Richmond Base Ball park at the head of Clay Street.[41] The following year the Peabody club, the Baltimore champions, visited Richmond and defeated the local club and "a negro base-ball club" that was in all probability the Swans. The "rough" men of the Peabody club beat up a Richmond club member so badly that the ringleader of the mugging was fined $10 and given a ten-day jail sentence, while four other members of the Baltimore club were fined $5 each.[42]

Bud Fowler was a key player for the Swans and is prominently mentioned in an 1883 report on Richmond's road trip to the nation's capital and Baltimore: "Richmond, Va., April 22 — The Swans base Ball club of Richmond will leave for Washington in a few days. The club is composed of colored men, all excellent players. Fowler, of Boston, who is said to be the champion colored player of the United States, and Moses Lewis, a well-known colored player of Boston, will join the Swans at either Washington or Baltimore."[43] The Swans' road trip featured a close win over a college nine in D.C., 9–6,[44] and a drubbing by the Washington Manhattans, 20–5.[45] Well-funded by the black social club of the same name, the Manhattans frequently vied with the Orion club of Philadelphia for recognition among the east coast African American baseball teams of the early 1880s.

After his brief sojourn in the South, Bud Fowler played on all-black independent teams the following year and was part of an unsuccessful attempt at organizing a national black baseball league. Having moved to St. Louis in the winter of 1883, he and local politician Henry Bridgewater worked together to organize the proposed league. Fowler also signed with and trained the St. Louis Black Sox before leaving the city in mid–May. In fact, Bridgewater's hiring of the African American player was a central element in establishing the credibility of the magnate's baseball bona fides: "[Bridgewater] has secured a team of the very best players to be found amongst the local colored clubs, and will have a notability in the person of Fowler, the famous colored pitcher from New Orleans, who has been playing in the Colored League games, and is a most [talented] man in the position, he having also pitched for several white nines in Canada."[46] Later in the year, Fowler played with distinction for the independent Niles (OH) Grays.[47]

While Bud Fowler was struggling to find a club to play for in the early 1880s, baseball was continuing to expand and grow in popularity. In fact, baseball reigned supreme in the 1880s. Everyone in America was playing, attending, reading or talking about the national pastime. The combination of athletic and strategic skills and its American lineage remained key elements in the game's popularity. The reformers "enshrined the values of skillful competitive struggle for victory as the dominant ethos of organized baseball"[48]; however, they did not eliminate the traditionalists who played for the love of the game.

Women in ever-expanding numbers played the game in the 1880s, especially at women's colleges in the northeast. Whenever female teams played the game, their attempts were treated light-heartedly by the sporting press and described in a patronizing, quasi-comic, stereotypical tone and language. One such contest pitted teams of blondes and brunettes who were chosen from a pool of 900 applicants. The women's uniforms, appearance, and backgrounds (variety actresses and ballet dancers were barred from participation) were mentioned in agonizing detail, as were the women's inept physical and strategic skills. The women were all praised as intelligent and prepared ("They [the women] all knew the rules of the game") but were perceived to be overmatched by the physical demands of the game ("their bruises increased" and "they were evidently sighing for the end of the season"). This "burlesque of base-ball" drew 1,500 fans to the Manhattan Athletic Club's grounds with the unexpected statement that such fun and games would occur again the next day:

> When five innings had been played and the back hair and the brains of the girls appeared to be in a hopelessly demoralized condition, with a tendency on the part of their hose to follow suit, the game was called. The girls heaved long sighs of relief, started for the dressing rooms, and like an unsubstantial pageant faded, left not a pin behind. The score was

54 to 22 in five innings in favor of the brunettes. They play again tomorrow.[49]

The late 19th century's love of the odd and bizarre was also played out on the ball fields of the era. There were games arranged pitting the fats versus thins, the Russians versus the Turks, the doctors versus the dentists (who then would tackle the druggists), and the one-armed versus the one-legged. Fans would also gather at local games to hoot and holler at the expense of "muffins," players who either did not know how to play the game or were especially inept. Such games frequently were employed as fund-raisers to aid charitable causes, support striking workers, or encourage women to attend games. One such representative game promoted the theme of fun at the ballpark:

> Boss Base-Ball by Butcher Boys — One of the most exciting games of base ball yet seen will take place at Richmond park this evening. The contestants will be select nines from among the butchers of the First and Second markets. Many of these have not used a bat for years, and the force of a ball has not been felt by some since the days of boyhood, when the old-fashioned games of "cat" and "chumbley" caused them to untie their legs and send before the wind.
>
> There will be a crowd to witness this sudden ebullition of interest in base-ball and what with arkwardness [sic] and earnestness they will be sure to evince, a rich time may be expected. The catching and batting, the falling down and pitching forward, may not be up to the rules laid down by the regulations adopted by the National Base-Ball Club, but there will be enough dash and accidental occurrences to supply all deficiencies. The proceeds of the game will be given for the purpose of supplying the grounds with a pavilion wherein the ladies can be more comfortably accommodated as lookers-on. The game commences at 4 o'clock P.M. Come out and see the butchers on a base-ball bender.[50]

With the advent of professional baseball as a mainstream leisure activity having blossomed into an insatiable demand for the national pastime in any form, the entertainment value and sheer zaniness of the pairings were seminal elements of many matches. Philadelphia, an early hotbed of baseball in its infancy, played host to many such unconventional matches:

> Novelty games were particularly prominent in Philadelphia; ethnic teams, "colored" male and female ball teams, Native-American nines, crippled clubs, and so on. John Lang, a white barber from Philadelphia who had "temporarily deserted lather and razor" to organize pioneer

black baseball clubs such as Orion, found his true métier in New York with his Chinese teams. In Chester, Pennsylvania, Lang also created a fetching nine of "colored girl" professional players.... Of the players of the Snorkey Club of Philadelphia (named for the one-armed hero of the drama *Under the Gaslight*), one had an arm off at the shoulder, another had a paralyzed arm, the rest were minus a hand; their opponents in a game on May 23, 1883, were the Hoppers, who were all one-legged or on crutches. In a reminder to the readers of the brutalities of the industrial age in America, both sides were said to consist wholly of former employees of the Pennsylvania Railroad.[51]

Finally, in this politically incorrect age, a group of ex–Confederates in Pulaski (TN) created a baseball team at the local chapter of the Ku Klux Klan and boasted of their desire to take on all comers. In a like manner, there was an explosion of the sport's popularity in the fall and winter months with the playing of parlor games, songs, polkas, and even, in this time before ice hockey and basketball were established, baseball on ice skates during the Hot Stove League period.[52] Baseball games were played on roller skates and indoors; even the seeds of fantasy baseball were sown in the 1880s with Thomas Lawson's "Base Ball with Cards" Tournament.[53] In the off-season, baseballplayers who were diamond stars or good copy were lionized in the sporting press and often performed in vaudeville skits at community music halls and opera houses to supplement their incomes and to trade on their popularity.

In the 1880s, baseball became firmly engrained in American popular culture as a mania for the game took hold of the country. To further this obsession with baseball, the advent of tabloid journalism with its focus on those juicy aspects of universal interest to the American public—sex, crime, and sports—underscored newspapers' major role in fanning nationwide interest in the game. The baseball crank, the devoted supporter of the local nine, became a recognizable figure in the culture.

In 1888, Thomas Lawson also wrote a small satirical text that was the first work devoted to the baseball fan. A businessman of the first order and a copper baron who partnered with, among others, John D. Rockefeller, Lawson wrote *The Krank: His Language and What It Means*, in which he describes in a somewhat tongue-in-cheek manner a typical fan's day at the ballpark and provides a detailed and humorous glossary of terms and phrases employed by the krank. (Five years earlier, Lawson had created a baseball table game of 32 cards that "directed players what to do next."[54])

Baseball was so ubiquitous in the era that many humorous newspaper articles purported to provide the uninitiated with a "new" set of baseball terms: "a good catch" = "one of the Rothschild girls"; "a base hit" = "a blow below the belt"; "the right field" = "the field of duty"; "put out on first" = "the man who gets April fooled"; "never reaches his second" = "the man who refuses to fight a duel"; "the champion pitcher" = "the pitcher that goes to the fountain and remains broken."[55] Bottom-of-page anecdotes based on jokey (and hokey) puns littered the pages of local newspapers: "Some boys undertook to play base ball in a field where a ram was feeding recently. He butted the short-stop through a picket fence, and forced all the rest to make a home run. The boy who was butted through the fence was the only one who scored, and he carried his score with him."[56] Even the Bard could not escape the baseball fever of the day, as is evidenced in the following list of "baseball" references in Shakespeare:

Shakespeare as a Player (of Ball)

Old Bill evidently played baseball occasionally. At least he knew all about it, if the following quotations be accepted:
Now let's have a catch — *Merry Wives.*
And so I shall catch the fly. — *Henry V.*
I will run no base. — *Merry Wives.*
After he scores. — *All's Well.*
Have you scored me? — *Othello.*
The world is pitch and pay. — *Henry V.*
These nine men in buckram. — *Henry IV.*
What works my countrymen?/Where go you with hats and clubs? — *Coriolanus.*
Let us see you in the field — *Trolius and Cressida.*
I will fear to catch — *Timon.*
More like to run the country base — *Cymbeline.*[57]

The decade also saw refinements of Frances C. Sebring's "Parlor Base-Ball Field," which had first been sold in 1866. This game was spring-actioned with the pitcher hurling a coin to a batter who swung. Outs were recorded when the coin was swallowed by holes in the board, while hits were made by avoiding the holes and landing on base hits marked on the game board. This particular game evolved into the more sophisticated versions found in the penny arcades of the early 20th century.[58]

Baseball in this era, however, did not offer equal opportunities for all Americans. Close proximity with such "different" groups such as immigrants and African-Americans caused traditionalists to feel threatened, especially in light of the very turbulent economy of the decade. The "other" became not an object of curiosity but one of fear. Such attitudes were the mindset of a people very uneasy with the rapid social and cultural changes that were redefining what it meant to be an American.[59] A period of social confusion resulted in the ascendancy of a Jim Crow mindset and, soon to follow, segregationist practices.

Bud Fowler's opportunity to play integrated baseball and to become an elder statesman among African American ballplayers was not only a matter of talent, perseverance, and character. It was also a matter of timing. With the color line not yet firmly drawn, he was given openings into organized baseball, and he took advantage of them.

In the 1880s, the segregationists of the baseball world took the first clear steps that ultimately led to near total victory over the integrationists by the middle of the next decade. Increased player complaints and threats of work stoppages combined with newspaper reporting that was insensitive, crude, and inflammatory to create a hostile environment that culminated in the elimination of African American players from club rosters. These developments, coupled with the absolutely undeniable success of blacks on the diamond when playing with and against white players, fueled racial thinking that contributed to the establishment of the color line in baseball.[60]

The question remains why no owner or general manager balked at the color line for the near half century that saw no African Americans in organized baseball. The answer may lie in the monopoly created and enjoyed by the major leagues. The most likely reasons for the exclusion of blacks from the national game were either that a small coterie of influential financial Brahmins didn't care to alter a successful enterprise to accommodate talented minority ballplayers or that the white public simply didn't care enough about the issue of racial equality to lobby for changes in the basic structure of the national pastime.[61] Until the creation of the Negro National League in 1920, African American ballplayers were acknowledged for their abilities on the field and even, at times, for their strategic and administrative skills, but they were marginalized by limiting their contact with white ballplayers to off-season barnstorming exhibitions.

The control of the major league owners over all of organized baseball ensured that baseball executives would never have to directly vote to exclude blacks from the major leagues, yet could still keep the color line intact. As Brian McKenna observes, "Like today, the road to the majors went through the minors. If African Americans were not permitted in the minors, how could they make the senior circuit?"⁶² The treatment of African Americans on the baseball diamond in the 19th century was a classic example of the creation of a second-class citizenry based on racial bias:

> Blacks were consigned to an inferior caste, treated the same in some superficial respects but rebuffed them whenever they asserted their equality. Baseball was as good an example of that institutionalized discrimination as existed in America. From the major league teams in the country's great cities to the marginal clubs in the small towns of the low minors, no one wanted black players.⁶³

1884 — Minnesota

As the sport continued to expand in the midwest in the mid–1880s, Bud Fowler headed to Minnesota to participate in integrated organized baseball for the first time since his brief appearance in the International Association five years earlier. The African American played for Stillwater in the second year of the Northwestern League, which was comprised of 14 teams from Indiana, Michigan, Wisconsin, Illinois, and Minnesota.⁶⁴ The increased demand for talented baseballists led to recruiting throughout the baseball world and black players were hired in this pre–Jim Crow year, especially in places such as Stillwater, which was on a major rail line and which had the smallest population base — 15,000 — in the league.⁶⁵ The Stillwater chief operating officer Chris Gregory signed Fowler among other easterners with proven track records on the baseball diamond. Hiring an African American player, even one of Fowler's talent level, was a risky social and financial maneuver that was done in order to put a competitive team on the field.⁶⁶

The need for talented ballplayers was aided by the rapid expansion of baseball on the major league level in the 1880s, a development that bled the minors dry of decent ballplayers. The 1880s saw the rise of a second major league to rival the National League (NL) (founded in 1876). The American Association (AA)⁶⁷ was formed to challenge the supremacy of the stodgier National League, which catered to the middle-class fan. While the AA agreed to honor the NL's contracts, it targeted the working-class spectator, who preferred and enjoyed a more high-spirited entertainment. The AA reduced the standard ticket price from 50 to 25 cents and served alcohol at its games. Beginning in 1884 and continuing for seven consecutive years, both professional leagues met in a final championship series with the NL winning four times. As economic pressures mounted, the AA was dealt a fatal blow with the appearance in 1890 of a third professional circuit, the Players' League. As a result, player salaries rose and instability in the baseball marketplace was such that both the Players' League (1890) and the American Association (1891) disbanded, leaving the field to the better financed and organized National League.

The American Association, however, had a lasting legacy on two major aspects of the future of professional baseball. Four AA teams that moved to the NL — the Dodgers, Pirates, Cardinals, and Reds — still have franchises in today's National League; on the other hand, only two charter members of the NL from 1876 — the Cubs and Braves — still have teams in the senior circuit. A much-less recognized historically important decision by the AA was to allow African Americans to play on integrated teams as early as 1884, over 60 years before the appearance of Jackie Robinson. Finally, the demise of its professional competitors allowed the tightly controlled, more buttoned-down National League to expand the 1883 reserve clause to the entire roster, thus restricting player salaries and movement.[68] Ownership had free financial rein until the Dave McNally and Andy Messersmith arbitrator decision in 1975 effectively ended the reserve clause and opened the door to player free agency.

Bud Fowler became an invaluable member of the Stillwater nine. He was a versatile player, manning all eight fielding positions during the year and taking his turn on the mound. However, Stillwater got off to a horrendous start that included a 4–0 shutout on the road to the Northwestern League leaders Bay City (MI) on May 16.[69] Ten days later, a Minnesota newspaper characterized two league franchises — Bay City and Grand Rapids — as strong and five others — Quincy, Saginaw, Milwaukee, Minneapolis, and St. Paul — as improving. The same newspaper offered the downtrodden Stillwater team some harsh advice: "Stillwater still insists on guarding the rear and moreover continues to play steadily just far enough behind to lose every game having a record of 16 lost and none to its credit, having appeared in all its games scheduled to date. Nor do we expect to see this record materially broken for the present. The club must have a change in several positions before it can even hope to successfully compete with even the weakest of the league's teams."[70]

There was one bright spot in the team's disastrous 0–16 start — all of the games had been played on the road due to Minnesota's late spring. Finally, Bud Fowler broke into the Stillwater starting lineup as a hurler and was responsible for five of his team's six consecutive wins in an early season turn-around beginning in mid–May. His 7–5 victory over Fort Wayne on May 24 was so well received by the Stillwater management that he received $10 and a new suit of clothes as a gift for his fine play.[71]

When Stillwater opened its home season on June 9, its record stood at 6–20. The locals lost, 3–2, to Minneapolis whose pitcher beat his African American counterpart by allowing only three hits and striking out 17 batters. Throughout the month, Fowler played at a high level and was a versatile player for the beleaguered Stillwaters. During a 12–8 road loss to St. Paul on June 13, he gave up no earned runs and a wild pitch before switching to third base in the fourth inning due to an injury to the starting catcher that necessitated a number of player position shifts. He fielded the hot corner flawlessly for the rest of the game and was in the midst of his team's scoring action, going 3–for–4 with a triple and three runs scored and a "splendid [rbi] hit in the fourth." The African American's team, however, continued to struggle: "There has been another Waterloo as far as the Stillwater Base Ball club is concerned. They cannot get down further. They had better to sleep for a while."[72] The sports reporter further noted that league weak sisters Minneapolis and St. Paul each had beaten the Stillwater nine two out of three games during the week.

A week later in an 8–2 home loss to Quincy, Fowler had another fine day at the plate, going 2–for–4 with a run scored and also contributing in the field with eight putouts, three assists, and no errors. However, there are suggestions in both the game analysis and the box score that the African American's versatility may have affected his throwing accuracy and had a direct influence on his switch to second base for most of the rest of his career. A heavy rain had made the Stillwater field very soggy prior to the game. After enduring a heavy pitching load over the previous month, Fowler played both right field and third base, both positions where a strong arm is also a basic requirement. Then he replaced his team's injured catcher, a move which would further tax his arm. The local reporter pointed out Fowler's very uncharacteristic four passed balls, attributing his uneven play in part to his playing directly behind the batter: "Fowler had a hard day of it, but kept close behind the bat ready all the time, and it was no wonder he had several passed balls."[73] It seems likely that Fowler suffered some minor injury to his throwing arm that affected his accuracy on long throws and limited his future pitching appearances to rare emergency relief ones.

Fowler got a measure of revenge in early July, when as a catcher and right fielder, he had two of his season's ten doubles in a victory at Minneapolis.[74] However, the honeymoon between the local media and the African American import appeared to be over, as his play became spotty and it became clear that he was not the savior who could single-handedly transform Stillwater into a winning ball club. In a July 4 home loss to Muskegon with nearly 1,000 fans in attendance, Fowler caught and batted second, going 1-for-5. However, it was his play behind the plate that drew criticism from the game observers. In describing the Stillwater battery of McCue and Fowler, both players, especially the latter, were called to task for some uninspired and lackadaisical play:

> The pitching was not as effective as Quinn on the previous day, nor was the catching of Fowler anything equal to that of Dealy. The errors on both sides were about equal, but the passed balls by Fowler either advanced bases or let runs home.
> Fowler got hot balls enough from McCue, and they appeared to daze him. Although he is an excellent and rapid thrower, it looked as if it were hard work for him to throw from the plate to Peters at second base.[75]

Since Fowler was a rival for McCue's position as Stillwater chief pitcher, he may have been crossed up by McCue throwing what he wanted rather than what his African American battery mate signaled so as to undercut the latter's value to the team. Such selfish (and racial) behavior was a characteristic of the Stillwater club and played itself out more openly at the end of the season.

On the following day in a 4–3 home loss to Muskegon, Fowler had been dropped to eighth in the batting order and was playing left field. His failure to deliver at the plate in three of four opportunities to advance runners and drive in runs was duly noted as typical Stillwater baseball, while the influence of new manager Johnny Peters was being praised as a hopeful sign: "Today they [Stillwater] were not overmatched and should have won. The way the men back each other up shows that they are profiting already by Peters' instructions. The attendance was good.... Again three of the times that Fowler went to bat men were on bases, but he was unable to advance them a peg, his strikes being directly into the hands of the fielders."[76]

On July 14, Fowler's wing must have felt good enough for him to make a long relief appearance, entering in the third inning of a 6–3 home loss to Bay City. Giving up two walks, three wild pitches but no earned runs, Fowler's work was summed up as follows: "Fowler pitched somewhat wild, but his balls were hard to hit."[77] Despite a brief streak of 4 wins in 5 games at the end of July that still left the club in tenth place, the Stillwater fans became upset by the losing ways of the home team and the league's numerous franchise replacements stayed away from the local games in droves.[78]

Stillwater continued its mediocre play and its descent in the league standings, never rising higher in the standings than tenth place. The local fans became so disenchanted that team management began playing games at Great Bear Lake, but the downward spiral continued. Team morale and stability were further damaged by three managerial changes in less than six weeks. The owners underwent financial losses, and, as a result, players began to come and go.

The Stillwater Base Ball Club officially disbanded on August 4, 1884. A poem that appeared in several Minnesota newspapers in early July of 1884 could serve as a fitting epitaph for the Northwestern League's misguided attempt to place a club in such a small town that suffered from poor weather, a lack of financial resources, and no discernible baseball tradition:

> Our left fielder is sick and our catcher is lame;
> Our shortstop is playing a very poor game;
> Two pitchers are used up, the other is wild;
> The baseman can't play when the weather ain't mild;
> The man in the right field is suffering from chills;
> Our captain has a strange combination of ills;
> Just what bothers our manager the D___l can't tell;
> But in other respects we are feeling quite well.[79]

The Northwestern League folded after its final game on September 17. Bud Fowler did some barbering in the area until Manager Johnny Peters helped him get a contract with Keokuk of the Western League for the following year.[80] Fowler also earned high praise from the newspapers throughout the midwest. "The Stillwater club has a colored player named Fowler who pitches, catches, and plays left field in good shape," observed the *Cleveland Herald*. The *Milwaukee Sentinel* added: "Fowler, the colored player, made one of the finest running fly-catches ever seen on the grounds, and was compelled to doff his cap several times to the enthusiastic plaudits of his many admirers."[81]

However, 1884 was not an unqualified success for Bud Fowler. He was spiked at home plate by a sliding white player, was knocked unconscious and missed three games due to a pitch that hit him in the ribs, and was fined 50 dollars and suspended for two weeks (reduced to two days due to team injuries) for refusing to catch newly signed pitcher Bradley, who, it was reported, would not take signals from a colored man.[82] (The difficulty between Fowler and Bradley may have been more than racially motivated. Bradley was replacing Fowler as the team's #1 hurler and there may have been distrust on both players' parts about how committed each was to the team.)

Eighteen eighty-four was the first year that the African American had played a significant number of games (48) in organized baseball. Fowler had a productive season, hitting .302 with 57 hits in 48 games, while also leading his team in runs scored, doubles, and slugging percentage. He posted a 7–8 pitching record (on a team that ended with a winning percentage under .400) despite suffering a mid-season sore arm.[83] As there were no restriction on pitching in 1884, overhand throws became the dominant mode of pitching. This major change may have led to Fowler's arm troubles or, as he was always known for his speed and wildness, he may have been hampered by an inability to master the new style.

1885 — Iowa

Eighteen eighty-five was a truly nomadic year for Bud Fowler as he traveled the country looking for a place to play. He began in Keokuk, where businessman Nick Curtis had signed Fowler in the off-season, at least, in part because of his potential as a gate attraction. Keokuk only had 11,000 inhabitants and needed 800 fans a game to break even financially. However, it also had an 11 percent African American population, rather high for an Iowa town in the late 19th century.

Bud Fowler (back row, middle) with the Keokuk (Iowa) club in 1885. Fowler was 27 years old and in his second of the seven consecutive years he spent in minor league integrated organized baseball (National Baseball Hall of Fame Library, Cooperstown, New York).

The team, known simply as the Keokuks, began the season with energy and enthusiasm. They played their games in Rand Park which was established just two years prior. On Sundays Keokuk had an ordinance against ballplaying, so the players and fans would take a boat across the river to a field in Crystal Glen, Illinois. The team uniforms were both patriotic and colorful: gold shirts, blue pants, red and blue stockings, and red, white, and blue caps.[84]

Keokuk, however, began the 1885 season not as a full-fledged member of the Western League but as an "alliance" team, which meant that league clubs would play 30 games at the Keokuks' home park. The Iowa team was at first denied entrance to the league because the other teams — Cleveland, Indianapolis, Kansas City, Milwaukee, Omaha, and Toledo — were from large metropolitan areas with much larger fan bases. Inclement weather brought economic hardship to the Keokuk owners and soon the team's finances were in disarray. Never a shrinking violet and clearly a rising talent, Bud Fowler actually went on strike over unpaid salary for a few days.[85] Always an advocate for players' rights, Fowler joked about how the reserve clause favored ownership: "When a player signs a league contract they [management] can do anything with him under its provisions but hang him."[86]

In late May, the Omaha Omahogs folded and the Keokuk franchise was invited to enter the Western League. The timing was opportune as the Keokuks were in the midst of a 13-game winning streak with an overall record of 29–8. Receiving national and local accolades, Bud Fowler was the most popular player on the team and duly noted for his superb play, including six innings of one-hit, no-run ball in his only pitching appearance. He also earned praise for his strong work ethic and his proper conduct; one observer described him as "...a good ballplayer, a hard worker, a genius on the ball field, intelligent, gentlemanly in his conduct and deserving of the good opinion entertained for him by base ball admirers here."[87] The respected *Sporting Life* noted that the African American ballplayer was having a superb season: "Those in the know say that there is no better second baseman in the country."[88] As if to prove this observation, Bud Fowler had an unassisted double play as a second baseman at Milwaukee soon after his team's acceptance as a full-fledged member of the league.

Fowler's reputation established during his brief tenure in Iowa has lasted into the 21st century as is evidenced by his cameo appearance in Marilynne Robinson's Pulitzer Prize–winning novel *Gilead*: "Once my grandfather took me to Des Moines on the train to see Bud Fowler play. He was with Keokuk for a season or two. The old man fixed me with that eye of his and told me that there was not a man on this round earth who could out-run or out-throw Bud Fowler. I was pretty excited."[89]

However, financial problems continued to plague the league and by late June only Milwaukee and Keokuk were financially solvent. The team officially disbanded on July 7, 1885, by which time Bud Fowler had already secured a position with Pueblo of the Colorado State League.[90]

Reports state that he was offered positions by the Philadelphia Orion — "Fowler the crack colored player is wanted to manage and play with the Orion (colored) club of Philadelphia, but is yet undecided as to what he will do"[91] and Milwaukee, both of which he apparently never took; he did play a few games for St. Joseph (MO) Reds, signing with the club in late August,[92] and then played for Portland (ME) of the Eastern

New England League.[93] Bud Fowler must have been burning up the railroad tracks in the summer of 1885 because in early August he was living in St. Louis and looking for a position on the diamond and working as a barber: "John W. Fowler, the noted color player, late of the Northwestern and Western League clubs, is in St. Louis without an engagement."[94]

Colorado

In August of 1885, Bud played only five games for the Pueblo Pastimes in the Colorado League, a league that consisted of the mineral resource towns of Denver (gold), Pueblo (coal), and Leadville (silver and lead) that were linked by the railroads. In spite of favorable press from The Rocky Mountain News (Denver)—[Fowler is a] "crack ballplayer ... [who is] an excellent runner ... and is popular with his team"—he was released due to reported racial tensions initiated by his teammates.[95]

Fowler's quick departure from the Pastimes may also have been connected to his play and to other less stressful opportunities that were open to the African American player. He pitched complete game losses in two of the games he played for Pueblo that month and was never the same effective and often dominant hurler after pitching regulations allowed any type of delivery the previous year. There is also some speculation that Fowler spent time with the Pueblo Blues, Colorado's first semipro all-black baseball club, also organized in 1885. Finally, the Pastimes were clearly a contentious group. In late August, the team refused to extend the pennant series and was boycotted by the other league members Denver and Leadville which, in essence, forced the Pueblo team to disband. In the same newspaper account, the reporter noted that John W. Fowler had opened a barber shop in Pueblo.[96]

We know Fowler was looking for employment that winter from an advertisement he placed in *The Sporting News*: "John W. Fowler, the famed colored second baseman, is now traveling through the Northwest giving walking exhibitions against skaters and running exhibitions. He is said to have walked a mile in 8m 30s, and to have run a mile in 4m 50s. He can be addressed in care of *Western Sport*, Denver, Col."[97] Fowler kept busy in Denver that winter by barnstorming, participating in a few running exhibitions, and operating a barber shop.[98] Bud Fowler was offered the position of captain of the Cuban Giants during their 1885 tour of Cuba.[99]

A mid-season comment about Fowler's overall baseball skills should not be forgotten in the maze of his 1885 travel and rotating in pursuit of a game: "He [Fowler] is one of the best general players in the country, and if he had a white face would be playing with the best of them."[100]

1886 — Kansas

Bouncing back from his worst year at the bat in his long career in baseball (.222), Bud Fowler in 1886 played up to his usual stellar standards for the Topeka (KS) Capitals of the Western League, a circuit composed of significant railroad towns with long baseball histories — Lincoln (NE), Leavenworth (KS), Leadville (CO), St. Joseph (MO), and Denver (CO), along with the Kansas capital.[101] Baseball in the west was a source of extreme civic pride as is evidenced in a newspaper sparring session between two major Kansas dailies: the *Topeka Daily Democrat* argued that "when it comes to trying to outrank Topeka, all the inflation, blow and puff of the [*Wichita Daily*] *Eagle* looks childish and silly. Yes, there is no doubt about it, Wichita is jealous, because she has no league base ball club."[102]

It was reported in the national sporting press that in the off-season that the wily veteran had signed with Guelph (Ontario), a city he had played in earlier in his career and where he had experienced racial hostility from his own teammates. However, Fowler never reported to the team but instead joined a few ex–Pueblo teammates in Kansas.[103] Fowler played the entire season in Topeka and had another productive season. He played in 58 games, had 77 hits, batted .309 (11th in the league), and led the league in triples with 12. His slugging percentage was boosted by his 16 doubles and three home runs. His 12 steals for Topeka signaled a new emphasis for the African American speedster, who became a prolific base stealer in future years.[104]

Fowler was at the center of the action while at Topeka. In July, he led his club into the Mile High City with his team playing its best ball of the season, having won 11 of the last 12 games. Unfortunately, Topeka "ran into a brick wall when they struck the Denver Club. The home team outplayed them in every particular." They lost a four-game series to the league leaders by an aggregate score of 54 to 25. Topeka committed a breathtaking 66 errors in the series, including 25 in a 12–9 loss. In that same game, Al Bauer, the new Topeka southpaw who had been picked up from the Black Diamonds, added to the traffic on the base paths with seven bases on balls, several hit batsmen, and a wild pitch. Fowler added to the fun with a home run and a double. On July 11, Denver defeated Topeka by a score of 14–7 with "both sides playing poorly" and both teams "slugging the ball hard." The veteran African American was back at his customary position at the keystone sack after a few games in right field and contributed a triple. Fowler had eight hits and six runs scored in the sweep but committed nine errors.

In a four-game series at home in August against St. Joseph (MO), Fowler's Topeka club won a laugher (11–4) and lost two two-run games and one three-run contest. Fowler kept up his slugging with eight hits in the four games, including one four-hit game (all singles), a double, and two triples. Furthermore, Fowler apparently had settled in on defense with only two errors in the four-game series. He and his fellow infielders were singled out for their play in the field: "'The Little 4' of Sullivan, Fowler, Butler, and Bill Miles work together tip top..."[105]

Nevertheless, at the end of the season, Fowler and most of his teammates were without a position for the next year. New management had been brought in after the lackluster 1886 season: "W.H. Goldsby, the new manager of the Topeka League Club, arrived here from Evansville, and will at once begin the work of organizing the new team. Jake Kenyon, Topeka's catcher of last year, has already been engaged and will catch for the team this year. Kenyon is the only member of last year's Topeka team who will play here next season."[106]

After the season, Fowler returned to St. Louis to play for a black team. He also pitched for the New Orleans Unions in a series against the New Orleans Cohens for local supremacy in black baseball. The Unions were a charter member of 1886's first black minor league, the Southern League of Colored Base Ballists (SLCBB). However, it was the Cohens who were the dominant team in the Big Easy, having beaten the Memphis Eclipse, the strongest club in the SLCBB. The Memphis pitcher was a superstar of that 1886 season, with the *Memphis Appeal* reporting that: "Renfroe, their crack pitcher, has won every game he's pitched but one, averaging 12 strikeouts a game for nine. In his first game against Chattanooga he struck out the first nine men who came to bat. He has great speed and a very deceptive down-shoot.[107] On the recommendation of Fowler, Renfroe joined him in signing with Binghamton of the International Association for the 1887 season.

Four

The Color Line Emerges (1887–1889)

1887 — New York

The 1887 season found Bud Fowler back in the east playing for the International Association's Binghamton Bingos (the Binghamton franchise was also referred to as the "Crickets" which was a long-term designation). In 34 games for Binghamton, he hit for the highest average of his career (.350 with 55 hits, including 12 doubles, 42 runs scored, and 30 steals) against some of the toughest competition in the minor leagues. However, racial tension was becoming more common and open. On June 27 in Binghamton, Milt West and William E. Dillworth asked for and received their releases, refusing to play with African Americans Fowler and William Renfroe. Then nine more Bingo players rebelled and signed a petition that stated: "We, the undersigned members of the Binghamton Base Ball Club, hereby refuse to play ball if the colored players, who have been the cause of all our trouble, are not released at once."[1]

Prior to the 1887 International Association season, club owners had apparently been open to signing African American talent to build competitive teams. Five of the ten teams in the International Association that year had black ballplayers on their opening day rosters. Bud Fowler was eager to begin play in the International Association and wintered in Binghamton, supporting himself by working as a barber. In the 1870s, Binghamton had had a very small black population, with fewer than 1.5 percent of its inhabitants being African American. This lack of familiarity was further fueled by the baseless weekly newspaper rumors of intended black atrocities to be committed against whites.

Yet prior to the season, Bingos manager Henry J. Ormsbee had been quite positive about signing the experienced Fowler: "In selecting our men we have special attention to ball playing and deportment; and believe by the combination of good character and ball playing we have a lot of fellows that stand in both above criticism. Today I met with Fowler, the colored player, for the first time in my life, and am satisfied that he comes within our ideal."[2]

However, at the first sign of an economic downturn in revenues, the owners retreated from their pro-integration stance and declared the inclusion of African Americans a failure. Management feared the racially motivated threats of their white players and the negative response of fans and the media. Furthermore, the hostility of fellow league owners led to the demise of integrated play in the high minor leagues.[3]

During a highly successful pre-season in which the Bingos went 6–0, the seeds of racial discord on the Binghamton squad were sown. With high praise for his fielding at second base and his base running, Fowler saw his reputation grow perceptibly. However, when he made two relief pitching appearances, he "hurt the team's cohesion because the pitching was the white players' preserve in an era of partial integration ... [Fowler's pitching] aroused the jealousy and resentment of his teammates."[4]

Bud Fowler was lauded by local fans and reporters and little mention was made of his race in game reports. In fact, it appears that there was little vocal or professional animus within the league against him. Binghamton's chief geographical rival Oswego hired African American infielder Randolph Jackson on Fowler's recommendation. Equally important, Fowler won a prize offered by F.F. Billings of a life-sized portrait of a Bingo who had the highest batting average during a home stand in late May. Ten teammates hit over .300 that week, but Fowler won it by going 8 for 16 (.500): "One would hardly expect that such a gift would have been given to a despised member of the community. After all, even 'official records' could have been altered, but there seemed no reluctance in awarding the prize to Fowler." Yet even this award was tainted by the racism and insensitivity of the press, which headlined an account of the African American's winning of the prize as follows: "Fowler Gets the Award: A Life-Size Picture of the Leading Batter Won by the 'Coon.'"[5]

Bud Fowler, in fact, began the 1887 season on a tear, leading a team that would end its season 19 games under .500 to a 5–5 start. The African American International Association rookie seemed to be at the center of events, whether they were positive or negative:

> [On May 4, 1887, in a 26–8 rout over Utica,] Fowler's second inning single contributed to a 7-run outburst. On May 9, Buffalo's Mickey Walsh was the victim of a 7-hit first inning explosion. Fowler was in the middle of the rally which, reported the [Binghamton] *Daily Leader*, gave Walsh a "dose of *nux vomica*." Binghamton finished its first home stand 5–5. A trip to Oswego netted three wins in four tries, and the Bings scored 47 runs. Fowler was the starting pitcher and loser in Oswego's 12–10 win. He gave up five runs in less than two innings, causing the *Daily Leader* to remark: "Fowler has hitherto been the packhorse between a lame arm and victory. He didn't get there yesterday." Two days later, Fowler "got there." The Bings beat the 'Sweeps 8–3, with Fowler the batting star. In the fourth, "Fowler stepped to the plate, and meeting the second ball pitched fairly in the nozzle drove it over the right field fence for a four bagger."
>
> ... The Bings first June contest was a 12–11 win over the Syracuse Stars. Fowler's two-run double in the eighth provided the winning margin. For the day Fowler was 4–5, with 3 doubles, each good for "two Ottomans."[6]

June marked an ugly turn of events in which International Association African American players, some of whom were the stars of their teams, were marginalized or left unsupported by their white teammates. Pitchers Robert Higgins of Syracuse and Will Renfroe of the Bingos were victims of intentionally poor play that in one case saw Binghamton's dominant portsider lose a game in 11 innings, 7–6, in which none of the seven runs were earned. Just a few weeks earlier the two African American hurlers had met in what may have been the first time in organized baseball that two black pitchers faced one another.[7]

Disgusted by the racial turn of events in the period beginning with the threatened team mutiny in Utica on June 24, Bud Fowler apparently asked for and received his release effective June 30, with the management proviso that he not play for another International Association team that season. In a letter printed in a local newspaper on July 2, the African American star performer provided for the record a reasonable, if false, explanation for his actions:

> To the public: I take this occasion to announce that I have this date respectfully petitioned the Board of Directors of the Binghamton Base Ball Association for my release, which has been kindly granted. The reason for this step is that I received a flattering offer from the management of the Cuban Giants, which I am desirous of accepting. I wish to thank the Board of Directors for the gentlemanly treatment displayed towards

me since becoming a member of the above organization, and to state that I entertain the pleasantest regard for them. Thanking the baseball population of this city for their kind and courteous treatment of me at all times, I am respectfully, John W. Fowler.[8]

The gentlemanly resignation letter of Bud Fowler was primarily for public consumption as explanation for the club's release of its most talented player. Fowler did not join the all-black Cuban Giants and Milt West, the suspended co-instigator of the team rebellion against the African American players, was reinstated and played for the Bingos one day prior to release of the letter. So the letter may simply have been a public relations ploy to avoid any further controversy that would prove bothersome to an already shrinking fan base.[9]

Two months later, the rival *Binghamton Daily Leader* printed the actual series of events that led to Fowler's departure from the local team:

> [Director] Kattell opened the exercises by stating succinctly that the work of the team had not been satisfactory; that aside from poor playing, members of the club had been intoxicated; that others had played poker in their rooms until a late hour, and to crown all, nine members of the team had been guilty of insubordination.
>
> This last accusation had been based upon a paper, signed by three players, and forwarded to the Directors from Utica in the latter part of June, requesting the release of Fowler, the colored second baseman. This paper was followed by a telegram ... stating that the white players would refuse to go on the field unless their wishes on the matter was consulted. These matters were rehearsed [sic] to the players by Mr. Kattell, who formerly notified them for that breach of propriety a fine of $50 upon each player signing the telegram had been imposed.[10]

Such protests were not just confined to the playing field, where white players would intentionally try to maim black opponents. Players would not sit for team portraits or participate in team promotions if African Americans were involved. Productivity and ability meant little in the highly charged racial atmosphere of the times.

The local press was clearly divided in its editorial attitude toward African Americans on the baseball diamond. A *Binghamton Daily Leader* headline for July 12 read "Coons Gone — Fowler and Renfroe." Yet a few lines later Renfroe was described in generous terms: "he will return to his home in Memphis, whence he expects to join the Topekas of the Western League [where Bud Fowler toiled the previous year]. Renfroe is a gentlemanly fellow, who deserves to do well."[11]

It is quite probable that Binghamton Bingos players and ownership employed the race card to deflect attention over the team's declining attendance and poor play. When Binghamton slipped behind local rival Oswego in the league standings, there was talk in the newspapers of a public meeting to be held in mid–July to address the possibility of moving the Binghamton franchise to Allentown (PA).[12]

Racial lines hardened and gained national attention on July 14 when the celebrated Cap Anson and his Chicago White Stockings refused to play the integrated Newark Giants team, unless African American pitcher George Stovey was scratched from the starting lineup. Adrian Anson was notorious for his racism. Black baseball historian Sol White claimed that the star first baseman had prevented Stovey from signing a contract with the National League's New York Giants earlier in the year. In 1888 during Albert Spalding's world tour of baseball, Anson referred to his own employee Clarence Duval, who was a singer, dancer, and clown, in virulently racist terms.[13]

In light of Anson's position, the directors of the International Association agreed to no longer tender contracts to African Americans after the 1887 season. The American Association and National League soon followed suit.[14] However, racial segregation was not yet universal and there was much discussion and gossip during the hot stove season that the International Association would allow teams to sign one African American per team for the 1888 season. Buffalo re-signed Frank Grant, who had hit .346 to lead his club in batting for the third consecutive year. However, a major concession was made to the vicious treatment Grant received from base runners intent on injuring him when he was moved on a permanent basis to right field. Pitcher Bob Higgins had another all-star caliber year, going 20–7, before becoming so dispirited that he returned to his home in Memphis. Fleet Walker was also signed by Syracuse and won his second major championship in five years. History repeated itself on September 27, 1888, during an exhibition game in Syracuse, when Cap Anson again refused to allow African American players to take the field against his Chicago White Stockings and Walker was prevented from playing. Such racial bias had become so commonplace and such a "non-story" that this incident was not even published in the white press.[15]

Cap Anson was not the only influential baseball man to agitate for the total elimination of African American from organized baseball. Toronto manager Charlie Cushman was at the center of the maelstrom in Ontario on May 23, 1888, which featured famed black catcher Fleet Walker and Canadian fans:

> ...a Syracuse player complained about the overflow crowd seated on the edge of the playing field in Toronto. Cushman responded by peevishly insisting that everyone not wearing a uniform — including the injured Fleet Walker, who had been seated in civvies on the Stars' bench, be turfed from the playing area. Subsequently, the irate Walker got into a confrontation with some fans out beyond the stands. According to *Sporting Life*, he "flourished a loaded revolver and talked of putting a hole in someone in the crowd." Another version of the story said that Walker's threats were directed towards Cushman, and that a police detective found a pistol in his pocket. In any event, Walker's gun was impounded, and he spent the night at No. 4 police station.[16]

Within the world of baseball, then, strict segregationist attitudes began to take hold in the late 1880s after years in which the sport had encouraged (or at least tolerated) signings of African American players as gate attractions and as immediate and affordable means to improve the talent level of teams. The Anson incident in 1887 helped establish and extend the color line and hastened the banishment of all African American players from integrated teams by the end of the 19th century. The final result of the "Gentlemen's Agreement" was the total elimination of all African American ballplayers from organized baseball from 1899 until 1946, when Jackie Robinson debuted for the Montreal Royals.

Adrian "Cap" Anson occupied a unique position at the pinnacle of the baseball world in the 1880s. He was a great player — the first player to reach the 3,000 hit plateau — and master baseball strategist who had enormous success as a baseball manager with his Chicago entry, winning five National League championships in the first seven years of the decade. He was admired by baseball fans for his fierce competitiveness and his adherence to the traditions of the game. (Cap Anson was such an old school adherent of the game that he continued to play first base without a glove long after it was accepted practice to do so.) Furthermore, Anson's public persona was burnished by Chicago president and owner A.G. Spalding, an early star hurler who then established an extraordinarily successful sporting goods business and became a tireless promoter of the national pastime, even taking the game on a world tour to such locales as Australia, England, Egypt, and the Sandwich Islands. The Chicago White Stockings had become such a national institution that a single game played against a local nine could ensure a profitable season financially for that local team. Furthermore, simply taking the field against such a wildly popular championship team would increase a team's profile, serve as a valuable tool for fan development, and encourage more talented players to consider signing with that club.

Yet, for all the praise he received from an adoring press as a shining emblem of late–19th-century masculinity, Anson was a very limited man who kept grudges and guarded his reputation religiously. His antipathy toward blacks was grounded in not allowing an "inferior race" to beat him on the field of play. Such a happening would be unthinkable, so Anson never played against African American ballplayers. Anson had difficulty with other minorities and did not limit his animosity to African Americans; he held life-long grudges against the Irish-Americans who dominated the rosters of his championship teams in Chicago but flouted his authority as captain. Anson's influence and authority in baseball was so unquestioned in the 1880s that his private disparagement of blacks in derogatory and demeaning terms was never widely disseminated by the baseball world or the sporting press. It was Anson's mere refusal to acknowledge the existence of African American players that aided the social movement toward complete separation of the races.[17]

Baseball team ownership was a financially precarious endeavor in the economically depressed late 19th century. A delicate balance among disparate groups — teammates, other team owners, local businesses, potential paying customers, and the press — had to be achieved in order to ensure a profitable return on one's investment. If one of the groups had even a few objectors to the hiring of an African American ballplayer, team management listened. This economic anxiety when added to the indifference and avoidance of African Americans at the highest level of the game led to the abrupt shift in perception of the black ballplayer from potential benefit to source of conflict and financial instability. The strict enforcement of the color line in baseball was more than open hostility to African Americans; it was also built on the fear of possible conflict that might hamper gate receipts.

Vermont and New Hampshire

Bud finished the 1887 season playing for Montpelier in the New England League and Laconia in the New Hampshire League. While he played only eight games for Montpelier, he hit an astounding .429 with seven steals. Moreover, he served as co-captain of the team, the first (and only) African American to serve in that position in organized integrated baseball in the 19th century. What is surprising about the veteran's appointment to this role is how un-controversial such an action was in Vermont in the racially charged 1880s.

Furthermore, Fowler was enormously popular with the Vermonters, as reported in the August 24, 1887, edition of the *Rutland Herald*:

> Captain Fowler of the Montpeliers is a colored man and a first class ball-tosser in every respect. He played a brilliant game yesterday on second and made two of the four runs for his club.... Fowler seemed to be the favorite with the spectators and was greeted with applause every time he stepped to the plate.[18]

Bud Fowler's impact on the woeful Montpelier Capitol City club was immediate. In an August 6 home loss to St. Albans, 3–2, the veteran's running abilities were noted. However, the professionalism and energy that the African American baseballist brought to his new team was of primary importance: "The game here this afternoon between the St. Albans nine and the home team was one of the hottest games of the season and the excitement attending it was intense."[19] The following week the cellar-dwelling Montpeliers went 2–3 against Malone, St. Albans, and Burlington with Fowler continuing to be the talk of the league with his fine fielding — "Fowler, the colored second baseman, captured the crowd by his fine playing" — and especially with his team leadership — "The improvement showed in the Montpelier team is the subject of much favorable comment."[20] Continuing this theme of praise for the newcomer's positive additions to the team ("[The Montpeliers have been] greatly strengthened the last two weeks"), reporters never failed to praise Fowler's offensive contributions to his run-starved team. In an August 15 rare rout for the Montpelier club, Fowler went 3-for-5 with 2 runs scored, 2 doubles, and a stolen base: "The features of the game were the hitting and base-running of Fowler...."[21] However, Bud Fowler's highly successful tenure in Vermont came to an abrupt end as the local fan base continued to refuse to support such a losing team: The game between Malone (12) and Montpelier (9) on August 22nd was apparently the last straw: "The contest was witnessed by about 250 people who regarded it as a miserable exhibition of base ball."[22]

The tireless African American veteran was also a prominent figure in the new black baseball movement of the 1880s. In 1887, Bud Fowler also organized the black barnstorming club the New York Gorhams based in Newburgh (NY). In addition, the National Colored Baseball League, a legitimate minor league organized under baseball's National Agreement for which Fowler served as a representative of the Cincinnati Browns, began play but folded after two weeks on May 23, 1887, due to sparse attendance and lack of substantial ownership financing.

It was clearly established by the late 1880s that African American ballplayers had the talent and drive to be successful on the highest levels of the national pastime:

> It was clearly demonstrated that colored players possessed major league qualifications when such players as Fleet Walker, Geo. Stovey, Frank Grant and Bud Fowler as members of the International League [sic], back in the eighties, were stars of a class "A" organization. All of these men would have been drafted by the National League or the American Association had they been of the opposite complexion. When Stovey and Walker were paired as a battery, they were considered the stars of the country. Grant and Fowler, as infielders, had no equals in the International League [sic].[23]

Nevertheless, having begun the 1887 season with 20 African Americans playing in integrated organized baseball, only eight black players were left in organized baseball by the end of the season.[24] The seeming inexorable tide of segregation was sweeping the country in all areas of the country; it also had a devastating impact on integrated baseball as well. Effectively, the end the 1887 season marked the closing of the door on African American participation in organized baseball with a few minor exceptions.

Frank Grant — perhaps the very best African American baseball player of the late 19th century, starring on integrated teams in the International Association. Bud Fowler was the only rival to Grant's acknowledged position as the best black second baseman of his day (National Baseball Hall of Fame Library, Cooperstown, New York).

1888 — Indiana

In the winter of 1888, Lafayette (IN) signed Bud Fowler to play for their entry in the Central Interstate League, apparently sight unseen:

> John W. Fowler of Utica, N.Y., arrived in Lafayette Saturday night, having been engaged to fill the position of pitcher for the base ball club of that place. It was thought that Fowler was a white man, and quite a surprise was in store of the Lafayette players when they discovered that he was a genuine darkey. The manager of the club concluded that he would only take strawberry blondes, and the contract with Fowler was annulled.[25]

The newspaper followed up the next day on Fowler's return to the midwest by naming names and uncovering the African American's new league destination: "He [Fowler] didn't suit Will Simpson and one or two other blondes. Fowler will probably play with the Crawfordsville (IN) club."[26]

In a marked departure from his diplomatic response to racial bias the previous year in Binghamton, Bud Fowler commented on this ugly incident in a very public manner in early April in a dignified and unequivocal response in the local newspapers:

> J.W. Fowler, the colored ballplayer who came from Binghamton, N.Y., to accept a place with Lafayette and also was refused a place on account of his color has called *The Crawfordsville Journal,* bitterly roasting the Lafayette management for their course. He intimates that as a body of businessmen, who contract with players and pay them advance money, they ought to know enough to find out who and what they are getting for their money. He also gives them a big blast on race prejudice. He claims he asked for his release as soon as he discovered that the city and the club's board of directors [along with local "patrons of the game"] was full of race prejudice.[27]

By early April of 1888, Bud Fowler was practicing with the Crawfordsville nine, whose ownership was looking to make significant changes in its 1888 season. Bud Fowler soon became a central figure in the upgrading and promotion of the franchise. Originally named the "Athenians," the club underwent a complete makeover:

> The Crawfordsville nine will be known as the "Hoosiers." The new uniforms of the club will be navy blue pants and shirts with white caps, belts, and stockings. A large letter "C" will be worked on the breast. The uniform is like that of the Chicagos [trading on the popularity of Cap

Anson's Chicago White Stockings]. Fowler, the colored player, is the only all-around player in the club, being a splendid catcher and pitcher, but he will be put on second, and those who have seen him play say there is no better second [baseman] any place.[28]

Prior to the season opener on May 1, hopes were high for a successful season for Crawfordsville. Bud Fowler's play was a major factor in such prognostications: "Bud Fowler is playing a great game at second ... little gets by him and [he] is predicted to be one of the best in his league at his position." Further, the local reporter, with little apparent self-consciousness, felt comfortable in also stating that Fowler was "called the coon" by his teammates.[29]

The one caveat of the Crawfordsville supporters was that the team did not have enough practice time prior to the opening of the season. Bud Fowler's last-minute hiring and lack of work with the club may have had an impact on his game. In an early two-game split with visiting Peoria, Fowler's fielding was uncharacteristically uneven. Batting sixth and playing second base, Bud went three-for-nine but made three errors in the second game: "But for Fowler's wretched play at second base, this [4–3 home win] would have been a model contest."[30] However, such play was far from typical. At least six times in the next month, Bud Fowler's fielding was praised in the brief game notes that accompanied late–19th-century box scores: "In one of the most exciting games of the year, Fowler carried off the fielding honors"[31]; "Fowler's work at second was the best feature of the contest"[32]; and "Fowler, the colored second baseman of the visitors played a brilliant game and won repeated applause.[33]

At this point the situation gets a bit murky. Crawfordsville was sold to Terre Haute investors in early June. Previously, the Dubuque (IA) club of the Central Interstate League moved its operations to Terre Haute due to poor attendance.[34] It was later revealed that Dubuque's demise — the team disbanded when the Central Interstate League reorganized in early July with Crawfordsville finishing with a record of 21–21[35] — was due to debt and the conduct of its fans, the bugbears of baseball management in the 19th century. The club owed its players over $500 in unpaid salaries and "the character of the hoodlum audiences of last year has not improved" and "the rampant element in the 'bleaching boards' and grand stand [still remains]."[36] Such rowdy behavior necessitated the creation of "Ladies Days" to ensure the safety and sensibilities of the fairer sex. To attempt to start with a clean state in Indiana, the new Terre Haute management invalidated all the contracts of its Dubuque players.

To further complicate matters, the newly formed Terre Haute team was not composed of Crawfordsville players with one notable exception: "The Terre Haute alleged base ballists expressed themselves as much surprised that they had been advertised in the city as the old Crawfordsville league team sold to Terre Haute. James, the mute, is the only one of the old team."[37] Apparently hoping to avoid law suits for unfulfilled player contracts and to finesse any other legal entanglements that resulted from the franchise sale and relocation, the new Terre Haute owners released all the Crawfordsville players from their contracts and signed new players, perhaps some from the now-disbanded Dubuque team, to play for their new team. Such tangled legal and financial affairs were an all-too-frequent occurrence in late–19th-century professional baseball. The only recourse for players was to pursue all options to sign with another club, which itself was often in an equally precarious financial situation. If the reserve clause made players indentured servants, baseball mismanagement made them itinerant laborers.

When the final Central Interstate League statistics were published in the fall, it was clearly established that Bud Fowler had a successful half-season with Crawfordsville. His statistics were near the top of the league in both hitting and fielding. He had a productive year at the plate (.294, which was tenth in the league) and had 22 steals in a half-season of play. His fielding average (.913, which was good for fourth among league second baseman) was certainly among the upper echelon of everyday players, as was his handling of 355 total chances.[38]

However, by July of 1888, he and his fellow Central Interstate League colleagues were on the open market and scurrying to land contracts to finish the season.

Many of the recently released players from the Central Interstate League had also played in California and the Western League, which served as prime scouting areas for the Las Vegas and Albuquerque entries of the newly established New Mexico Baseball League. These clubs began signing players as early as May of 1888. When Santa Fe retaliated by signing players to upgrade its roster and become competitive with the newly bolstered clubs in the NMBL, at least two current members of the Capital City team — pitcher Lookabaugh and outfielder O'Neill —

had competed against Bud Fowler and could have provided scouting input on the African American as a potential signee.

New Mexico Territory

On the field of play, baseball was undergoing minor but significant changes in the late 1880s. In 1887, the batter could no longer request a high or low ball, a longstanding practice. Equally important in this era of unrestrained fan support, umpires now had the power and discretion to call a game based on unruly crowd behavior. The major changes in 1888 were less dramatic with the pitcher (again) receiving an error for a walk (which in 1888 was five balls, changed to four in 1889), wild pitch, hit batsman, and balk. A walk was not considered a hit and there was no charged time at bat, but a hit by a pitch was recorded as a base hit. Also, if a runner was hit by a ball, the batter would receive a base hit. Finally, in recognition of the changing nature of the game, any ball hit over a fence that was less than 210 feet from home plate was not a home run but a ground-rule double.[39]

The national pastime was also in a state of change and development, moving westward as the railroads and the United States military brought the game from its eastern roots to the ever-expanding America. By 1888, baseball was so firmly established in the New Mexico Territory (and the Southwest) that perennial champ Santa Fe played teams from Las Cruces, El Paso, Fort Seldon, Silver City, Socorro, Raton, Las Vegas, and Albuquerque, the latter two teams being charter members with the City Different in the only year of the New Mexico Baseball League.[40]

As it continues to be today, New Mexico in the 1885 Territorial Census was a large (77,568,640 acres) but sparsely populated (154,141 residents) land. Santa Fe was itself a rather small community with 160,000 acres and approximately 8,000 inhabitants.[41]

The arrival of the railroads in 1880 created a boom town mentality that pitted the modernizers against the antiquarians in a pitched battle over economic opportunity and growth that continues in Santa Fe to the present day. The city fathers and local businessmen desired continuance and expansion of the rail lines and the financial investment that would inevitably follow. This group had postcards printed that focused on Santa Fe as an "Eastern" city. In a similar vein, the Plaza portals were taken down as too "foreign" in an attempt to sell the City Different as not-so-different from its US counterparts.[42] The antiquarians fought back by emphasizing the uniqueness of the local architecture and of the Spanish and, especially, Native American cultures. In a small victory for traditionalists the portals on the Santa Fe Plaza were replaced a few years after they were initially taken down.[43]

The political and aesthetic tug-of-war between civic progressives and romantic traditionalists was heightened with the creation in 1880 of a Bureau of Immigration to increase tourism and "sell" the state to investors. To ensure against economic downturns, the territorial officials placed progress and Americanization side-by-side with antiquity in the incipient interest in the "cliff dwellers," which would slowly morph into the town's characteristic Pueblo style. San Miguel Church was the most popular tourist attraction in Santa Fe, yet, at the same time, nearby stucco buildings were painted to make them appear to be constructed of stone.[44] Santa Fe fought so fervently the Albuquerque assessment of the capital as a "dusty adobe town" that local supporters even contemplated building a two-and-a-half-story courthouse in the middle of the Plaza until cooler heads prevailed and the unique character of the municipal and commercial area was retained.[45]

In the 1880s, Santa Fe was poised for economic growth, which it saw as an essential step in its desire for statehood. The territory had to overcome the perception that life there was too dangerous and too idiosyncratic in order to be admitted to the union, a development that local government felt would ensure prosperity. Baseball was an integral part of an Americanization plan for New Mexico. Tourism, then, had a double-edged (and ironic) purpose: to draw more visitors and immigrants to a territory because of its differences from the nation as a whole and to be certain that these differences were "tame" enough to encourage emigration and investment. This Americanization strategy eventually worked and the people, dollars, and statehood followed.

By the mid–1880s, the Santa Fe Baseball Association was fully manned and financially secure. It was led by Manager George Preston, Assistant Manager John W. Olinger (who served as a combination general manager and traveling secretary), Treasurer Abe Gold, and Chief Scout A. M. Deulebach.[46]

The Santa Fe Ancients grew out of a long-standing tradition of strong ballplaying in northern New Mexico. The 1888 season began with the Capital City as the four-times running Southwest baseball champs (how official these claimed titles are is open to debate). The town had nine baseball clubs and juvenile teams, as well as teams from St. Michael's College. The Ancients began the season winning their first 15 games in the spring, including a two-game sweep of rival Las Vegas at the Meadow City (April 29 & 30),[47] a clubbing of Albuquerque (12–6) in the Duke City in early June, and a three-game demolishing of visiting Tombstone, the reigning Arizona Territory champs, on May 25–27, by a total run count of 22–5.[48]

Weak organizational structure(s) was often a harbinger of future troubles in newly formed 19th-century baseball leagues. The NMBL did not escape this pitfall in 1888. The league suffered an almost fatal self-inflicted wound in late spring in what the local newspapers referred to as the "Hapeman Imbroglio."[49] Revolving, or jumping to new teams during the season, was a major problem for management in creating team stability and loyalty and a supportive fan base. The owners exacerbated this situation by releasing players after a poor game. The prevailing "get-rich-quick" ethos of the day and pervasive problem of gambling undermined the sacredness of a signed contract. With little league structure and few league sanctions that were enforceable, baseballists and management alike overlooked legal niceties and jumped from team to team seemingly at will.

Hapeman was a pitcher for the touring Tombstone team that Santa Fe trounced at the end of May. What follows are facts that are not in doubt:

- Ancient star outfielder O'Neill spoke to Hapeman about playing for Santa Fe.
- Santa Fe Manager Preston offered Hapeman $5 more a month to play for the Ancients.
- Hapeman asked for and received permission to play for his old Tombstone team for one last game at Las Vegas before reporting to Albuquerque on May 30 to play for his new NMBL team.
- Hapeman received seven dollars from Santa Fe in expenses to go by train from Santa Fe to Las Vegas.
- Hapeman signed another contract to play for Las Vegas (!) and went to the Duke City with his even newer teammates.

- Albuquerque Manager Crawford was warned that he'd be fined $100 under NMBL by-laws if Hapeman took the field against Las Vegas.
- Las Vegas and Albuquerque played an "exhibition" game on Sunday.
- Las Vegas withdrew its claim on Hapeman.

The local Santa Fe newspapers made it clear who they thought were the offending and offended parties in this dispute: After a virulent attack on Hapeman's character and past record — he was currently being blacklisted by the San Francisco (CA) Pioneers for hippodroming (throwing games) — Santa Fe manager Preston was praised for "his just and manly stance on the Hapeman case." The Santa Fe sportswriters quoted their Albuquerque counterparts in their disparagement of the former Tombstone hurler: "Everything passed off pleasantly except some ungentlemanly conduct on the part of Hapeman who proved himself a very inferior portion of humanity [*Albuquerque Morning Democrat*]." In the same article, the City Different reporter argued that "It seems to have been a most fortunate thing that Santa Fe didn't secure Hapeman, late pitcher for the Tombstones, after all." He added:

> *The Albuquerque [Daily] Citizen* says of his conduct in Sunday's game: "Hapeman, the blacklisted player, is the most disagreeable player in New Mexico. He has associated himself with eight gentlemen of the Las Vegas club, and his presence among them almost disgraces the whole nine in the eyes of respectable people. Hapeman, besides being blacklisted in New Mexico, is a Californian who has been blacklisted there. He is crooked in every sense of the word.... The sixth inning was remarkable for the kicking of Hapeman, and the air around the pitcher's box was blue from his profanity. It hurts him to have his great curve caught onto by the home team."[50]

The case made against Hapeman signing with Las Vegas and for honoring his signing with Santa Fe was a mish-mash of legal reasoning:

- Hapeman was NOT drunk when he signed his Santa Fe contract.
- Since the NMBL does not recognize contracts outside its own, Hapeman was free to sign with Santa Fe.
- Santa Fe did not delay in informing Las Vegas of their official blackballing of Hapeman. Well, actually the "notice" was late

but Assistant Manager Ward, an Ancient reserve catcher and outfielder, was totally at fault for this "minor" infraction.
- Albuquerque would refuse to play Las Vegas on June 9 and 10 if Hapeman plays.

The Santa Fe reporter summed up the argument against Hapeman's second New Mexico contract as follows: "Las Vegas should cease its childish behavior." As early as late June, Hapeman dominated Albuquerque in a 5–1 victory at Las Vegas during a three-game series that introduced the Duke City hurler Vogel to high stakes baseball: "Vogel with a little head work would develop into a crack left handed twirler."[51]

After official NMBL play was resumed following the Hapeman controversy, the Santa Fe Ancients fell into a deep slump from June until mid–July with most of their losses being by five or more runs. The team began making an inordinate number of errors and players who had been successful in competitive leagues in the past, such as Howard of the Western League, were tried out, found wanting, and dropped from the team.[52] Such a drop-off in performance raised suspicions among the fans and management particularly since many of the baseball imports had checkered careers in the past and were using the NMBL to seek a second or third chance at baseball redemption in order to return to superior (and more lucrative) leagues in the midwest, east, and California.

By early July, the Santa Fe Ancients were undergoing further internal problems and even had difficulty in fielding a team: "Owing to the fact that three members of the Santa Fe base ball team were on the sick list and the new battery not materializing in time, the games arranged for Thursday and Friday were postponed."[53] At the end of July, the NMBL standings showed Santa Fe in the league cellar with a 3–11 league record; Las Vegas led the circuit at 11–4, with Albuquerque at 5–4.[54] Hopes for Santa Fe grabbing a fifth consecutive New Mexico Territory championship pennant were looking bleak.

Following the example of their fellow league members, Santa Fe searched beyond territorial boundaries for replacement players to make their club more competitive. Bud Fowler, recently released when his Indiana Central Interstate League club disbanded, was part of these imports in what was a significant overhaul of the Ancients: "Fisher, the new 3rd baseman, and Fowler, the 2nd baseman, will arrive at Las Vegas to-night and play in Sunday's game (June 13, 1888). Fowler, one of the new players that Santa Fe sent for, is a colored man whose skin is exceedingly black. He has a fair record." Lookabaugh replaced the ill Favour, who returned to his Milwaukee home, and took over chief pitching duties for the Santa Fe nine.[55]

The new additions began to pay immediate dividends. In describing a weekend two-game split with Las Vegas, a few of the home-standing Ancients were singled out for their play: "The features of the game(s) were the catching and general playing of the new men Fowler and Hill; the fielding of Clark and batting of O'Neill and Joanes."[56]

Only a few weeks after his arrival in the New Mexico Territory, Bud Fowler gave an extraordinarily candid interview to a local reporter about his views on race, the player-owner relationship, and what was essential for the future success of the national pastime:

"A representative of *The Herald* met Mr. Fowler to-day, the second baseman of the Santa Fe Club, and talked with him about his experience at the Plaza Hotel in Las Vegas, where the African American ballplayer was not permitted to sit at the regular table. Mr. Fowler said":

> I came to the Territory, I wish to explain to those who visit the games. Before coming here I was aware of the fact that a prejudice existed among the players. We are as a color and represented in all national sports throughout the United States, and why should we be objected to in baseball? Do we not respect the National game?...we are "drawing cards" and add to the recipts [sic] of the game wherever we play. If those who control our clubs would have first class players at once, and not get "cast-offs," the good players would hold their positions and not be released on the slightest occasion. Colored players would be retained and there would be no chance for prejudice. We would have better games, better attendance and the game would be properly supported and made a success.... There are several players in the New Mexico league, that I have played with in other leagues and I would like to hear any one of those players speak his opinion and say if he has not found me a gentleman and a hard player.[57]

As a sidelight to this interview, Bud Fowler received plaudits from the local Las Vegas newspaper — "[his] second base playing was splendid" — in what was described as a "tiresome game for the most part, being too one-sided, and very few brilliant plays were made by either side" that was compounded by illegal and unacceptable behavior. Umpire McCue infuriated the fans by calling Las Vegas player Thomas out for interference and Santa Fe right fielder Howard out "for not getting to the plate in time."

The reporter also noted the home team's uninspired play and described it as "poor, whether purposely or not." (Only one of Santa Fe's eight runs in the game was earned.) The public was apparently divided on the issue of team effort since "the home team [Las Vegas] played very poor ball, as they always do when Hall is in the box." Though Lookabaugh pitched well for the Ancients, the key news of the day was the Capital City's hiring of a new pitcher for the stretch run: "A new pitcher [Frank Fudger] will arrive here [Las Vegas] to-night. He played in the western leagues last year and made a great record."[58]

The Ancients continued their improved play throughout August and September. During a weekend series with Albuquerque held at the State Fairgrounds, Fowler was the losing pitcher in a 7–4 defeat by the home team, though he had eight strikeouts and only one wild pitch; in the following day's game, Bud had his best day at the plate for the Ancients, going five-for-six with two doubles and two triples while scoring five runs in a 20–3 rout.[59] A week later, in return matches versus Albuquerque in the City Different, Fowler's clutch extra-base hitting was again singled out for praise.[60]

The Santa Feans seemed to come into their own as a team in early September when visiting Las Vegas. They lost the first game of a two-game set, 9–0, with Bud in the pitching box. He was called to task for his control: "Fowler was in the box for Santa Fe, and was very wild, keeping his catcher guessing all the time." Las Vegas twirler Behne limited Santa Fe to two hits with the "only error being an intentional one by [shortstop] Valley in order that Fowler may be put out and Hill be left on in his stead." Fowler's seven wild pitches and the Ancients' 16 errors (with Howard having five at shortstop) when combined with a nightmarish eighth inning turned a close match into a laugher: after single unearned runs in the second and third innings, "no more runs were made until the eighth inning when Santa Fe went to pieces allowing seven unearned runs to be made by Las Vegas. It was a comedy of errors, everybody who could possibly get hold of the ball throwing it wild. This sadly marred what would otherwise have been a close and exciting contest." Only center fielder Ward's throw from deep in the outfield to the plate and Lookabaugh's brilliant catches in right field merited positive comment by the Meadow City reporter. Finally, Bud Fowler's 0 for 4 day at the plate was mentioned in the game post-mortem: "Fowler hit the ball every time he went to bat, but never reached first base. Some mean fielders always threw him out."[61]

On the following day, the Ancients defeated their opponents in uncharacteristic fashion in a 15–5 pasting of the NMBL leaders. Though Las Vegas played well in the outfield, losing pitcher Hapeman was "very wild" and the victim of "uneven support." A recent arrival from California led Santa Fe to victory in a lackluster game: "Except for one inning, Fudger was very effective and demonstrated his ability to pitch winning ball.... As a whole, it was a poor exhibition of ball playing and was disappointing to the large crowd of spectators." The annoyed Las Vegas observer commented on the boisterous and litter-prone Santa Fe supporters: "The tie pile delegation shouted themselves hoarse for Santa Fe yesterday. If the railroad lumber yard should catch fire some time by reason of lighted cigars or matches being thrown around promiscuously, perhaps these people will be deprived of their cheap seats, but it looks as if that is the only thing that will bring about that result."[62]

Catching fire, the Santa Fe club finished the month by winning three of the last four games with Las Vegas and six of nine from the Albuquerque nine. Part of this revival was a new development in the season-long search for a dominant pitcher. Kid Browner started the season for the Ancients and was inconsistent; then Favour took his place and soldiered on, but he became ill and returned home to the Midwest. Next in the box on a regular basis was another refugee from the Central Interstate League, Lookabaugh, who was "batted hard" in a 12–4 loss to Albuquerque and who received his release from his NMBL contract to join Beatrice (NE) with the proviso that he play for the team in its upcoming games with Las Vegas. Lookabaugh never kept this commitment and was replaced by Frank Fudger. The Santa Fe papers were unanimously sanguine that such a move was certain "to worry our enemies." As usual, Bud Fowler was at the center of the action. Reporters speculated that if Fudger missed his connections to Las Vegas — which he did — Bud would start the upcoming game. He was also praised for his play in the loss to the Duke City combatants that marked Lookabaugh's last NMBL appearance.[63]

Fudger's presence in the pitching box was a key ingredient in the Ancients' push for the championship. The team jelled and the praise for the local nine was loud: "On careful inspection of our base ball team we have come to the conclusion that there is not [flies] to be discovered on any one of them. *No hay moscas sobre nosotro!* They can play ball and propose to do it and this pennant is yet in the future."[64]

The local sports reporters began to employ a heightened mock heroic voice and satirical style as the fortunes of the Santa Fe Ancients improved on the diamond and fan expectations for a winning season increased. In a week of baseball between Santa Fe and arch-rival Albuquerque, the New Mexico capital's newspapers had a field day mocking the home team's uneven play and the always unexpected nature of the national pastime:

> Well, we've got another one! It was not a very big one, but it was bigger than the game that Albuquerque got on Wednesday. The fact is that we are too generous by half. We presented the game to Albuquerque on Wednesday in the eighth inning. We tried our best to present the game to them yesterday [Friday], but they would not or could not accept it. Probably professional base ball courtesy intervened and told them not to take it. No, by no means, take it. It would be too bad for the Ancients. Bless their hearts! They were so kind.
>
> The base ball game yesterday between the Albuquerque and Santa Fe nines was a hotly and closely contested one all the way through. The final score stood 11 to 10 in favor of Albuquerque. At the end of the 2nd inning Santa Fe with its 4 runs to Albuquerque's none, looked like a probable winner, and when in the 3rd inning the Albuquerque men became apparently oblivious to the fact that there were any persons on the grounds besides themselves and started in on a practice game of throwing and muffing the ball while Tippy O'Neill was quietly trotting around the bases, it seemed like a more certain victory for the quondam giants. Indeed it was dollars to doughnuts that they would win, with their clear lead of five runs. But there is nothing so absolutely certain to occur as the unexpected.[65]

In a two-game series with Santa Fe on September 8 and 9, longstanding NMBL umpire McCue played a prominent role. He made the decision to stand behind the pitcher to better call balls and strikes. He was praised by the local Las Vegas newspaper for urging the players to "get a move on" but he was chastised by the reporter as well: "McCue made a good call but acted the baby by threatening to call the game."[66] The Ancients must have found fault with McCue's actions or detected some real or imagined bias against the Santa Fe team because in late September it was announced that McCue had umpired his last game for the NMBL: "Mr. G.C. Preston [Santa Fe manager] said it was possible that Mr. McCue will not umpire any more games for New Mexico League, and that Williams may be engaged to fill his place."[67] That was indeed the case for what was left of the league season.

Bud Fowler continued his timely hitting throughout September with a clutch double on a Ladies' Day game defeat of the Albuquerque nine. In typical fashion, the women in attendance were praised for their knowledge of the game and appropriate behavior: "It was ladies' day and the grand stand was filled with Albuquerque's fair. They were excited and deeply interested, applauded good plays and criticized poor ones, proving conclusively that they understood the game thoroughly."[68] In another defeat of the Duke City squad the following week, the Ancients continued their success in NMBL games. Despite the tightening of the league pennant chase, a lack of paying fans was worrisome late in the season. Albuquerque responded by adding more "ladies' day" games at the Albuquerque Fair Grounds with the goal of boosting attendance by both sexes.[69]

The Ancients' return to respectability was evident in a game in which Bud collected three hits. The reporter was relentless in his derisive comments about the home team's listless play: "...the [Albuquerque players] are too religious a community by far to play base ball on Sunday, so they didn't play the game. If anyone thinks they did they are mistaken. They simply didn't. If a balloon had been anchored on the home plate, very few of our boys would have hit it...."[70] After a 7–4 victory over their Albuquerque rivals at the State Fairgrounds on September 30, the Santa Fe team needed a win on the next day to create a flat-footed tie for the NMBL lead with games the following weekend in Santa Fe determining the pennant winner.[71]

The season ended with two major bombshells: the Las Vegas club disbanded in mid–September and then on October 1, Albuquerque followed suit: "On Monday last the Albuquerque ball club disbanded for the season, leaving Santa Fe to play out the remaining games with herself if she so wishes. This undoubtedly gives that club good grounds on which to claim the championship, there being no other club organized in the Territory."[72]

A local Santa Fe newspaper, reprinting an article from the *Las Vegas Optic*, provides a concise history of the major events of the 1888 NMBL season: "The history of professional base ball in New Mexico this season has been an eventful one. At the start Santa Fe won eight straight games from the Las Vegas team. Then the Hapeman embroglio [sic] came up, and the league for a time ceased to exist. Afterward a new schedule was arranged with three clubs in the league. For a time the Las Vegas club had things all its own way, winning game after game in quick succession."⁷³

Las Vegas then led the way in recruiting good ballplayers from established leagues in the midwest, the east, and California:

> Then Albuquerque strengthened her nine, and commenced rapidly to climb the stairs, Santa Fe all the time being haplessly in the rear. When Albuquerque and Las Vegas were pitted against each another, close and exciting games were nearly always the result, the teams being pretty evenly matched. Up to a month ago [the Ancients] were putting up an inferior article of ball, but at that time new blood was infused into the nine [including stars Fowler and Fisher along with pitchers Lookabaugh and Fudger], and they braced up a little. The Las Vegas club, for want of proper support, disbanded three weeks ago, when it was leading in the race, thus abandoning the field to its competitors...."⁷⁴

The Santa Fe Baseball Association was still looking at this late date in the season to improve its club by tendering contract offers to now unemployed Las Vegas club members for the upcoming games with Albuquerque. For example, Las Vegas twirler Frank Behne apparently made a deep impression on the Ancients. By the third week of September, Behne was on the roster of the Santa Fe nine in their final scheduled showdown with Albuquerque:

> The Santa Fe Base Ball Club will leave tonight for Albuquerque and will play there to-morrow and Sunday.
> The Las Vegas Club has disbanded. Frank Behne their pitcher has been wired to meet our club at Lamy [a rail station the Ancients would pass through on the way south to Albuquerque] this evening.
> Albuquerque will play here Friday Saturday and Sunday of next week, and the possibilities are that a regular rate of fifty cents will hereafter be charged for admission to the grounds and grandstand.⁷⁵

In a financial move that flew in the face of the reality of decreasing attendance figures, Santa Fe team management, blinded by the improved won-loss record, attempted to cash in by raising the price for admission to NMBL home games to 50 cents.⁷⁶

Unlike the financial demise of the Las Vegas entry, Albuquerque disbanded because of another of the endemic problems of professional baseball in the late 19th century:

> ... now Albuquerque has gone under. The principal reason for the disbanding of this club, as near as can be ascertained, was too much "boozing" on the part of the players causing a lack of interest in their behalf

on the part of the citizens. Thus, Santa Fe, which did not stand the ghost of a show before, stands alone on the diamond field, claims the coveted bunting, with no one to oppose her, although with the aid of some ex–Las Vegas men, they have been playing great ball lately.[77]

Santa Fe supporters had a different take on the 1888 season, though they agreed on the chief reason for the folding of the Albuquerque Greens. While praising Manager George C. Preston's leadership as "aggressive and courageous," the Santa Fe reporter crowed that Las Vegas and Albuquerque "faced disbandment or ignominious defeat and that the local nine have claimed the title of Southwest baseball Championship for the fifth consecutive year." What is not in question is that Albuquerque manager Bayse and the team owner were suffering financial problems and "had only three sober players left on the club.... Demoralized, the players were released on October 2, 1888."[78]

The final Albuquerque accounts of the team's demise were refreshingly less rancorous and negative than may have been expected considering the competitive nature and boosterism of the reporting of the period:

> ... Albuquerque has disbanded. The players that belonged to the best team in New Mexico [Albuquerque] can feel proud of the fact that they played good ball generally here and the citizens that supported the team are well satisfied that most of the boys will return to their eastern homes but can feel assured that should they ever turn up in "Sunny New Mexico" they will find many of their old friends will be glad to see them.[79]

In spite of the inconsistent level of play, the often unsavory behavior of the players and fans, and the tragicomic nature of the 1888 NMBL season. America's game was now firmly established in the New Mexico Territory and in all points west of the Rocky Mountains. However, the game remained a very roughshod experience for many potential fans and this was clearly a significant factor in the dwindling late-season crowds:

> "The [Santa Fe] management is determined to stop some persons in the audience from talking to players and guying them in any way. Hereafter this rule will be strictly enforced.... A few hoodlums turned a deaf ear to their [Ancient players Tip O'Neill and Mackay's] silvery words and rather sat down on them. This is not right.... A number of hoodlums acted discourteously toward the Santa Fe visitors on the base ball grounds yesterday, yelling and hooting. The officers of the association should eject such characters at future games" [*Albuquerque Daily Citizen*].[80]

Even in the enthusiasm of an opening day win over Las Vegas, Santa Fe newsmen had pointed out the seeds of discord that would haunt the NMBL in its only season of existence: "The game was a good one, but was spoiled by the wrangling which took place. It would be a good idea to form a league which would adopt rules giving the umpire power to fine such small plays as throwing the ball at the man. When this is done base ball will become more interesting and more profitable to the stockholders."[81]

The 1888 campaign was the first and only season of the NMBL and also was Santa Fe's only professional baseball team in its 400-year history. The league grew out of the spirit and enthusiasm of the age and expired as a result of the excesses that were the dark underside of the competitiveness and enthusiasm. At the midpoint of his playing career, Bud Fowler brought his talents on the diamond and his unquenchable desire to tread his own path to Santa Fe. He once again demonstrated both the tenacity and spirit needed to succeed in the brave new world of professional baseball.

It is ironic that one of the final baseball stories of the 1888 season covered by the Santa Fe dailies was the much ballyhooed upcoming tour of the world by the National League Chicago and American teams that were traveling across the country en route to their final destination across the Pacific Ocean.[82] While Bud Fowler was looking for a team to hook on with to continue his baseball career, Al Spalding and Cap Anson, who had been driving forces in the movement to ban African American players from organized baseball, were traveling in a luxurious rail car and receiving adulation and tributes for expanding America's national pastime beyond the country's borders.

In November of 1888, in conjunction with the international tour to promote America's national pastime, a leading sports weekly of the 19th century published a highly laudatory biographical profile of Anson that was representative of the press coverage he received. The author praised Anson for his All-American character and unmatchable accomplishments:

> ... he is the greatest baseball general on the ball field. In private life he is as pleasant a companion as one could wish to meet. Should Capt. Anson conclude to leave the Chicago Club, he could undoubtedly command the largest salary ever as an exponent of the national game. His record as a team captain is the most brilliant in the history of the sport. "The old

man" is bluff and direct in his methods of management, but his discipline has been healthy, and it has resulted in a career whose success has been the wonder and the envy of other great cities which have struggled in vain for years to obtain the proud position so often gained by the Chicago Club.[83]

There was not a word about his prominence in establishing and promoting the color line in baseball, which was becoming more firmly entrenched at the very moment that the sport was being packaged internationally as the American Game.

One further irony occurred in 1888 that underscored both the soaring popularity of baseball in the mainstream culture and the further marginalization of African American players within the confines of organized baseball. On June 3, 1888, in the *San Francisco Examiner*, Ernest Thayer's poem "Casey at the Bat" was first published; on August 15, 1888, this paean to the national pastime was presented by DeWolf Hopper (who went on to recite it 10,000 more times) before the Chicago and New York National League teams in a New York theater and it soon became a beloved part of American culture.[84] One day before that recitation, African American baseball player, promoter and pioneer Bud Fowler had been released by his Central Interstate League ball club, which led him to head west to play ball for the Santa Fe team of the New Mexico Baseball League. That a talented and experienced player of Bud Fowler's caliber was reduced in playing in a first-year three-team league of has-been and never-were hired guns in the New Mexico Territory is more an indictment of the national pastime itself than of any deficiency in either Bud Fowler's character or his game.

Bud Fowler's brief tenure in Santa Fe also revealed a tolerance among the City Different's populace that was atypical of the time and place. In late September of 1888, Bud entered into a business partnership that suggested he planned to become a full-time Santa Fean: "Second Baseman Fowler, he of the Santa Fe team whom everyone delights to see play ball, is going to settle down as a permanent resident of Santa Fe. Yesterday he and Barber Haskins formed a partnership and bought out Johnny Alire's Capitol City barber shop. Fowler is said to be as handy with the blade, clippers, and shears as he is with the ball and bat. He is a clever fellow all around and deserves success."[85] A week later, after the Ancients backed into the NMBL pennant, Fowler was reported to have spruced up his new business: "Haskins and Fowler, the barbers, have had their place of business brightened with many stripes, and given it a thorough over hauling and altogether it presents quite a neat and pleasant appearance."[86]

Another significant event that happened in the 1888 New Mexico baseball world reveals a more accepting attitude toward blacks subsequent to Bud Fowler's arrival in the territory. Manager Tom Wade of El Paso, a city that once disbanded its team rather than participate in a baseball game with mixed-race players, had turned over a new leaf by 1888: "[New Manager Tom Wade] does not object to colored players and wants to make dates with Santa Fe [for whom African American Bud Fowler was then playing]."[87] As the color barrier was descending on organized baseball, Santa Fe was employing an African American whom other local teams were eager to compete against on equal terms. While New Mexico was striving for statehood in the 1880s, it was demonstrating, if not a more enlightened view on race than much of the rest of the United States, then at least a tolerance of (or indifference to) the "other," which was a label under which many of the inhabitants of the territory themselves suffered.

Bud Fowler's short but productive run in the NMBL was to be extended by a trip to the West Coast to play a series of games in California with a touring team of league all-stars, including fellow Ancient players Chouquette (catcher and right fielder), Hill (third base), O'Neill (left field), and Fudger (pitcher). The team would be led by Santa Fe manager Preston and funded by local contractor and developer James Duncan (whose Las Vegas Opera House is still in use today as a movie theater): "The team will have a special car and the suits [uniforms] will consist of old gold and maroon trimmings while across the breast will be the words 'Duncans of New Mexico.'"[88]

In late December of 1888, it was reported that John Fowler, "the colored second baseman," was discussing playing for the San Bernardino entry in a proposed South California League prior to signing with the Quincy (IL) Ravens of the Central Interstate League for the 1889 season.[89] However, there is no evidence that Fowler ever played integrated ball in California in the fall of 1888.

The Southern California League, which did play in 1886 with two teams from San Luis Obispo and one from Tulare City, did not officially reorganize until 1899. There was a major collapse in land values in 1888 and the citrus culture that became a signature industry for California did not hit full stride until the mid–1890s. Equally telling is the fact that the Santa Fe newspapers did not mention the proposed NMBL All-Star trip to California that they had trumpeted at the end of the 1888 league season. Baseball was still enormously popular in the capital city and ignoring a barnstorming trip to California with many Santa Fe Ancient players would have been unthinkable. As with many endeavors in which Fowler was involved throughout his career, the proposed tour apparently never materialized.[90]

However, Bud Fowler did make it to the San Bernardino area in the winter of 1888-89. By January, Fowler was wintering in southern California and playing for a San Bernardino team with former teammates and opponents from his earlier career stops.[91] During a summary of players who were in California over the winter and were returning to the east and the midwest for the 1889 season that included his former Santa Fe Ancient teammates Fudger and Goodenough, Bud Fowler was mentioned as leaving California in early March to coach the amateur Beaumont (TX) team for two weeks before heading to Michigan to open the 1889 season. Fowler was enthusiastic in his praise of the potential of the Texas club: "...the Beaumont Club has some good material and will be heard from this summer and will make all the amateur clubs hustle to beat them or win a ball."[92] Though only 30 years old with many years of playing the national pastime at a high level still ahead of him, the veteran Fowler, besides grooming himself for the leadership roles of captain and team manager, was also demonstrating his skill (and generosity) in evaluating young talent. Buck Freeman, later a star slugger in the major leagues, remembered the advice he had received as a 16-year-old portside flame thrower from the African American professional who had just seen him hit two home runs in an 1888 amateur game. "I never gave batting a thought until Fowler tipped me off," Freeman said. "You have pretty good control of the ball for a left-handed pitcher, kid," Freeman recalled that Fowler had told him. "But batting is your hold. Keep on practicing with the stick. It will get you more money."[93]

1889 — Michigan

Though a few sources had suggested that he would sign with the financially stable Quincy Ravens for the 1889 season, Bud Fowler did not end up playing there, nor in Peoria, where another erroneous report had placed him.[94] Instead, for one of the few times in his career in organized baseball, Bud Fowler spent the entire 1889 season with the same ball club, Greenville of the newly formed Michigan State League.

Bud Fowler's heady play was commented on early in 1889 by local reporters who helped establish the persona of the experienced, crafty African American veteran that served him well from age 30 on:

> Fowler, the colored second baseman of the Greenvilles, is a tricky player. When at the bat he turns his head occasionally and catches the sign made by the catcher to the pitcher and lays his plans accordingly. [The catcher] discovered the act yesterday and fooled him several times. It is said he has played in nearly every state in the union, coming here from Texas. He has a peculiarity or, perhaps a superstition, about striking at the first ball over the plate and always strikes at it whether over the plate or over his head.[95]

Bud Fowler's 1889 season with Greenville saw him compile career highs in games played (92 out of the team's 100 games), at-bats (426), runs scored (93), and hits (129), while stealing 46 bases and hitting .302.[96] With John Foster as manager, Greenville finished fifth in the league in 1889, going 42–58. The team had the leading hitter in the circuit, Joe Katz, who batted .364 and had 154 hits.[97] In fact, the "mystery" indicated in the following late-season assessment of the Greenville club's lack of success on the diamond had a decidedly mundane solution: "One of the mysteries is why the Greenvilles can't win. Fuller, Raymond, Drummond, and Fowler are putting up good ball, but like the Kazoos, they seem to be hoodooed."[98] The answer is that, while Greenville led the league in hitting, it was next-to-last in fielding. Even the usually sure-handed Fowler was fifth of six second basemen in the league with 70 errors and a .886 fielding percentage.[99]

Greenville was a small railroad town on the Detroit, Grand Rapids, and Western line, and 1889 was its only year as a league member. In 1890, the Michigan State League continued in existence and even "signed the articles for qualified admission to national protection"[100] on March 6, 1890, in Louisville. However, Greenville did not make the league lineup — instead, there were new franchises in Port Huron, Manistee, and Muskegon.

The 1889 season also marked the heating up of a Bud Fowler self-promotion blitz that continued throughout the baseball pioneer's involvement with the national pastime. He inflated his age, claiming to be the oldest active ballplayer in baseball. Moreover, he romanticized his career by inventing (and inflating) narratives of playing ball in the wilds of Canada, the Western Territories, and California.[101]

As early as the late 1880s, it was being argued that the proper model for American business was poker. Baseball's monopolist practices of the late 1880s and 1890s led to counter-maneuvers that were perhaps too fraternal (and utopian) by those opposed to the reserve clause. Soon syndicate baseball (where more than one team was owned by an ownership group that then could manipulate the teams)[102] reared its ugly head and threatened the very essence of baseball's appeal: "The secret of the success of base ball is that it is on the square. The game that is bought or bargained for will destroy the nine, or the league, if it were once even hinted about in the homes of the people. The games that we play best in this life, those we win, are, every last one of them, if they give us any real good, won also 'on the square.'"[103] There was no room available for African American players, even those of the intelligence and talent of a Bud Fowler, in such a tightly controlled financial system.

In the final analysis, the 1880s saw professional baseball become a big business:

> [In 1890, there were] about one hundred professional clubs giving employment to about fifteen hundred players ... the average salary is about $1,000 a season making for a total of $1,5000,000.... [When one considers the Brotherhood clubs who existed outside the aegis of the National Agreement] the grand total is 1,620 players and $1,750,000 in salaries.... These clubs travel 6,300,000 miles by rail ... at two and one-half cents a mile not counting sleeping car accommodations [the cost would amount] to $157,000.... [Based on an eighty-day seasonal booking], hotels would earn not less than $200,000 [a season].... Probably $100,000 would be a small estimate of the rents paid by their clubs for their grounds and certainly $200,000 would not more than pay the miscellaneous expenses, such as sleeping-car fares, carriage hire, advertising, salaries of ground employees, treasurers, and gatekeepers, and the purchase of supplies.
>
> [Together, the costs would average] nearly two and a half million dollars.... [while profits would be] a quarter of a million dollars [with total attendance] of about eight million people....
>
> ... Every day during this summer five million Americans will examine the columns of their favorite newspapers to find the result of the professional base-ball games of the previous day.[104]

Professional baseball was an unqualified success as a business proposition in the 1880s. That success was built on the enormous popularity and worldwide spread of baseball to such diverse venues as Canada, the Sandwich Islands, Cuba, the southern, western, and northwestern states and "far-flung San Francisco." Feeding the age's desire for "authentic experiences" and appreciation of physical activity, the game's primary national appeal was that baseball offered relaxation and excitement in a characteristically American manner:

> ... nothing affords more pleasure than a ball game. Here he [a business man] can throw off all cares and troubles. He forgets to think about them in the relaxation he enjoys in the excitement of a close contest, and he goes to his home feeling all the better for the few hours spent in the air. It is a medicine to him and a tonic, and it with a zest that he afterward partakes of his evening meal. The game, too, is purely and thoroughly American, entirely characteristic of our race and times.... [The American] is quick and active, nervous and energetic, and he wants his sport to answer the requirements of his temperament. Base ball has answered his purpose admirably....[105]

Equally important, the 1880s were a relatively peaceful and prosperous period in which a cohesive capitalist social order was coalescing into increased demand for the consumption of goods and services, including mass-produced leisure activities such as baseball.[106] By the last decade of the 19th century, baseball was a professional business enterprise that met the simple demands of the sport from its earliest inception: "headwork required" and "action demanded." The patriotic myths of the national pastime as an American idyll and as a signifier of all things great and American were giving way to the realities of the business of baseball.[107]

— Five —
Shut Out
The Independent Years (1890–1899)

1890 — Illinois and Iowa

After spending the winter of 1889-90 in Toledo, Bud Fowler signed with Evansville (IN),[1] but his contract was sold before the season to Galesburg (IL) of the Central Interstate League. Since the Illinois club was using an infusion of $1000 or more to boost civic morale, management pursued the African American infielder in a manner that reflected the community's desire to have a first-rate ball club: "Second baseman Fowler, who has been wintering in this city [Toledo], has joined the Galesburg, Ill., team. Galesburg purchased his release from Evansville, paying $500, Fowler getting a share of the purchase money."[2]

As was becoming a recurring pattern in his career in integrated organized baseball, Fowler performed extremely well for Galesburg, but his team found itself in the cellar at the end of May, playing sub-.300 ball at 7–17. The team lost series with Terre Haute, Peoria, Evansville, and Burlington and was shut out twice. The reasons provided for Galesburg's failures on the diamond were legion: "The home team [Galesburg] would not have been shut out had the coaching been properly done" (May 23), "The visiting [Galesburgs were] overpowered in everything but fielding" (May 22), and "[Galesburg suffered from] a few unlucky plays and a little demoralization" (May 21).[3]

Bud Fowler, on the other hand, was thriving for his new team. He had at least one steal in three-quarters of the games in May as well as having only one multi-error game (which he experienced in the shutout loss to Evansville). He was even more productive at the plate: in nearly two-thirds of Galesburg's May games, the African American baseballist had either a multi-hit game and/or an extra-base hit.[4] Early season batting highlights of his two-month stay in Galesburg included a mammoth home run on April 29, and on May 2, in his team's home opener, a six-hit, five-runs-scored game in a crushing defeat of Peoria, 31–5. One home observer summed up Fowler's prowess at the plate as follows: "[It is interesting] to see the visiting fielders move back when Taylor, Weddige, and Fowler go to the bat."[5]

After Galesburg folded at the end of June, Fowler caught on with Sterling (IL) of the Illinois-Iowa (Two-I) League for a month.[6] Fowler got off to a fast start in early July with a number of steals, a three-hit game, and the usual plaudits for his keystone sack play: "Our [Sterling] new second baseman, Fowler, caught the crowd by his field work, and put up the finest game at second ever seen here."[7] In an extra-inning 12–10 victory over Cedar Rapids on July 11, Fowler doubled to center in the tenth inning, stole third base, had the game-winning RBI and scored an insurance run.[8] In spite of Fowler's contributions at the plate, by late July Sterling was firmly ensconced in last place with an 18–49 record. In a rare victory in which Fowler contributed a key double in a winning rally, the local newspaper's headline excoriated the losing Iowan team for its 5–3 loss to Sterling: "The Canaries Allow the Boys from the Sucker State to Take a Game from Them by Loose Playing."[9]

Yet the African American veteran had some difficult moments in the field: "Fowler muffed a throw at second from [Sterling catcher] Wirsche."[10] Later in the month, in a game in which Sterling had seven errors on fly balls, Fowler was at the center of the action: "Some mistakes were made in calling players for fly balls. For instance [Sterling center fielder] Mackey was brought in nearly to second and muffed the sky-scraper after a hard run which Fowler could have reached without an effort. Fowler could have gotten one or two of Collins', also, and as he does not use gloves he is much surer on those high twisters."[11]

Fowler's two miscues in this game may suggest that the African American's teammates would call him off the ball in circumstances where he could easily handle the chance. In the same game, Fowler was called out on a disputed ruling by the umpire that may also reveal a double standard of treatment of African American players on midwest diamonds:

> The crowd thought that we [the Sterling club] were robbed of a run in the third when Fowler ran home after Barnes' high fly was caught in right field, and the umpire declared him out at third because of leaving the base before [the] ball settled in Hughes' hands. The umpire's inten-

tions were good but he was not in as good position to watch base runner and ball as those in the grandstand, and to them it seemed that Fowler waited long enough. This retired the Sterling's as well as cutting off the run.[12]

One intriguing account, however, did shed light on Bud Fowler's impact on his fellow African Americans:

> *The Dubuque Telegraph* says: "It was amusing to observe the awe with which Fowler, Sterling's second baseman, was regarded by his colored brethren in Dubuque. When he came into a crowd of them every chair was vacated and the former occupant of the one he condescended to accept could not conceal his gratification nor the others their envy. They fall all over themselves in their haste to hand him a fan, and more than one watermelon was cut in his honor."[13]

The Sterling franchise was somewhat shaky financially and the owners tried to fill their coffers by playing exhibition games that were also intended to advertise the upcoming league games. In early July, for example, after a listless victory over the visiting nine from Dixon, the team management expressed their displeasure at the level of play: "Several of the stockholders of the Sterling Association criticized our club for not playing a better game, as to better advertise the league games here [Sterling] — well, the Sterlings didn't half play and yet won very easily."[14]

At the end of July, 1890, the African American baseballist found himself heading back to a newly resuscitated Galesburg franchise, now relocated to the Two-I League. The new Galesburg management began August with a burst of enthusiasm:

> Once more Galesburg has the proud distinction of owning a ball team, having purchased the franchise and team of the Sterling association. The news will be hailed with delight both by the other Illinois-Iowa teams and the enthusiasts. The new team contains many new faces, Fowler, Weddige, Relman, Barnes and Sullivan having been members of the old Inter-State team. Captain Wirsche will be remembered as having played with the Monmouth team last season. With a little weeding out the club can be made to stand up well in the race.[15]

The reborn Galesburg franchise grasped its second opportunity and ran with it, playing an exciting brand of baseball that was led by Bud Fowler. In a game in which he had four hits against league rival Dubuque, Fowler was praised for his play and, in keeping with the temper of the times, his race was duly noted: "And how some of them [the Galesburg players] ran the bases, especially that man Fowler. Just think, five stolen bases ... in one game. If only he had been painted white, he would be playing with the best of them."[16]

However, by the end of August, while Fowler continued to hit and field at an all-star level, the Galesburg team was in the league cellar. More tellingly, the team was playing a number of benefit games and taking part in running and throwing field competitions with league opponents to raise cash. (One such game with Dubuque "raised nearly $35."[17]) Fowler finished a desultory fourth in the running-the-bases competition; however, perhaps his mind was on more weighty personal matters since it was also reported that week that he filed a lawsuit for racial discrimination: "*The Aurora News* says Fowler, the colored second baseman in the Galesburg nine, has brought suit for damages against the Ottumwa Ballingall Hotel. During the races they would not allow Mr. Fowler to eat in their dining room, hence the suit."[18]

Bud Fowler's response to the institutional and overt racism he faced on and off the ball field changed dramatically in the period from 1887 to 1890. Never one to passively accept racist treatment from teammates, the African American pioneer moved from quietly accepting his departure (and perhaps receiving a financial incentive) in New York in 1887 to commenting loudly and publicly in the newspapers about racial bias when he resided in Indiana and the New Mexico Territory in 1888 to filing a legal suit for racial discrimination in Iowa in 1890. As the country suffered through a deepening economic crisis and segregation became the accepted social order, Fowler found his opportunities to play in integrated organized baseball severely curtailed after the 1890 season. Only his physical presence in Nebraska (1892) and in Michigan (1895) as a talented performer and recognizable name on touring all-black teams when coupled with the desperate need for new leagues in their first year of existence to immediately build their skill level and gate attractiveness led to Fowler making brief returns to organized baseball.

After another financial fiasco in Galesburg, Bud Fowler ended the season in Burlington (IA) in a further league reshuffling. The well-traveled veteran hit .322 for Galesburg in the first half of the season and .314 for three teams in the second half. Fowler also had a productive season with regard to extra-base hits, garnering a total of 17 doubles, 5 triples, and 2 home runs.[19]

A mid-season 1890 controversy over African Americans playing in organized baseball sent a loud and clear signal that the continuance of blacks in integrated white baseball was in grave jeopardy. The great star Frank Grant was signed by Harrisburg (PA) in the Atlantic Association but his presence in the league was objected to by Baltimore, Wilmington, and Jersey City. (In the same year, the African American Cuban Giants represented York [PA] in the Eastern Interstate League.) The following reasoned and reasonable argument for allowing Grant to play for the Ponies fell mostly on deaf ears and is representative of the strength of the anti–African American sentiment in the last decade of the 19th century:

> Composed as these places [Baltimore, Wilmington, and Jersey City] are with a colored population of considerable magnitude, no harm could possibly result from his [Grant's] playing and the attendance would be increased instead of diminished as claimed. There is no class that caters more to amusements than the colored folks and every effort is made by them to do so. This has been demonstrated in this and other cities and would be the case in the places mentioned. If a man is a good mechanic, whether colored or white, he does not lack for patronage in any place. Grant is a good ballplayer and it is not his color but his "style" of handling the ball and bat that causes the trouble.[20]

Again, it is the allegedly ostentatious on-field behavior of the African American player that is blamed for his harsh treatment at the hands of his racist tormentors.

Bud Fowler's hectic travels and almost endless movement among teams in 1890 pointed to the rather shaky condition of baseball as the decade began. Since the birth of the National League in 1876, it had face several challengers): one-year wonders the Union Association (1884) and the Players' League (1890), and the American Association (1882–1891). Yet all of these rivals had succumbed to the bluff and bluster — one might be tempted to say the hardball tactics — of the more established National League. The players fought back to win a share of the increased revenue made by improving ticket sales; nevertheless, profits of 15 to 33 percent a year were often made after salaries were reduced by the creation and extension of the reserve clause.[21]

By the 1890s, baseball management regained dominance over the ballplayers. Their greed and arrogance led them to the creation of a monopoly that they equated with security but which was in reality a means of controlling costs. The tools of this monopoly included the reserve clause, which bound a player to his club even after his contract expired — the player could either play for a salary dictated by management or not play at all. The draft and the option were further tools that ensured that non–National League clubs would be subservient to the major league organization. National League clubs could draft any player from a minor league club for a fixed amount that "had no relationship to the player's value on the open market." Thus, non-National League teams could develop young talent but would not be able to keep such strong players or benefit economically by selling them to major league clubs. Finally, the option allowed National League clubs to "send players to non-League clubs, subject to recall."[22] The effect of the owners gaining such complete control of the industry can be summarized as follows: "The reserve clause, the draft, and the option were championed for years as necessary for the economic stability of baseball. In truth, they were necessary only for the economic advantage of the league owners who could undermine leagues that tried to resist." The creation of a monopoly for major league baseball did not bring tranquility to the national pastime but sparked unrest and rebellion.[23]

The owners also succeeded in creating the myth that they were the guardians of the national pastime and that the players were its selfish and undeserved benefactors:

> These pieties express the orthodox view of American baseball that insists the sport is not really a business at all but a pastime provided to the public through the owners' generosity. Because the owners are not interested in money, players who apply pressure for higher salaries are spoiled ingrates. Worse yet the players' union is a radical threat to the goose that is laying the golden egg. Since baseball is not really a business, antitrust law need not apply, and communities should show the proper feudal spirit by building stadiums for their sports franchises.
>
> This orthodox view is pure Babbitry at its finest, as the executives' own statements demonstrate ... the real game [of baseball] until the 1970s was the game of the owners controlling players.[24]

Furthermore, with the reserve clause in standard player contracts severely restraining player movement and keeping player salaries artificially low, and the endless labor disputes being a major contributor to dwindling fan enthusiasm, both players and fans alike were in need of a psychological and emotional boost as the country entered the last decade of the 19th century.

1891–1894 — Ohio

In the 1890s, difficult economic conditions and a prevailing attitude that was decidedly anti-multicultural and racist made it extraordinarily difficult for African American ballplayers to find work in integrated leagues.

Bud Fowler spent five years of the decade—1891, 1893–94, 1896, and 1899—playing at least part-time for and later working as a part-owner of an independent integrated team, the Findlay (OH) Sluggers (or various incarnations of this team).[25] The 1891 season was a particularly difficult one for Fowler to find a position. In the off-season of 1890, the African American veteran, who had connections with black baseball organizations in Nebraska, was angling for a position with Plattsburgh: "Bud Fowler, the crack colored second baseman, wishes to sign with the Plattsburgh team. Fowler is one of the best men at his position that can be found and would be a good acquisition to the team."[26] Instead he caught on with independent clubs in St. Louis, Wisconsin, and Ohio, leaving him out of organized baseball for the first time in seven years.[27]

1892 — Nebraska

Eighteen ninety-two was the first year of play of the Nebraska State League (NSL), which also was the only league in organized baseball that signed African American players that year. Bud Fowler had ended the previous year playing for the great black baseball team, the Lincoln (NE) Giants; he and a few other stars from that team moved over to the NSL. As early as the winter of 1891, the veteran ballplayer was angling to play on an integrated Nebraska team.

In 1892, Fowler signed on with the Lincoln league entry to modest fanfare: "Bud Fowler, the old Leadville, Colo. second baseman, will shake the barnacles off his frame around second base for Lincoln."[28] Before the season began, there was little hint of the racial unrest that would emerge as a result of the financial and organizational stresses the Nebraska State League would undergo. In fact, prior to the season, little mention was made of the race of the two potential star signees: "Castone is getting into shape at Lincoln along with Bud Fowler and will bear watching this season, as he is one of the best in the association."[29] However, inclement weather and a very weak fan base doomed the Lincoln franchise, which by mid–May had relocated to Kearney. A light-hearted but insightful editorial laid the failure of baseball in the state capital at the feet of the fairer sex and with the ownership for not understanding women's importance to the national pastime:

> It was not a flattering commentary upon the capital city that she has allowed her base ball team to go hence in distress, and were it not for the insufferable weather that has been vouchsafed this section the ladies of Lincoln would certainly be required to bear their share of approbrium [sic]. And no inconsiderable share would it be. No base ball team can thrive in any city unless it receives the support of the ladies, and even the cranks among Lincoln's fair ever lent the encouragement of their presence in appreciable numbers at a game this season. Under such circumstances of course the team could not play ball, and of course, also, very few of the sterner sex found time and inclination to attend. In sport, as in work, the presence and approval of the fair sex stimulates the zeal of the champion and develops hidden merit. The base ball manager who placed a few dummies in the grand stand clad in resplendent millinery had a head so level that a chequerboard [sic] would fit it. Should a western association team come to Lincoln something must be done to revive the interest of the ladies in base ball if it would live in Lincoln.[30]

The Lincoln franchise first transferred to Kearney: "In the Nebraska state league the Kearney team will play the schedule dates of the defunct Lincoln team until June first. A new schedule will be arranged for games after that date."[31] However, the schedule maker need not have gone to such trouble, as the Nebraska State League folded by mid–July: "The Hastings base ball club has thrown up the sponge and disbanded without finishing the season. This is the last relic of the Nebraska State League."[32]

Bud Fowler had a difficult year both on the field and in the clubhouse, as he had to deal with the open hostility of his opponents and several teammates. His year's statistics were substandard by his past high levels of achievement. He hit .273 with only 8 extra-base hits in 172 at-bats.[33]

Bud Fowler's future in organized baseball in the early 1890s was partially determined by a major nation-wide economic depression and bank run that led to a major contraction of the minor leagues.³⁴ The same time period saw two famed black baseball clubs — the Cuban Giants and the New York Gorhams — with whom Bud Fowler had had some involvement enter as an entire team in otherwise white professional leagues (Middle States League [1890], renamed the Eastern Interstate League [1891], and finally the Connecticut State League [1892]) as a last-gasp effort for survival prior to their demise in 1892.³⁵

Playing up his veteran status to the hilt, Fowler claimed he was 48 years old (when he was actually much younger) so he could be perceived as older than the "grand gentleman of the nineteenth century game, Adrian 'Cap' Anson,"³⁶ with whom the African American pioneer was, consciously or unconsciously, competing for national recognition and paying fans for his on-field appearances.

After a contentious half-season on the Great Plains in 1892, Bud Fowler returned to Findlay and to Galesburg to play independent baseball after the Nebraska State League disbanded in mid–July. He stayed on with the Sluggers but was playing with Galesburg again in 1893 when he was the second baseman for "the best independent team in the state" (Illinois). A story datelined from Galesburg of August 30, 1893, entitled "Possibility of Two-Eyed League Reorganization," described "...a wonderful revival of baseball in central and western Illinois ... [Galesburg] has won sixteen out of twenty-one days...."³⁷

In 1894 he played on a team with hometown Findlay sensation, Grant "Homerun" Johnson, a 21-year-old college graduate who was a prodigious power hitter. There were many reports that Johnson hit 60 home runs that year, claims that entered the young slugger into the realm of legend if not verifiable fact. The rookie star and the veteran looked for the financing for a club to be named the Findlay Colored Western Giants but could not find investors. However, in 1895, Johnson and Fowler became involved with the Page Fence (Colored) Giants, a landmark black touring baseball club that was a major turning point in African American baseball in segregationist America.³⁸ A major factor, perhaps, in pushing Fowler to pursue management opportunities at this time was a report at the end of 1894 that he suffered a debilitating injury that may have signaled to the African American veteran that his every day playing career was nearing its end: "It was reported about town [Lima] last night that Bud Fowler, the crack colored second baseman of the Findlays, had his leg broken yesterday."³⁹

1895 — Ohio and Michigan

While playing for Findlay (OH), Bud Fowler placed an enigmatic ad in the national publication *The Sporting Life* that hinted at the next stage of his baseball career. As his playing days neared an end due to the aging process and the open racial discrimination of the 1890s, the African American baseball pioneer was looking to the management side of the game: "First class colored players can hear of something advantageous by addressing Bud Fowler, 822 North Main Street, Findlay, O."[40] His ambition was to create a touring team of African American players to be called the "Findlay Colored Western Giants"; however, the local funding fell through and Bud turned to entrepreneurs in the midwest and east.

However, at the end of August of 1894, Fowler's plan to relocate to Adrian (MI) and organize a national first-class black baseball club began

Bud Fowler (middle row, far right) with the Findlay (Ohio) Sluggers (1894). In 1894 Fowler, now 36 years old, was to play one more half-season on an integrated team (1895) with the rest of his playing career being spent in independent baseball and on black touring clubs (National Baseball Hall of Fame Library, Cooperstown, New York).

to take shape. On the 27th and 28th, the Findlay Sluggers defeated the Detroit Tigers of the Western League, 8–7 and 9–5. While in Adrian on the 29th, Fowler's club won a doubleheader, 6–0 and 19–9, and he gave an interview to the local newspaper about his 1895 plans: "Bud Fowler, the efficient second baseman of the Findlay ball team, is anxious to locate in Adrian next season. He wants to organize a 'Cuban Giant' team, composed of the best colored talent in the country, and will made [sic] Adrian his headquarters if our citizens will guarantee him $500 and fix up good grounds."[41]

On the following day, Fowler elaborated on his plans regarding this Adrian-based all-star team, which was to feature southpaw George Wilson on the proposed "Adrian Cuban Giants":

> Bud Fowler's sceme [sic] for organizing a ball team here next season, composed of colored players, is growing. Secretary Hoch, of the Association team, has it in mind to take one-half of the $500 stock necessary, and to have suitable grounds fixed up. The scheme unfolded is to secure a special car, with compartments for 15 to 18 people, let the team live in the car, do their own hotel work there and work on the percentage. Fowler states that he can get a team equal to the famous Cuban Giants, and $500 would start it. Nothing would advertise Adrian as that, and we could become the ball center of the state, if not of the west.[42]

Within a month, it was being reported that the Page Fence Giants would be a reality starting with the 1895 season:

> The organization of the colored base ball club for the season of 1895, with management and headquarters in this city, is a settled fact.... L.W. Hoch has conducted the negotiations between all the parties interested.... When the famous company of players departs from this station in their special car in the early spring, to seek conquests with the best material on the diamond, they will go forth under the title "The Page Fence Giants of Adrian, Michigan."
>
> This alone removes every obstacle of doubt as to the feasibility of [and] practicality of the enterprise. It is bound to be a success. The Page Wire Fence Co. is always progressive and wide awake, and success with them is the watchword which never fails. The Page Fence Co. will not be directly identified with the management of the association, their interest being continued to making it an advertising medium in the cities and towns where the Fencers make their appearance. The entire concern, however, will be in the hands of the Adrian people — men who have the enterprise and ability necessary to bring abundant success.
>
> Thirteen of the finest ballplayers in the country have already been secured, and will be under contract immediately after the close of the

present season. "Bud" Fowler, who is favorably known here, for twenty years as one of the best drawing cards on the diamond, will be the manager of the team. Grant Johnson, the famous home run short stop of the Findlays, who delighted the audience by his brilliant work in the Findlay and Delphos games, will be captain. Every other member of the club will be of the same high grade....[43]

Bud Fowler made good on his commitment to the Adrian community by moving there on October 12, 1894, to work "at his trade as a barber. He likes Adrian, and will very likely take a chair in Steve Craig's shop." That predication came to fruition the following month:

The Oriental barber Shop, under the management of Craig & Reid, live, young, energetic business men, whose Tonsorial manipulating work is done in first-class style, have engaged for the winter, Mr. Bud Fowler, formerly of the Findlay base ball club, now here organizing the greatest colored club ever in the field, "The Page Fence Giants," which will be an advertisement for the City of Adrian, (equal to the greatest Findlay club, which was an excellent advertisement for that city), as the Page Fence Co. never do business by halves. Bud will be pleased to meet his old friends at any time.[44]

The November 1894 national sports papers were filled with specifics about the upcoming Page Fence Giants:

- [The Page Fence Giants will be based in] Adrian, Mich., the home of the Michigan Amateur [Baseball] championship [and will be a] colored rival for the eastern Cuban Giants.
- The colored professionals Page Fence Giants are booked through June 1 [1895].
- [The Page Fence Giants will visit ten states] in their own special [railroad] car, giving bicycle parades before each game.... Bud Fowler, late of the Findlays, will manage the Giants....
- [The Giants] will be used as an advertising card for their [Page Fence Wire Co.] wares.
- [Bud Fowler states that the Giants] will be the strongest colored aggregation ever organized.[45]

The sporting press employed much of the promotional copy of the Page Fence Giants in its discussion of both Bud Fowler and his strong African American roster:

Bud Fowler Organizes Another Big Colored Club
(Findlay, O., Oct, 22) Bud Fowler, an old colored League player, who played second base for the Findlay Base Ball club the past season, has organized a color[ed] ball team for next season. It will be backed by a wire fence company of Adrian, Mich., and a bicycle company from Massachusetts, and will be used as an advertising card for their wares. A special traveling car will be secured and fitted up as the home of the team. A bicycle parade will be given prior to each game. Fowler says his team will be the strongest colored aggregation ever organized. He has the players under contract as follows: Bud Fowler, Findlay, manager and second base; Grant Johnson, Findlay, captain and short stop; Roscoe Graham, Dubuque, Iowa, and Edward Kelly, Stockville, Miss., catchers; George Miller, Dubuque Iowa, George Hopkins, Chicago, and Bob Higgins, Memphis, pitchers; George Taylor, San Francisco, first base; Fred Patterson, Stockville, Miss., third base; Ed Brooks, Chicago, center field, Tom Kelley, Stockville, Miss., right field. The season will be opened March 27 at St. Louis, with the Browns of that city.[46]

During the winter, the national sporting newspapers continued to report on the management team of the Page Fence Giants and Bud Fowler's specific involvement with the team:

This city [Adrian, Michigan] has gained prominence enough among enthusiasts in the Northwest, so that the Page Fence Giants, colored professionals have been organized, undoubtedly one of the strongest teams in the country. [The Page-Fence Giants] will travel to 10 states during the season of 1895 to their own special car, giving bicycle parades before each game. Bud Fowler, late of the Findlay, O., team will manage the Giants, and is now booked up to June 1.[47]

In a final significant development during the Hot Stove League months, Bud Fowler used his relationship with his former team to good advantage. Findlay manager Charles A. Strobel invited his former star player to open the season at his new ballpark at the Wigwam grounds: "The grounds will be opened on Decoration Day with the Colored Page Fence Giants, of Adrian, Mich., with Bud Fowler, Findlay's last year's second baseman, as manager."[48]

The 1895 Page Fence Giants were wildly successful on the field, going 118–36–2. Johnson and Fowler were so encouraged that they planned a series with the premier black ball club, the Cuban Giants: "Arrangements are being made to play the Cuban Giants five games, three in different cities of the State and two in New York, for the colored championship of the world. All clubs wishing dates in New York State can communicate with Bud Fowler, Adrian, Mich."[49]

Bud Fowler also became involved with a Lansing club that had postseason designs on the international baseball market: "The Lansing Colored Capital All-American team was organized and incorporated this Saturday by R. N. Pearshall, owner of the Lansing State League Club, and Bud Fowler, of the Page Fence Giants, who organized the Giants. The club will consist of several of the great Page Fence Giants and two of the Cubans [Giants]."[50] A month later it was reported from Lansing that the touring African American team was being assembled: "Some of the players signed include 'Bud' Fowler who will act as manager; Clarence Williams, catcher; Robinson and Seldon, pitchers, Jackson, fielder, and Grant short stop, all of the Cuban Giants; Graham and Wilson, of the Adrian team, will report at the close of the State league season."[51]

The first barnstorming plan after the above proposed "colored world championship" was to play 40 games in England between the Page Fence Giants and Minneapolis of the Western League. This plan was then replaced by an even more ambitious one: a nine-man all-star team from the Michigan State League would travel with the Giants and play for a month in Honolulu. This would be followed by a barnstorming trip to Australia and New Zealand, where they would play for three months! However, neither of these plans ever came to fruition. With his hyperbole, Fowler got what he wanted from this interview: the reporter's enthusiastic encouragement to his readers to go out to the ballpark the following day to see Bud's team play baseball.[52]

Fowler was also making increasing use of a gambit that became a personal trademark. He inflated his age to such a degree (usually by 11 years)[53] that his appearance in the line-up on even an occasional basis seemed miraculous and allowed him to be compared to the national pastime's grand old man, Cap Anson. Fowler employed this promotional tactic to varying extents during his barnstorming years with such clubs as the Page Fence Giants, the All-American Black Tourists, and the Colored All-Americans:

> Anson has a rival. Bud Fowler, the second baseman of the Colored Page Fence Giants, is forty-eight years of age. He has been playing since 1869.
>
> Bud Fowler is still in the business, playing second base and organizing the Black Tourists. Bid McPhee and A. C. Anson are spry young lads compared to Fowler.

> Bud Fowler, the veteran ballplayer, is now 55 years old but still plays ball.[54]

In spite of the enormous critical and financial success of the all-black touring club he organized and played for in 1895, Bud Fowler abruptly left the Page Fence Giants in mid–July to play for the Adrian Reformers in the revitalized Michigan State League (where six years earlier he had a strong season with the Greenville franchise). The lure of playing integrated baseball against the best competition was too great a temptation for Fowler to pass up. He was replaced as the Giants keystone sacker by Sol White, the pioneering black sportswriter and a star player in his own right.[55] After a few games with Adrian, Fowler landed in Lansing with the Senators, where he had another stellar season with an impressive combined set of statistics in 31 games — 46 hits, including 11 doubles and a triple and 40 runs scored and a .331 batting average. Fellow African American George "Lefty" Wilson dominated the league with a 29–4 record and a .879 winning percentage, while Fowler's teammate Jack Daly was equally dominant at the bat, hitting .397 with 143 hits, 124 runs scored, and a prodigious 25 home runs.[56]

Immediately after the MSL season ended, Bud Fowler planned to hit the road with a black touring team that was organized by his Lansing owner:

> The Lansing Colored Capital All-American team was organized and incorporated by R. N. Pearsall, owner of the Lansing State League club and Bud Fowler of the Page Fence Giants who organized the Giants. The new team will start from Lansing, Mich., for New York, playing en route, and will sail for England for two months, joining the Minneapolis team of the Western League. The club will consist of several of the great Page Fence Giants and two of the Cubans. Arrangements are being made to play the Cuban Giants five games, three in different cities in the state and two in New York, for the colored championship of the world. All clubs wishing dates in New York State communicate with Bud Fowler, Adrian, Mich.[57]

Yet, in spite of the banner year he had on the diamond, this was Bud Fowler's last year in organized baseball; he never received another contract offer to play integrated baseball. He was through as a player at 37 years of age due more to the temper of the times than any deteriorating skills on the ball field.[58]

1896–1899 — Ohio and the Midwest

After his departure from the Page Fence Giants and the conclusion of the Michigan State League season, the public was interested in where Fowler would land in the 1896 season. He headed for Northeastern Ohio, which was his default destination in the last decade of the 19th century: "'Bud' Fowler, the old time colored ballplayer, has been spending a few days in the city [Cincinnati]."[59] As the 1896 season opened, Fowler, who had organized the black club the Muncie (IN) Londons (which was actually the relocated Rock City [TN] franchise), was managing and playing first base for the new club. Muncie folded early in May because of attendance woes and because many southern teams would not play the team. Fowler apparently headed back to Ohio just one step ahead of the law:

Bud Fowler Skipped Out
Muncie's famous Creole baseball team has disbanded owning to the fact that the people would not patronize a colored team. The club was taken there from Nashville, Tenn., where it played for years as the Rock City Club, and as such was the champion club of the South. Many of the southern teams would not play them, drawing the color line. Last Friday the club played Alexandria, and Bud Fowler, the manager and first baseman left that night for parts unknown, with the gate receipts, amounting to $25. Fowler is 49 years old and has been playing for 29 years. He is a great player.[60]

While he continued to be successful on the diamond, the veteran infielder was finding it nearly impossible to make a living in the professional game: "It was hard picking for a colored player this year [1896]. I didn't make a living; I just existed."[61]

In December of 1896, Fowler was contacted by a management group in Galveston (TX) to organize a team and an African American baseball league. Fowler was named manager of the Galveston Flyaways and was the driving force behind the Lone Star Colored Baseball League of Texas: "A Texas colored league is also being organized here. Bud Fowler, formerly with some of the noted colored teams up north, is the leading spirit of the organization. Clubs will be located at Galveston, Houston, Palestine, Cameron, Beaumont, Austin, Waco, and San Antonio."[62] The African American baseball pioneer was apparently quite sanguine about the prospects of the Flyaways and the Lone Star Colored Baseball enterprise:

Colored Baseball Matters

Yesterday afternoon Bud Fowler, manager of the Flyaway baseball club, had the boys out practicing in their regular uniforms. A match game was played between the Flyaways and a picked team, which resulted in a victory for the Flyaways by a score of 7 to 3, nine innings.... The game was a good one, and some clever ball playing was done.

Manager Fowler will have the team practice regularly hereafter. W.H. Noble, the financial manager of the Flyaways, was looking at the boys playing, and when they get their new uniforms they will make a good appearance on the diamond. [The reporter then lists the players already signed by Manager Fowler and three municipalities — Dallas, Beaumont, and Shreveport (LA) — which were clamoring for entry into the Lone Star League.]

However, though Fowler's energy and enthusiasm were key elements in the proposed league's early organization, there is no further public mention of the Lone Star Colored Baseball League after January 25, 1897.[63]

Fowler returned to the midwest and played a few matches with the Findlay and Lima (OH) ball clubs. He was still a drawing card and playing a very respectable second base during a down cycle in which the national pastime was not thriving financially. One Ohio newspaper described a mid–September game briefly: "The Wheeling, West Virginia, ball team defeated Lima, yesterday. Score 12–9. 'Bud' Fowler, the colored player, who has been in the diamond for 25 years, was on second for Lima." The local Lima paper had a fuller account of the same game, including the odd occurrence of the banning of stealing in the game, before reporting on Fowler's stellar play in the field:

Played Without a Mask

The spectators were discouraged at the outlook when the first inning opened and the Wheeling catcher refused to go behind the bat with the mask that was on the grounds. The visitors had no mask of their own, and the one that Lima afforded was broken. The teams agreed to play the game without stealing bases and it looked as though the game was very much school boy, but when the playing had fairly commenced, the brilliant fielding made the game interesting.

... and second base was covered by the old time Bud Fowler of Findlay fame and ebony color. The stops and catches made by Eichler [the regular Lima shortstop] and Fowler in the field and the exceptionally fast fielding done by Jennett, Honeyman, and Boise in the outfield were both frequent and perfect.

In November, Bud Fowler was named manager of his former Findlay (OH) club for the following season.[64] However, in keeping with the many disappointments he experienced in his baseball career, the African American pioneer did not manage the following year as Findlay never fielded a team in 1898.

In May of 1898, the African American veteran was playing second base for the Cuban Giants in a victory over the Utica (NY) of the New York State League. He went three-for-five at bat and knocked in the winning run and was praised for "his general play," while the entire team was commended for making "things lively with their coaching and [running] the bases cleverly."[65] Apparently, Fowler also found time to umpire an upstate New York game between Athens and Philmont.[66]

Fowler also suffered continued personal misfortune in 1898. After playing with the Cuban Giants in New York, he hopped a train, planning to visit his family in Fort Plain in upstate New York. He was set upon by four muggers who beat him "savagely and brutally."[67]

He spent the winter in Findlay, where he began planning for the upcoming season: "Findlay, O., will have a team next season managed by 'Bud' Fowler, the colored second baseman. Sunday games will be played at Cygnet the home of 'Dusty' Miller."[68] The winter of 1898-99 brought threatening economic clouds to the baseball world as a whole, but the aging African American was working hard in Ohio to build a competitive team for the following spring:

> Notwithstanding the unsettled condition of the base ball world, and the possibilities of a change all around, Manager Strobel [Findlay] is signing new talent for 1899, talent which he hopes will be strong enough for any league he may be in. Among the players signed are two pitchers. One Wilts by name, was recommended by the venerable "Bud" Fowler. Patrons of the game will remember Pitcher Engle, who was with the Jackson team in the Interstate League. He has been signed. Tim O'Connell, the shortstop, will also be given another trial.[69]

One month later, the tireless Bud Fowler had leased the playing grounds in Findlay, had established an early season schedule, and had assembled a truly national team:

Fort Wayne People Getting Anxious—
Findlay Will Have a Good Team

A dispatch from Findlay says: This city, after being without base ball for two years, will once more have a club. Bud Fowler, the veteran colored player, known in base ball circles ever since the national game attained any prominence, has leased grounds and now announces the signing of the following team: Catcher Mack, of the Canadian League; pitchers, McIntyre, of the Texas league; Wagner of Ashtabula; Porter, of the New England league; Lindsay, of the Cincinnati Shamrocks; first base, Heistand, of Terre Haute; second base, Fowler; third base, Richards, of Ashtabula; shortstop, Kelley, of Jacksonville, Ill.; left field, Bissel of Wapakoneta; center field, Myers, of the Cincinnati Shamrocks. The average weight of the members is 160 pounds. The opening games will be played at Toledo April 22 and 23 and Toledo will return games here April 26 and 27.[70]

Eighteen ninety-nine was to be a watershed year for Bud Fowler. As the only African American on the Findlay club, Bud Fowler was a part-owner, manager and starting second baseman and he served in the same roles for another reincarnation of the Black Tourists team. His partner in both endeavors was respected local white businessman Dr. William H. Drake, who apparently provided most of the financial investment in the clubs. As usual, Fowler provided the diamond expertise, enthusiasm, and promotion for the project(s). Early in the year, Fowler was recruiting the top tier of African American players in the country: "Findlay [which] was the first [baseball club] to have its semi-professional team organized" had Bud Fowler solicit the services of such black stars as Sol White, Clarence Williams, Fred Grant, Selden, and Jackson (Cuban X Giants), George Wilson (Page Fence Giants), and Billy Holland (Chicago Unions) — "Address letters to Bud Fowler at once."[71]

Six months later, the white players on the Findlay club were in revolt, demanding that Fowler be fired or they would withhold their services: "The white members of Findlay's ball club have drawn the color line and demanded of Dr. Drake their backer, that Bud Fowler, colored, be ousted from the team. They will quit if their demand is not heeded. The management is also two weeks behind in their pay."[72] Drake acquiesced to the white players' threats; however, Drake's relationship with Bud Fowler apparently remained positive as within two weeks the two partners announced an ambitious off-season tour of the midwest, west coast, and southwest by the Black Tourists:

> Dr. W.H. Drake and Bud Fowler, the organizer of the famous Page Fence Giants will take a team [Black Tourists] to California in September, playing through Ohio, Indiana, Illinois, Missouri, Kansas, Colorado, Utah, California, returning through New Mexico....
>
> [The team] will be composed of the best colored players in the United

States.... The great feature of this club will be their daily parades, which will be made in full dress suits, black pants, white vests, swallow-tail coats, opera hats, silk umbrellas and, by request of different managers, will play the games in full-dress suits.[73]

However, Fowler could not catch lightning in a bottle a second time by reprising the promotional strategies he employed with the Page Fence Giants. The ambitious western tour envisioned by the African American entrepreneur ended ignominiously: "A base ball team composed of colored men organized by Bud Fowler for a trip to the Pacific coast, disbanded at Decatur. Fowler played in this town [Delphos] some years ago with the Lima club."[74]

Bud Fowler's days as an everyday player were nearly over. While he continued to make appearances in games throughout the first decade of the 20th century, they were usually limited to brief appearances to spur gate receipts. In 1899, Fowler was 41 years old (though he frequently claimed to be 11 years older). His many nagging injuries suffered from the hard (at times vicious) play of white opponents and the wear-and-tear of the running game that was his forte, combined with the constant travel, and the normal process of aging to make it clear that the African American star would need to find a new role if he were to continue in the national pastime.

Along with his playing ability and character, Bud Fowler had impeccable qualities as an organizer, coach, scout, and owner. What he lacked was the financial capital needed to run a first-class professional baseball team. The racism he experienced in Findlay seems to be of a piece with all the prejudice he faced in the game in that such behavior could always be traced to economic factors. Usually his white teammates either objected to the inclusion of African American players on integrated teams because they feared the loss of their positions or losing face by being beaten by an inferior race, or they employed racial issues as a means to escape from one-sided contracts or untenable team situations. The inability of Drake and Fowler to meet the payrolls for both the 1899 Findlay Sluggers and the Black Tourists in a timely fashion, for example, would be reason enough for both whites and blacks to rebel.

The only avenues still open to African American involvement with the national game were the black touring circuit, or, if economic investment could be stabilized in an improving financial environment, the dream of an African American major league. Bud Fowler had been intimately involved in black baseball almost from the beginning of his baseball career. Moreover, his national success with the Cuban Giants and the Page Fence Giants as well as experiences with clubs of lesser repute made him a magnet capable of drawing superior players to his black teams. Finally, Bud Fowler recognized the entertainment value of the game and the wishes of his African American audience, so he added popular comic routines and fashion plate garb and cycling parades to make games more appealing to the casual fan looking for a fun evening. The end of the 19th century coincided with the full blossoming of Bud Fowler as a black baseball entrepreneur.

With baseball coverage now a central focus of national and local reporting and a key element of building civic pride, newspapers did their part in reviving flagging interest in the national pastime. They did so by discussing new variations of the game and by referencing two of the oldest selling points of baseball — that it is a captivating game and that it is America's game.

Indoor baseball, which evolved into the sport of softball, was highly praised for its intensity and dangerous qualities. In direct opposition to baseball's vast outdoor spaces, the cramped, limited nature of the playing area was viewed as a positive in a female's account of an indoor game in Chicago:

> Chicago has one advantage over our city. Now this is not saying that it hasn't more than one, but I am willing to vouch for this one, personally. It is the great and glorious game of indoor base ball. I attended my first two games last week, and mourned because I had not the opportunity to see the third. Imagine yourself in a room about the size of Temple Hall, on the floor of which is a painted diamond, so constructed that the field [lies now to the] west. You observe that there is no centre [sic] fielder, but that the second baseman plays quite far back. The left and right fielders play close up to the line, while the short stop and the ninth man, whom one expected to see in centre [sic] are called the right and left short-stops and maintain their positions on either side, inside the side lines, about halfway between the box and the plate. One's first impression is that no batter could ever get a ball past all these persons crowded together. This game started in a peculiar way, the idea being originated by a man who batted a boxing glove with a broomstick. The ball used is about six times as soft. It is not a perfect sphere, and is very hard to hold. The willow is but little larger than a broom handle. Never was I so excited at a ball game as I was last Friday evening, when the far-famed "Catlin" nine played for the championship against the La Grange team, in the pretty little La Grange club house. Everything seemed so haz-

ardous. I sat in the gallery and held my breath for fear the first baseman, the one I was most particularly interested in, would fan out, or, if he hit the ball, that it would sail up in my direction. When a Catlin boy would come to bat I almost prayed that he'd get to first base; once there he was as good as across the plate, for he slides!—slides did I say! It is too mild a word. A toboggan is not to be compared with him. At the first pitched ball he starts on a dead run; when he gets about two jumps away from first he wildly casts himself on the floor and scoots on to second where, clutching second, the two continue their mad career until stopped by a wall or some other little obstruction. In the same way he reaches third and home. Between pitches the whole nine repairs to the immediate vicinity of their respective places, where wet rags lie upon the slippery floor. They jump on these with both feet and fondly imagine that it helps them to maintain their equilibrium. Perhaps it does; at any rate it is invaluable to a poor batter. He steps up to the plate and wildly saws the air. The crowd jeers and so, instead of standing there all embarrassment, calmly leaves the plate, rubs his feet over the wet rag, walks back and tries again. The Catlin pitcher struck out eight men of the nine who came to bat in the first three innings, and the Catlin enthusiasts, of whom I was the only feminine member, fairly raised the roof. The famous seventeen inning game with Minneapolis was not more interesting, and the score—11 to 1—was vastly more satisfactory. The La Grange women would have taken pure [joy] surely in throwing me out of the window that evening. One was constrained to pity them for they had nothing to applaud. La Grange, I believe, has decided not to play any more ball this season. The catcher for the Catlin's is a little boy about twelve years old, but he can hold this ball. It was worth the price of admission to watch the left short-stop. As soon as the ball would leave the pitcher's hand he would start at the batter, taking little short steps and pounding his feet hard. It was no wonder that his opponents lowered their batting average, he just simply scared him so they couldn't bat. The La Grange team has a professional pitcher, and many were the cries of "How's that for a raised ball, Mr. Umpire!" the rule being that the ball must be delivered underhand *sans* curves. But I imagine you are weary of this dissertation, so will change the subject.[75]

Lest the potential ticket-buying cranks forget the joys of the city game, editorials such as the following rite-of-passage narrative appeared throughout the country to create an instant nostalgia for a sport that was barely out of its infancy:

BASEBALL IN CITY STREETS

It has its delights and difficulties and it produces good players.

Let us see whether you will not learn from these boys some games to take to your friends out of town.

First and foremost comes baseball. If anyone doubts the universal popularity of this game, one afternoon upon the street will convince him that the American boys' love of baseball has become hereditary. It seems as if these boys no sooner left the cradle than a base ball found its way into their hands. They commence to play as soon as they can roll a ball across the pavement. From a real game, with nine "men" on a side and three bases, we shall see everything in ball playing, down to the solitary youngster who rolls the ball up an awning and catches it as it returns to him. And these boys can play baseball too. I hesitate to admit it, for I was a country boy, but I'll warrant you that from the inhabitants of a block I can select nine boys, none of whom shall be over ten years of age, who can beat the best nine of thirteen-year-old fellows your village can produce.

They play in the streets; they play on the sidewalk; and they go at it with a vim and earnestness one grows enthusiastic in watching. They pitch "curves," and why their catchers' intent and mask-less faces are not more frequently damaged by the bat they "catch off" of, no one can say. All this remember, on the cobblestones, with slippery car tracks dividing the "field," and wagons, drays and cars constantly passing by.

On any field a quick and practiced eye is required to measure the arc of a "fly ball," and to select the spot from which it may be captured; but when the ground is a crowded street, and there is added the more or less rapidly passing vehicle, the chances are even that the fielder may get under a horse's hoofs and the descending "fly" at the same time. Many narrow escapes have I seen, but somehow the active little bodies always managed to be missed.

But the cars and wagons and pedestrians are as nothing; the players look out for the former two, the last must care for themselves if they wish to avoid a batted ball or a runner making a frantic dash for "first." What these boys really mind, because it is an effectual preventive of ball playing, is the blue coated policeman, known by the boys as a "cop." An abbreviation of "copper," the origin of which name is uncertain.

Here is a game in active progress; there is intense excitement; shouts of encouragement fill the air. Turn away your head for an instant. Now look again. Where are our players? Not one of them to be seen; only a few boys strolling along the sidewalk; not a bat nor ball in sight. What does it all mean? Truly, you have never seen so abrupt an ending to a game of ball. But look: coming up the street, a block or more away, in all the stateliness of blue uniform and brass buttons, idly twirling his club, comes the awe inspiring "copper."

For you must remember that it is illegal to play baseball in the street, and every player is liable to imprisonment. How would you have liked to have one of your games so interrupted? Is the game ended? By no means; wait a moment, this is only "time." Slowly the retreating blue-coat fades in the distance; then like magic each player resumes his place, and the game is resumed with all its former ardor.—Frank M. Chapman in *St. Nicholas*[76]

Baseball in all its youth, vigor, intensity, and excitement is being invoked in such encomiums. After a decade of court battles, franchise movements, business improprieties, betting questions and concerns and general fan and player discontent, a general baseball fatigue set in on the country, and a desire for more "innocent" earlier days became a nationwide quest. In a sport less than 50 years old (with a professional game just a bit more than two decades old), there was a nostalgia for an earlier, mythical "golden age" of baseball in which the inherent and inescapable tension between being a game and a business profession never existed. While noting the slump in baseball attendance and enthusiasm in the early 1890s, most newspapers tried to rally the public by arguments that in spite of the many recent changes in the game, baseball was and would remain America's pastime:

> If there is anything that plainly shows the peculiarity of the course of public opinion it is the base ball season of 1891. First-class players are just as numerous, and the great clubs are doing just as good team work as ever, but there is a notable lack of enthusiasm among lovers of the game. There is not the outpouring of the people to see a match game between the leaders that there was a few years ago, and which crowded 15,000 to 30,000 excited men and women in the old Polo Grounds, who could not have been more interested in the game if the fate of the nation was at stake. It is rather difficult to determine the reasons for this apathy. Undoubtedly the mistakes and quarrels of last year [1890] have had much to do with the indifference with which the public looks upon its aforetime favorites. Then the changes that have taken place in the teams, have had something to do with it. Men who have been accustomed to yell for "Johnnie" or "Buck," don't like the idea of seeing their favorite players in opposing teams. The sentiment of hero worship is still strong within us.
>
> It is safe to predict, however, that base ball will always be our national game, and the favorite outdoor pastime of the American public. There is a dash and spirit in the game which appears peculiarly to the American temperament. A successful cricket player may have as much skill and endurance as a good all-round base ballplayer. It is even possible to admire the fine plays in the noble English game. Foot ball is exciting enough, but does not admit of brilliant strokes that appeal to all the spectators. But there is nothing but base ball that will make a man dance on his seat, turn red in the face and yell like a Comanche Indian over a

home run or a three bagger. The base ball crank falls asleep over cricket, and considers foot ball "no game."[77]

The last paragraph of this editorial in praise of (and also in defense of) baseball could have been composed 35 years earlier in the game's infancy. Thus, from its very beginnings, baseball has inspired civic pride and invoked the virtues of an American ideal of youthful optimism and vigorous earnestness. The last decade of the 19th century proved to be a consolidation of changes in the professional game on and off the field, with such retrenchment leading to a continued growth in popularity of the game and, ultimately, to further expansion of the sport on the local and national levels.

Furthermore, in keeping with the "scientific" focus that 19th-century baseball advocates always invoked in discussing the game, 1890s sportswriters presented subjects about topics that would be familiar to 21st-century fans of the game. For example, in the ever-present wish to enhance the spectators' experience at the ballpark, baseball ownership invested in electronic scoreboards as early as 1891:

> Electric Power describes a new system of reporting baseball and other games by means of an ingenious electrical apparatus. The special object of the apparatus is to enable a full report of games to be made in sight of a large number of people and at the same time dispensed with one or more of the assistants now required in reporting such games. This device is intended not only to indicate the progress of distant games, but actually to be used at the opposite end of the ball field from the grand stand, in order to enlighten the spectators on many points on which they are liable to be momentarily in doubt. Spectators coming in late are often unable to ascertain the number of innings played, the striker at bat, the number of balls and strikes called, etc., and even those already on the ground sometimes find it difficult to determine whether the umpire has called a strike or a ball. All these weighty issues, upon which the baseball enthusiast expounds such intense solicitude, can now be cleanly and reliably recorded, and all anxiety and uncertainty can be removed by a glance at the exhibition board placed in sight of the spectators, the indicators on which are electrically controlled and operated by an experienced person located close to the diamond.[78]

With the complete triumph of the professional game over its amateur counterpart, baseball humor in the 1890s began to focus on the fan. The rabid rooter whose identification with his favored club is so intense that it clouds his judgment is a recurring anecdote in the sports pages of the decade:

"The Rooter's Mistake"

He was a rooter if there ever was one. His enthusiasm was at a boiling heat all the time. He rooted with joy when the home team scored, and he rooted with disgust when the opposing nine added to its score. In every movement of either team he saw an occasion for rooting. He knew the game and understood it — at least he thought he did. He made his comments whether those around him liked his complaints or not.

The rooter always claims the right to be the critic of everyone connected with the game, from the lordly umpire to the mascot who hasn't yet reached his teens, and including the barefooted, ragged urchin who gains admission to the game by recovering the ball that was batted over the fence. Our particular rooter exercised that right, not bothering himself a bit whether he was allowed or not.

The result of the game was in doubt, and the interest was intense. The Hardfords [sic] were in the field, and the opposing nine was at the bat. A batter made a "swipe" at the ball as it came like a shot from the hand of Vickery, winding into a graceful inshoot when it reached the home plate. The bat whistled through the air, but didn't come within hailing distance of the ball. Just then a sparrow rose from the turf and flew toward the left field. The death like silence was broken by the rooter shouting:

"Go for it, Petit!"

Every eye was turned toward the place from which the loud bass voice of the rooter came, and everyone wondered.

Bob didn't obey the command of the rooter, and this made the rooter mad. He began to abuse Petit, and for a minute Bob's reputation as a baseball player suffered.

"What did you want to have him go for?" asked a person who was sitting near the censorious critic.

"Why, the ball that that was batted into left field."

"The ball! Why, you blankety [sic] blanked chump, that was a sparrow," replied the other.

The rooter's rooting ceased —*Hartford Times*.[79]

While the game on the field was improving as a spectator sport with its increased emphasis on hitting and the increased press coverage, baseball club owners managed to make a mess of the game during a time of national financial depression. Raised in the Gilded Age era of unrestrained and under-regulated business wheeling-and-dealing, 1890s management groups were comfortable in employing monopolies and cartels to limit economic downturns. The decade ended on an ominous financial note for the national pastime:

> The 1899 season is a disaster on many levels. Boston or Baltimore has won all seven of the 12-team [National] League pennants so far. The

Temple Cup [an attempt at a post-season championship series] has been abandoned after 1897. Now the artificially strengthened Brooklyn team [Baltimore owners Von der horst and Hanlon bought into the Brooklyn club and transferred their best players there] wins the pennant by eight games over Boston, with Baltimore fourth, 15 games back. St. Louis, even with Cy Young added, rises only to fifth, while the stripped Cleveland Spiders compile a 20–134 record that not even the 1962 Mets will be able to match for futility. The attendance average inches back over 200,000, but it is concentrated almost entirely in seven solid cities: Chicago, Philadelphia, Boston, Cincinnati, and, with special player help, St. Louis, Brooklyn, and Pittsburgh. These account for 80 percent of the total.[80]

Six

A Boy's Game and a Gentleman's Agreement
The Tensions within Nineteenth Century Baseball

Bud Fowler had been a recognized presence on the national baseball scene by the 1880s. By the turn of the century, he had experienced more than two decades of success on the diamond and racism on and off the playing field. The sport itself was only about a half century old while the dominant professional league was little more than two decades in existence. The assessment of baseball as the national pastime was unassailable but its value and its potential for harm were constantly under review as its supporters and detractors continued to face off.

Baseball had been of paramount importance to the nation in the 1880s, as is evidenced in a front-page observation of 1888: "The two greatest interests of the American people at the present time are the baseball championships and the presidential nominations."[1] The popularity of the sport was such that references to baseball games were difficult to escape even when attending religious services — "It is alleged that base ball announcements are made in the various pulpits of Albuquerque on the Sabbath." This was especially the case for a rabid baseball fan: "A Philadelphia clergyman who is a great athlete and lover of base ball forgot himself once and said: 'Here endeth the first inning — let us pray.'"[2]

With its combination of fierce competition and necessary cooperation, baseball seemed the essence of the American experience. Every town needed to have a baseball team in order to "keep abreast of the time."[3] The numbers tell the story of the game's popularity in the 1880s and beyond:

Some idea of the magnitude of base-ball can be shown by these figures: There are twelve leagues and associations now under the national agreement. They are the National, International, Western, Northwestern, Southern, Eastern, New England, Ohio State, Michigan State and National Colored Leagues, and the American and Pennsylvania associations. Nearly a hundred clubs are in these leagues, and they employ nearly 1,200 players. As there are several other minor leagues in existence who will probably join in the national agreement, it is safe to say that there will probably be 150 professional clubs in the United States and Canada, employing about 9,000 players and paying at least $1,500,000 in salaries.[4]

It was also a matter of civic pride and a sign of a prosperous locality to have a large contingent of fans travel to away games: the numbers of such cranks, often inflated, were frequently printed in newspaper post-mortems of a particular game.[5] Baseball attendance in the 19th century became a means whereby a community could "objectively" evaluate its economic growth and its success as a municipality.

In its earliest years, baseball was embraced as an example of "manliness and modern America" rather than the "boyishness and old world" nature of the earliest ball-and-bat games.[6] The myth of baseball and Iowa corn fields is just that—a falsehood based on the egalitarian notion of democracy in America and the "common man" source of the game's beginnings. Thus the advocates of baseball were fighting a two-pronged battle for the acceptance of its sport as the national pastime (a term first used in a December 1856 issue of New York City's *New York Mercury*): on the one hand, baseball was a win-at-all-costs endeavor that was an apt metaphor for the rough-and-tumble capitalism of the Gilded Age; on the other hand, it was a middle-class activity that defined bourgeois sensibilities for a country searching for an American identity.[7]

Baseball and correct comportment in society were integrated into the 1880s psyche to the point that it was *pro forma* for newspapers, even in the wild and woolly New Mexico Territory, to comment on and praise the proper behavior of teams and their fans:

- The visiting El Paso team and fans were observed to be "gentlemanly."[8]
- Albuquerque praised Santa Fe as having a "solid business appearance" and its people as "generous and obliging."[9]
- Las Vegas lauded the Santa Fe team for "acting like gentlemen"

and stated that they were a "credit to Santa Fe," including being singled out for "their singing and their musical ability."[10]

Fans themselves celebrated team victories in spontaneous displays of civic exuberance and intense team pride: in the early morning hours of June 11, 1888, after a weekend sweep of the Santa Fe Ancients, an Albuquerque observer reported that "a procession from the train [snaked] up Rail Road Avenue to 3rd and Gold, up 2nd to Rail Road Avenue.... There were 1,799 people in the crowd." The journalist also took a final lesson from his hometown's exuberant embrace of the local nine: "[This is] proof that people [of Albuquerque] appreciate good ball playing."[11]

Such bonhomie, however, did not extend to the game itself. Town pride and the competitive spirit of the local populations led to highly competitive games, including some ludicrous game preparations that bordered on insanity. One such incident occurred as a result of a string of defeats of Cerrillos by Madrid, two mining towns just three miles apart: "The home folks, mostly roughneck miners were threatening rebellion.... [T]he coach [Harry Scranton] purchased 3,000 sheets of sticky flypaper to be worn on the catching mitts and the soles of the baseball shoes. If that didn't cut down on errors and boost the score, said the coach, he would resign.... A year later, he [Scranton] is reported to have still held his job. So the flypaper must have worked!"[12]

With the creation of the National League in 1876 and the American Association in 1882, professional baseball became a legitimate business and made the sport of nation-wide concern. The two leagues represented the class split in the popularity of the game: the NL attempted to clean up the game and make it acceptable to all by forbidding players to drink, banning all gambling, creating blue laws preventing baseball from being played on Sundays, and not serving beer at the ballpark. The AA either allowed or did not prosecute such unsanctioned activities; with the core of spectators being immigrants and workingmen who attended games as a form of recreation and socialization, the newer, less stodgy league actually outdrew the more established NL.[13]

Baseball's popularity was being championed throughout the country by the mid–1880s. Citing *The Philadelphia Record*, an Iowa reporter mentioned the need for the manufacture of more baseballs before launching into a detailed discussion of how the spheroid was made:

> There is not a city, town, village or country but what has its base ball club. Everybody plays ball now, from the seven-year-old boy to the gray headed man who has scored half a century of innings. Just for a moment consider how many balls are needed for all the clubs in season. How many are knocked out and lost. Nearly every member has one to practice with. And then [consider] the small boy. He can chew up a base ball with about the same celerity [as] a sausage machine chops up meat.[14]

As the game was continuing to grow in popularity, baseball began to have more "investigations" into the inner workings of the game, including the following piece on the manufacture of the standard baseball:

> How a baseball is made is something very few of the game's enthusiasts know. Millions of balls are turned out in a year. One factory alone manufactures 5,000,000. A force of 1,250 men, women and boys are employed the year around by the factory. It takes thirty minutes to make one ball.
> Here is how the ball is made.
> The ball goes through eight stages before it is finally ready for the market. In one room are a number of machines, each operated by a boy. Pure rubber balls, one inch in diameter, are put into the machine and wound with woolen yarn until the ball is two inches in diameter, when the machine automatically drops them out. They are then taken to the "dipper."
> The dipper stands before the vat containing a whitish liquid, about the consistency of water, into which he dips the balls and then lays them aside to dry. The fluid is a liquid cement to hold the yarn firmly together and to prevent the ball from being "batted out of shape."
> The balls are then taken to machines which wind on another inch of yarn, are then again dipped into the cement and dried. They are then ready for covers.
> The covers are made of an alum-tanned horsehide. This hide is near one-eighth inch thick. One horsehide supplied but eighteen ball covers, as only the strongest part of the hide can be used. The covers are all cut by the machine.
> The balls are stitched by men; women are not strong enough for the work. Cotton thread alone is used: silk or linen will not stand the wear. After sewing, the balls seams are rough, and the balls are put through a rolling process, first by hand and then in a machine, in which they roll seven or eight miles.
> Each ball turned out is five ounces in weight and three inches in diameter. To prevent having the ball too light or too heavy, they are weighed after each stage in their manufacture.[15]

Another Iowa reporter of the same year notes the great number of men making a living by playing baseball: "It is estimated that not less than a thousand men will make a regular business of playing baseball professionally this summer."[16] A third Iowan in 1885 provides a variation on the hoary joke of learning to play baseball rather than getting an education as a true American measure of success:

> Useless Accomplishments [cited from the *Norristown Herald*] — A man in New York who could speak Italian, Portuguese, Spanish, Greek, Turkish, French and English fluently, applied to the justice at the Tombs a few days ago for employment. While this unfortunate man was frittering away his valuable time mastering several languages he might have learned the art of pitching the curved ball, and would now be overwhelmed with tempting offers to become the pitcher of a score of professional baseball clubs.[17]

By 1890, baseball was firmly entrenched as a cultural given and symbolic display of American competition and cooperation. For example, during the 1888 Inter-State Fair in Fort Wayne (IN), there were a number of all-American attractions, including a huge cyclorama of the Battle of Gettysburg, a Georgia exhibit of the state's products that itself was worth the price of admission," and a series of "novelties from Commodore Foote's Collection of Curious Things" in the main exhibition tent. However, the big draws were the horse races, the balloon ascensions (with a woman aeronaut who jumped from a gondola and reached ground safely via a parachute), and the hit of the fair, a three-day series of "amateur" baseball with teams representing Cincinnati (the Shamrocks) and Chicago (the Kents). The Shamrocks were the class of the field, winning the $300 purse and supported, as were the Kents, by "a number of professionals sandwiched in."[18]

The national pastime was employed by communities to prove their patriotism and adherence to the American rules of fair play. For example, baseball was at the heart of the program in the New Mexico Territory that was planned for Independence Day in 1888. Baseball was first among equals in preparation of the "Glorious Fourth" celebrations in Santa Fe: "The great game of base ball on the Glorious Fourth, between the Santa Fe champions and the heavy nine of Albuquerque. Whether the rest of the programme is carried out or not remains to be seen."[19] Businesses were urged to expand the festivities in a show of support for the push for statehood[20] and to demonstrate Santa Fe's civic pride and ability to

Fourth of July celebration at Santa Fe (New Mexico) Plaza (circa 1890). Baseball games and related baseball-oriented competitions frequently constituted 30–40 percent of the patriotic activities at Independence Day celebrations in the late 19th century (courtesy Palace of the Governors Photo Archives [NMHM/DCA], 0112278).

welcome those outside of the local residents: "It is probable that fully 400 Albuquerque people will accompany the base ball team from that live city to Santa Fe, on the Glorious Fourth. The people of the Capital City will do their utmost to make it pleasant for the visitors."[21]

The July 4, 1888, celebration in Santa Fe was a full-fledged affair with the military band meeting the Albuquerque train at 11 A.M. with a parade down San Francisco Street, where the businesses were all decorated in "bunting, flags, and evergreens," to the Plaza Pagoda, which was decked out in red, white and blue.[22] Events as disparate as horse racing, bicycle contests, Indian dances and games, equestrian, and concerts were scheduled.

In its celebration of Independence Day, Santa Fe had baseball as a central focus of the official festivities. Early in the day at Association Park, a "kid team" (no one over the age of 15) defeated their rivals from Albuquerque, 14–4.[23] This youth game was followed by a pigeon popping (skeet shooting) competition in the nearby fields. The crowd then returned to the ballpark to watch contests of base running and long-distance throwing (won by Santa Fe Ancient starting players O'Neill and Clark respectively). A ball game followed with the locals defeating their Duke City counterparts, 9–5, with a good time had by all: "Both nines merited praise for good behavior and good playing." From there, the games and contests continued on the Santa Fe Plaza, where the 10th Cavalry Band performed "patriotic airs" prior to "the reading of the Declaration of Independence in both English and Spanish, political speeches by Governor Ross and Don Nestor Montoya (in Spanish), and fireworks at 8:30 P.M."[24]

The use of baseball as a symbol of the American character extended to Independence Day celebrations throughout the country, including our nation's capital:

> To begin with, let it be noted that this is intended as a perfectly unbiased account of a baseball game between Senator Murray Crane's Steam Rollers and a team made up of the newspaper correspondents here. Personal feeling has been laid aside and every statesman will get his due. The Steam Rollers won: score 14 to 11. They ran [President] Taft into the game in the eighth and final inning, but the newspaper men, or rather Mr. Taft's little son Charley, took care of him all right. It was Senator Murray Crane's slashing three bagger that did the business.[25]

In a brief few decades, baseball transformed itself from a form of childish play to the more formal level of a game, and then with the addition of spectators and adult participation and attention to a national sport. The combination of the sport's inherent dramatic nature and the emphasis placed on the game by the press led to intense fan interest.[26] Rooting for local teams and individual players was a form of local boosterism, vicarious wish fulfillment, and hero identification necessary in a

The 9th Cavalry Band (Buffalo soldiers) at Santa Fe (New Mexico) Plaza. African American soldiers often established bands and other artistic groups that served as social outreach programs for the communities in which they were housed (photographer: Ben Wittick [1880]; courtesy Palace of the Governors Photo Archives [NMHM/DCA], 050887).

society undergoing radical economic and social changes. Baseball was a reassuring cultural given within the first half-century of its introduction into America. In fact, its broad appeal served to unite, at least momentarily, Americans of opposing ideologies and all socio-economic classes in a shared cultural experience:

> Chief Justice Ruger and Justice Andrews of the New York Court of Appeals, live next to each other, on James Street, Syracuse. Judge Ruger is a Democrat and Judge Andrews is a Republican, and in 1852 they were pitted against each another on the state tickets. They are, nevertheless, the warmest of friends, and are always together in their hours of leisure. They are enthusiastic lovers of baseball and attend every game that takes place in Syracuse. They understand the game in all its phases, and often indulge in learned arguments regarding the decisions of the umpires.[27]

The last word on the popularity of baseball in the 19th century goes to Albert Spalding, the national pastime's most memorable Renaissance man. A star player, sporting goods entrepreneur, and visionary, Spalding penned a 1913 autobiographical history of baseball that captures the essence of the national pastime's mass appeal and beneficial impact on the individual. Spalding lauded baseball as a "patriotic" endeavor that was wholly American in character and easily "adaptable to the American temperament" (enthusiastic and eager) and to basic American values, such as "self-restraint and a strong work ethic."[28] Spalding spoke for all the sport's proponents who believed baseball was an essential element in the cultural process of becoming an American.

The Dark Underside of the Gentlemen's Game

Baseball was not universally embraced by the public in the 1880s. There were many objections to the game from the ludicrous to the practical to the metaphorical. One outraged reader objected to baseball because "it taught boys to steal."[29] Other opponents believed that baseball was "not a child's game" and should be banned from being played on city streets: as an unnamed journalist witnessed from his office window, some "careless boys almost hit a nurse and a baby in the narrow [Santa Fe] streets."[30]

One very modern complaint about the sport was the length of games and, at times, the indifferent attitudes and behavior of the players. One outraged and bored reporter pulled few rhetorical punches in describing his experience:

> [The games] were uninteresting and tiresome. In fact, we do not know why it should take two hours and a half to play a game of base ball [sic]. You wear out the seat of your trousers, waiting to see the finish, and you wear out your patience waiting to see a play. It reminded me of Tennyson's Brook "For men may come, and men may go, but I go on forever." When the Albuquerque pitcher, last Saturday, insisted upon rubbing the cover off the ball every time before he delivered it, and attitudinizing before the spectators in the grand stand, he simply tired them. He accomplished no other purpose, for he got knocked out of the box.[31]

Though baseball was extremely popular in the nineteenth century, it was not always competently organized and run. There were numerous reasons for fan unrest. There were a high number of late starts and last-minute postponements with excuses running the gamut of irresponsibility, including player illness and injury, failure to inform all players of game dates and/or starting times, and the mere threat of rain. In such situations, games would often be played with one team short-handed, undermining the competitiveness of the game in question. Equally important, baseball had no professional umpiring crews. A single arbiter, who only received travel expenses, was agreed upon by both team captains. (The umpiring pool in a particular locale could be rather limited as it was a requirement that any arbiter had to be a member in good standing of a National Association Base Ball club before he could officiate a game.) The results "were woefully uneven," resulting in further crowd displeasure. The umpire also made frequent use of the rule that he could ask spectators for help in making a decision, trusting in their non-partisanship. The obvious effect was to lengthen games by the to-be-expected "umpire baiting and fan heckling."[32]

The 1880s also saw financial liabilities mount and bills come due. In the NMBL, Albuquerque owed the Santa Fe club $156 at the end of the 1887 season for expenses by the visiting team for games during that year's New Mexico State Fair.[33] In the process of attempting to increase profitability, team owners engaged in the practice of luring the better players away from other clubs. The direct result was to weaken local involvement and identification with a team, since often the only direct community connection to a club was the ownership. The principle of teams being composed of local talent was replaced by a professional business ethos that was buried beneath an institutionalized mythic appeal to the conventional family. This exercise in nostalgia gave the lie to the reality that by 1883 ballplayers were effectively and legally indentured servants with the implementation of the reserve clause that limited player mobility and salaries.[34]

However, it was neither the nature of the game itself nor the economic stresses that most threatened the existence of baseball in the late 19th century. Rather, it was the rough-and-tumble nature of the players and the behavior of a certain type of obnoxious fan that were most in need of repair. A strongly worded editorial encouraged baseball to take a position against swearing and poor fan behavior: "Any player guilty of blasphemy should be fined, or, in the discretion of the management, be released. [Moreover, baseball must] do away with hooliganism and bring the national sport up to a standard of respectability."[35] Duke City residents coined their own term — "hoodlumism" — to describe the constant "hootings and yellings" of the boisterous spectators.[36] The *Albuquerque Citizen* never lost an opportunity to upbraid the behavior of the town's own supporters, calling for fan ejections and less hectoring of the visiting teams.[37]

There were many specific reasons for the often precipitous drop-off in general fan support of 19th-century baseball throughout the nation that resulted in many teams folding after a few years or even a few months. The swearing, the indifferent play, and the general hooliganism at the games all undermined the notion of baseball as a respectable adult, if not family, pastime. More problematic were the boozing, contract jumping, and hippodroming (actual fixing of games by players). The public was especially outraged at the cavalier attitudes displayed by both players and management with regard to signed contracts. There were many editorials that demanded more significant action with regard to breached formal agreements that threatened the industry (and very existence) of professional baseball:

> There must be something more than a common law punishment for violators of contract, and there must be something to punish clubs and associations for violation of contracts on either side of the issue other than a suit of damages. In the past it has been quite as difficult to keep the magnates in line as the players; indeed, more so in some respects,

and nothing short of the iron clad national agreement would have done it or will do it in the future. We have a specimen of what would happen without it when the clubs hustle to obtain the services of a new player who has made a mark, and the constant disputes coming before the board of arbitration show what most of the clubs would do if they had a chance. As for the players, the events of the last few months in the signing of contracts and the bargaining and "shenanigans" indulged in are good indications of the kind of practices that would become general were there not some iron bound rule to hold both magnates and players to a given line.

It is this baseball law that has made the national game such a prosperous financial institution and made it possible for ballplayers to get such princely salaries. Its destruction would mark the decadence of the sport, and make it unprofitably professionally without a tremendous reduction in salaries.

The natural result would of course be a return to this present system or something very close to it in time, but the experiment would be costly for he who now secures a living from the game of baseball [W. I. Harris].[38]

Though social drinking was a universally accepted social activity in private social organizations and celebrations, public drinking, including serving alcohol at ballparks, was frowned upon by the majority of the populace. The fear of disorderliness and uncontrolled partisanship flew in the face of the community standards of an "ascendant bourgeoisie evangelical culture of modesty and self-restraint" and class differences in the desirability of pursing of respectability. Far from being a "democratic mix," 19th-century baseball reinforced the segregationist, nativist, stilted Victorian code of conduct of middle-class white America.[39] Objections to alcohol within the national pastime often stressed the deleterious effect of drinking on the play itself: "[A local critic says that] ball and liquor drinking will no more mix than castor oil and croton water. Just as sure as the two keep company for any considerable period of time the liquor will come to the top and the ball playing drop to the bottom. A good ballplayer needs firm muscles, clear eyes, a good steady nerve, a healthy stomach and a brain which is never supplied with alcohol."[40]

The anti-saloon and temperance movements were in complete agreement in targeting the poor behavior of all alcohol imbibers involved with the national pastime. Both movements focused not on the drinker's moral weakness but the evils of drink itself and the dangers of smoking tobacco. Their "scientific" argument posited that while smoking was tolerated, it was a stimulant similar to alcohol and created an unnatural heat in the body that demanded adequate hydration. This ideal concept of the sober American citizen, in sharp contrast to the many boozing spectators at the ballpark, would have a profound impact on the initial success and ultimate failure of many 19th-century clubs and leagues.[41]

Much of baseball's "rowdyism" was fueled by gambling, by competitive capitalism, by the pursuit of wealth, and by striving for local, regional, and national recognition.[42] Fan distrust and fears of violence, either real or symbolic, were leading causes of the lack of consistent fan support, especially among women. As local business leaders contributed resources to sign better players as a form of cheap advertising and civic promotion, the imported players' behavior undercut the middle-class belief in baseball as a gentleman's game. The result was that baseball became somewhat disreputable to both the investor and the fan, with the entire community desiring a more efficiently organized and performed sport.

Furthermore, by the 1880s, no law or reform movement was going

Gambling in front of the Palace of the Governors (Santa Fe, New Mexico). Gambling was perhaps the largest threat to the integrity and continued growth of baseball in the 19th century (photographer: Jesus Cito Candelerio [1886]; courtesy Palace of the Governors Photo Archives [NMHM/DCA], 099588).

to eliminate betting on baseball. Gambling was both a respected business and an entertainment for the unskilled immigrant "who was out of options" and desired "the thrill of living on the edge."[43] Further, gambling was the essence of existence in the western expansion of the United States. Eastern immigrants gambled in coming to the United States territories, looking for open spaces or mineral wealth or business opportunities or just a fresh start. They gambled with their lives in their dangerous daily occupations, dealt with the unpredictable weather and shortage of water, faced the possibility of hostile Indian raids, and experienced a constant lack of adequate basic supplies. A gambling mentality was at the core of daily life for many of the inhabitants of 19th-century America.

Vice in general and gambling in particular served a specific social need and often had a positive economic effect on communities. Businesses such as hotels, barber shops, and clothiers flourished near a profitable saloon and the local economy boomed. Saloon and dance hall licenses paid for many of the public services in a success of a western town. For unskilled men with money in their pockets and time on their hands, there were few other options offered these sparks. Both in their few leisure hours and in their arduous lives, gambling provided needed excitement and wild dreams of the big hit. The bet was both a psychological and social activity intended to quell that personal yearning for an intensified experience.[44] Even newspapers caught the gambling fever and attempted to cash in on the excitement and popularity of gambling. Following the model of *The Police Gazette* with its focus on a "colorful sporting fraternity," the embryonic sportswriting guild employed "jargon, puns, exaggeration, classical references, and irony in creating a critical analysis, historical portrait, and humorous human interest story for every event."[45]

Gambling, however, made a mockery of the notion of baseball as a fair-minded and respectable pastime that developed positive role models for the community. The practice was lambasted in the press for making "a burlesque of the game." However, baseball's expansion and its transformation from amateur to professional status were so rapid that there was little time to create controls and sanctions for the gamblers. In an era of gross mismatches, gambling was employed to retain spectator interest and keep the fans in the ballpark when uncompetitive and uninteresting games were occurring, especially since the stated policy was that no refunds were made after the first inning was completed. Gamblers would hold sway in their own sections and operate openly. They would make book on the ratio of runs by which a superior squad would defeat a weak opponent; on the number of runs a strong team would score in a few innings against what an overmatched foe would score in the entire game; and on particular runs during a rally, particular at-bats, and even particular pitches.[46]

Pool betting was a major form of gambling in late–19th-century America. This complicated form of wagering involved bidding on teams and odds prior to a game with the pool seller taking a small cut of the bets (his "vigorish" or "the vig") and having the responsibility of paying off the winners. After National League president William Hulbert rid the ballparks of their "pool sections," the pools were most often held in saloons, with the room where the pocket billiards tables were located often the center of the action.[47]

As with the more complex and less traditional form of pool wagering, the targets of the policy gambling syndicates were the working urban poor in large cities where sports entertainment was generally located. The most popular version was the numbers game, in which bettors would choose three numbers — if they correctly matched the gamblers' threesome drawn the next day, they would pay off at odds of 100–1. Bookmakers in the 19th century would take wagers as low as one penny, so extending sports betting to the baseball-mad public increased both the bookies' take and his "vig." However, the setting and manipulation of odds and the fairness of winning payouts was ultimately decided by the gambling syndicates and thus were open to massive abuses and outright theft of successful bettors. Such behavior sparked newspaper crusades to rid the national pastime of the scourge of gambling:

> Some of the New York newspapers have taken up the agitation against the base ball pool. It is earnestly to be wished that all would do so. There is no form of petty gambling at the present time that preys so outrageously on a class that can least afford to gamble as the base ball pool. Policy in its worst days is no meaner a form of trying to get something for nothing. Policy took pennies from the wives of workingmen and sometimes took all of the pennies which they had. The base ball pool takes pennies from office boys and takes all they have. Its operation is as crooked as that of policy. In the latter method of gambling the operators, or rather the big backers of the game, could cheat as much as they wished and no one would be the wiser. No man or boy who INVESTS IN A BASE BALL POOL has the slightest guarantee that he will get a square deal and most of them do not. The operators of the

pools handle them as they please. Not only do they win their percentage, but it is possible for them to take any part of the principle [sic] which they desire and put it in their pockets, paying the deluded buyers of the pools pennies or dollars as they see fit.[48]

With the baseball mania of the 1880s linked inextricably with betting, fans and even casual followers of the sport were suspicious of any seeming oddity or final outcome that was unexpected. A Richmond reporter discussed this imminent danger to the national pastime, employing a recent three-game set between Ross (Chester, PA) and the local Virginia Base Ball Club:

> Eyes Opened — They think that Some "Gay Gambolier"
> has been Playing a "Short-Stop" Game with Their Nine —
> The Latter Indignantly Deny the Charge —
> Curious Betting and Lucky Winners
>
> Some time since the base-ball craze reached Richmond afresh. It took deep hold, and was much worse than the "Dolly Varden Dress," the cartwheel "Gainesborough hat," or any of the much-descried but innocent fashions that the ladies are so much satirized so much about by the lords of creation. The craze grew apace, and some of the best men — that is, if the best men are those who have comfortable bank accounts — set to work and organized a stock company. The number of shares to be held was limited to four, and the list of stockholders showed up a cheerful line of business-men, taking a range so wide that it covered callings all the way from gambler and bar-keeper to staid bankers and merchants. The Sunday-school teacher and the temperance man met, through the zeal for base-ball, on the same footing with the men who toil Sunday nights in pent-up bar-rooms, the front doors of which must be closed to the public because of the bad moral odor likely to escape thereby. Baseball was the common plane upon which this democracy could meet, shake hands, and readjust the business difficulties of the city. The jollification was great, the prospect pleasing. "Base-ball helps a heap," said a member of the Association. "See the number of hacks and wagons that make, every day a game is played, $3 or $4, to say nothing of the horse-cars, cigar-dealers, and many others. Why, I have known country merchants to stay over here a day in order to witness a game of ball. It is our only amusement in the summer, and deserves to be patronized by all. Even some of our preachers attend the games."
>
> The stunned reported mused over this strange announcement, which came from a gentleman for whom he held the highest respect. The remarks dazed him, not having forgotten which old Leigh Richmond said to his daughter when she declared that although a minister's child and a member of the Church, she could go to a ball and not suffer by it.

A coal of fire had fallen to the hearth and then died out, and Mr. Richmond asked his daughter to pick it up. Instantly it was held between her snowy fingers.

"Now let it fall," said the father, and Miss Richmond obeyed.

"Did it burn you?" he asked.

"No, sir," was replied.

"Ah, my child, but see how it smutted."

Bawling about Ball

These reflections were recalled yesterday, when at every corner of the street men were talking about the game Tuesday between the Virginia Club, of the newly-organized Association, and the Ross Club, of Chester, Penn. The latter club arrived here and played a game last Monday. They were heralded as the "champion amateur club of the country," and the announcement, although smacking of circus side-shows and theatre-comique handbills, was swallowed by the lovers of base-ball to the extent that nearly a thousand people paid 25 cents to witness the game; and this, too, when the ladies of Richmond cannot raise $50 to put into position at Hollywood cemetery a gate that will do honor to the heroic General Pickett and the brave Confederate dead who sleep near and around him.

Verily, mighty is base-ball—mightier than fame.

The game was played, and on the first inning the "champion amateur club of the country" allowed the Virginia's [sic] to make ten runs. The game closed in favor of the Virginias, the score standing 21 to 5.

It was clear to the initiated that our amateurs were more than a match for the visitors.

A Hole in the Skimmer

So plain was this that the great motor of base-ball excitement—betting—worked to its full extent on the game to be played Tuesday between the same clubs.

The Virginias had the choice, and heavy odds were offered on them. Presently these bets began to be taken, and before 2 o'clock Tuesday knowing base-ballplayers began to see that something was astir. The work of taking the bets on the Ross Club was conducted quietly, and by the time the game was called some $3,000 or $4,000 were staked on the game. As quietly, however, as this was done, some intimation of it reached the ears of the management, one of the Virginia Club having said to an officer of the Association, "The game has already been played and lost: we can do nothing," and this before an inning had been played.

Indignant Ejaculations

Yesterday morning when Richmond waked up and went about its business, it straightway commenced to growl.

"You just ought to have been up town last night," said a well-known gentleman to the reporter. "You never saw such a kicking. The tree-boxes and signs caught it badly. The boys who lost by betting on the Virginias swear that the game was given away." Another gentleman, an old base-ballplayer, said: "I rode into the base-ball grounds in a buggy with a friend. I had seen enough for me to know by 2 o'clock that something was wrong. At least I suspected it from various manoeuvres [sic] that I saw. Why, one man that didn't know anything about base-ball was going around staking a gambler who was betting heavy on the Ross nine. As soon as I got in the grounds I saw one play that satisfied me. I never saw a crowd so completely disgusted. If it was a trick of the gamblers, it was well managed, and there are a number of soreheads and empty pocket-books this morning."

The Loss by Betting

Vigorous inquiry showed that about $3,000 changed hands on the result. The unnaturalness of the termination of the game as compared with the judgment of experts is shown when it is stated that in the morning bets of 2 to 1 that the Virginias would beat the Ross 2 to 1 were offered and not taken. Mr. Ross, after whom the Ross Club is named, and who came on here with them from Chester, Pa., lost $50 on the result. To offset this, however, it is said that he has a bet in Chester of $1,000 that his club would win one game. One gentleman, it is said, lost $300, which amount is the largest bet heard of as being made by any one person.

The managers of the Association had no idea (until this storm-head cloud of indignation burst) of the extent of gambling involved in the game of base-ball.... At any rate, the management of the Association have determined that no more betting will be tolerated, and to this end have had large placards printed and put up on the grounds, which read: "No Gambling Allowed, Under Penalty of the Law."

Hunting the Guilty

The Association met the shock yesterday morning manfully. A leading member said: "I mean to sift this thing to the bottom. In my opinion it is a fight between the gamblers and the Association. We will either run them out, or I will take my name from the list. The Association was organized with a view to the benefit of Richmond, but when it becomes a gambling scheme it will be broken up before anything of the sort shall be tolerated. We have offered $100 for information and proof of the guilt of any one engaged in selling out the game. We have also appointed a committee who will ferret the matter to the bottom if possible; and we intend to spare no means to discover the guilty ones and fasten the proof upon them."

The Virginia Club indignantly deny the charges that they willfully "muffed" a ball, or done anything else to throw the game into the hands of the Ross Club. Any seeming effort in that direction, however plain it appears to the public, they charge to accident and natural causes. Yesterday morning Mr. F.D. Steger, a notary public, with the following paper, sought out each of the Virginia nine, and secured their signatures, &c., to the following:

> "It being announced that some members of the Virginia Base Ball Club were bribed to give away the game played with the Ross Club, of Chester, on the 31st of July, we, the undersigned members of the Virginia Base-Ball Club, hereby solemnly swear that such a rumor is false in every particular; that we have never received a dollar bribe for such a purpose and challenge any one to appear and prove any such rumor to be true. We not only have never received any bribe to throw away a game since we have been connected with the Virginia Base-Ball Club, nor will we ever countenance any one who should approach us for such a purpose."

Many skeptics continued to believe that "something had gone wrong in Denmark" and that members of the Virginia club were bribed to throw the second game of a three-game set. The proof would be revealed in the rubber game of the series: the Virginia club led by seven runs after the first inning and went on to an easy 25–6 victory.[49] Richmond learned an early lesson in the destructive potential of gambling and the national pastime.

The marriage of gambling and baseball was not confined to local teams in geographical and sporting backwaters. The first major scandal in the National League, one that threatened the survival of the professional game in its infancy, involved gamblers paying four members of the 1877 Louisville Grays to underperform. The plot was uncovered, a principal confessed, and the players in the conspiracy were all banned for life from organized baseball.

It should be noted that as working-class and immigrant baseballplayers used the game as a means of entry into the middle-class so, too, shady businessmen of questionable character tried to employ baseball ownership as a ticket to middle-class respectability. An often overlooked form of baseball ownership of the 1880s–1890s was an even more dangerous threat to the integrity of the game — syndicate baseball, in which one ownership group would control more than one franchise in a particular league. The possibility of unfairly tipping the competitive balance by player movement and team complicity was always a central fear during the late 19th century.[50]

The athletic creed of the late 19th century can be summarized as follows: "...physical prowess, manly character, and the best features of U.S. citizenship."[51] These attributes would serve the following goals for America: a toughening of the physical fiber of the white middle-class youth, a social control over the restive working-class, and a moral regeneration of the country.[52]

The dominant white population couched its racism toward African American athletes in a pseudo-scientific racialist theory and jargon. Such a belief, of course, denied or dismissed a black athlete's hard work, discipline, and motivation — those "manly" qualities so praised in the athletic creed. African American athletes who saw success in sports as "proof of equality, a mechanism for assimilation, and a platform for social mobility"[53] could thus be easily marginalized for not having the "right stuff" necessary to become the gentleman performer who is the true athlete and the true American.

African American ballplayers were not the only targets of group stereotyping. Native Americans and women suffered from "humorous" anecdotes that revealed white supremacist attitudes. As with African Americans, Native Americans were portrayed as morally lax and immature. Women were frequently portrayed as too dense to understand the intricacies of the national game: "It is said that Job never lost his patience. This warrants the inference that he never undertook to explain a baseball game to a woman."[54] Such twisted thinking led to excesses that went beyond discrimination of a class of sportsmen. The militarization of the notion of sport led to instances of the elimination of due process and a desire for swift and punishing sentences in American penal institutions. Worse yet, war fever and American imperialism were buried in a mock-heroic ideal of military strength and white superiority.[55] Sport, especially the ever-popular baseball, became a tool of the Americanizers. In the process, they subverted the tenets of fair play and equal opportunity that are the most basic axioms of the game.

Seven

Bud Fowler, Black Baseball Entrepreneur (1883–1913)

1880s

Undeterred by the limitations of the color line in baseball, Bud Fowler continued in the game until 1911 as a promoter of black players and black baseball. As early as 1883, while only in his mid-twenties, he tried to organize a league of black clubs. In 1886 Fowler pitched for the New Orleans entry of the Southern League of Colored Base Ballists (SLCBB) in a crucial post-season series against inter-city rival the Cohens. The SLCBB was the first African American sports league but had disbanded by August of 1886.

In the last months of 1886, the budding young baseball entrepreneur served as the representative of the Cleveland Browns proposed entry in the short-lived National Colored Baseball League (NCBL), which lasted only two weeks in May due to high travel costs and the absence of the high-profile Cuban Giants. Fowler was also asked to contribute to the writing of the NCBL constitution.[1] Then, in 1887, Bud Fowler helped to run and manage the touring all-black club, the New York Gorhams, which was based in Newburgh (NY) after being founded the previous year in Manhattan; he could also lay claim to being the winner of the first "colored championship" the same year when the Gorhams won a three-game series over the Cuban Giants.[2] The Gorhams were a well-respected team that was reviewed positively in the New York dailies from their earliest days:

> After today [August 8, 1888] the Cuban Giants and the Gorhams, the crack colored teams, will make a change of base from the Polo Grounds to Washington Park. The colored residents of the Harlem district have been given the chance to see their champions play on off days at the Polo

Grounds for a month past, and now they are coming to see their Brooklyn friends. The Gorhams will play the [Cuban] Giants, the Keystones of Philadelphia, and two other crack colored teams at Washington Park between now and the 23rd. Admission 25 cents, grand stand extra.[3]

The New York colored champions of the Metropolis, the Gorhams, are playing great ball at Washington Park. Yesterday they took the Brooklyn Athletics with ease by a score of 7 to 3. The first five innings of the game virtually gave it to the Gorhams by 3 to 0, the colored troops handling the ash in a style which opened the eyes of the Brooklyn team's players, who watched them from the grand stand, three model hits being made in the first inning.... The Gorhams' captain wisely sends his opponents to the bat first. They [Gorhams] do not fancy the Brooklyn team's pet rut of going to the bat first. They fielded finely yesterday and played the points like veterans, their battery work being first class. Those who fail to see them miss some very good ball playing.[4]

Bud Fowler's promotional skills almost single-handedly led to the instituting of a series for the colored championship of 1887. A master of publicity from his days as a competitive runner and walker in the mid-1880s, Fowler proclaimed his Gorhams to be the "State Colored League"

Cuban Giants (1888). The Cuban Giants were the first professional African American salaried baseball club. They were the "colored champions" in 1887 and 1888 (National Baseball Hall of Fame Library, Cooperstown, New York).

champions, though the sporting press did not know of such a league or where and against whom the Gorhams won such a pennant. Rising to the bait (and sensing a large payday), the Cuban Giants accepted the challenge and Fowler's team had immediate credibility on the diamond with their 1887 victory. The following year the Giants defeated the Gorhams along with African American teams from Pittsburgh and Norfolk. From 1889 to 1891, the two famed black teams were affiliated with white leagues in organized baseball. By 1893, both the Cuban Giants and Gorhams left the professional ranks and disbanded, with the Cuban X Giants rising out of the ashes of these once highly successful clubs.[5]

1890s

Not only was Bud Fowler active in the very beginnings of black professional baseball in the mid–1880s, but he also provided a successful business model for a floundering enterprise in the mid–1890s. While Fowler spent the decade proceeding his organization of the 1895 Page Fence Giants playing for integrated clubs, he was never far from the earliest efforts to promote and to establish opportunities for African Americans to play and to invest in the business of baseball.

Prior to Rube Foster's launching of the Negro National League in 1920, black baseball leagues were either abortive disorganized failures or financially doomed from their inception. These efforts started with the League of Colored Baseball Clubs (1887) and ended with the United States League of Professional Ball Clubs (1910), an attempt at a mixed league of teams with no color line. In between, there were several failed attempts to include black teams in essentially white leagues (1889 Penn League, 1891 Middle States League, and the 1898 Iron and Oil League). There was also a league that mixed black and white teams (the 1907 International League of Independent Professional Baseball Clubs) and a separate black league (1891). These leagues were unsuccessful for a legion of reasons, including "lack of leadership, unstable financing, the lack of a substantial urban black population, and the strength of segregation."[6]

A prime source for the earliest history of what was then called "colored baseball" was star player, manager, entrepreneur, and journalist Solomon White. In his seminal work, published in 1907,[7] White sketched the earliest endeavors at creating successful all-black professional clubs, beginning in 1885 with the African American employees of the Argyle Hotel (Babylon, Long Island) under the guidance of head waiter Frank P. Thompson. After the hotel season ended in mid–September, the team went to Philadelphia, where it defeated the Orions, 6–4. The hotel club immediately signed three star Orion players, making it the best independent team in the east. The revitalized Long Island team then went on to defeat the Eastern League champs from Bridgeport (CT), 5–4. At the end of the year, the team, under new management, renamed itself the "Cuban Giants" to lessen any fan or press opposition by avoiding the use of the terms "black" or "Negro" to refer to the team. Very few Cubans ever played for the various clubs that designated themselves "Cuban."

The Cuban Giants in various incarnations dominated black baseball for nearly a decade, fighting off the challenges of a number of highly competitive all-black clubs. In 1887, after the League of Colored Base Ball Clubs formed and folded within two weeks, the highlight of the Cuban Giants' season came when they defeated Cincinnati and Indianapolis of the National League and lost to reigning World Series champ Detroit, 6–4, and to the well-stocked all-black club Pittsburgh Keystones, 3–2. The New York Gorhams began to threaten the Cuban Giants' dominance on the diamond, which was settled in 1888 on the playing field with the Giants winning the silver ball as champion of a colored tournament in New York.

In 1889, both the Cuban Giants (representing Trenton, NJ) and the New York Gorhams (representing Easton, PA) joined the Pennsylvania League [Middle States League]. The latter club defeated the Giants two games to none to claim the eastern black championship. The following year, the Cuban Giants (representing York, PA, and reorganized as the York Monarchs) continued in the Middle States League until the league folded on July 5, 1890. By the end of that year, the Monarchs (the original Cuban Giants), the Cuban Giants, and the New York Gorhams were the only all-black clubs still in business. In 1891 and lasting only for that year due to an under-financed operation, the Big New York Gorhams formed an all-star ball club by signing all of the Monarchs along with African American standouts Charlie Williams (catcher), George Stovey (pitcher), and Frank Grant (shortstop). That team went 96–4 during the season, which is the best all-time record in black baseball history. From 1892 to 1894, the only all-black baseball club was the Cuban Giants

Cuban X-Giants (1895). Composed of many former members of the Cuban Giants, the X-Giants were perhaps the best African American baseball team during the first decade of the 20th century in the pre–Negro National League era (National Baseball Hall of Fame Library, Cooperstown, New York).

who were resuscitated in 1896 as the Cuban-X Giants. That ball club had a successful decade-long run.

In the Midwest, where Bud Fowler for the most part was pursuing a playing career in integrated, organized baseball, the top amateur club was the Chicago Unions, a team that began play in the mid–1880s and became professional in 1896. The first all-black club in the west was the Lincoln (NE) Giants, a team that played in both the Western and Nebraska State Leagues but, like so many professional teams in the 19th century, collapsed under the weight of financial debt. Bud Fowler's participation in the 1892 Nebraska State League was due, in part, to his connection with the Lincoln Giants in 1891 when he was recruited by Giants pitching ace Will Castone.

Fowler's successful organization of the Page Fence Giants in 1895 established his national reputation as the central figure in the black touring baseball world. When faced with white teams of poor talent, Fowler would have his team turn to vaudevillesque comedy routines to lessen any racial tensions and to ensure future support from an essentially white fan base for such games. Such routines included shadow ball, mock respect for the umpire, humorous coaching bits, nonsense speech, and general horseplay on the infield, including doing the cakewalk if the game situation called for comic diversion.[8]

There was frequently a standard promotional routine that barnstorming teams would follow as they traveled to the small towns throughout the heartland of America, which would most often pick up all expenses and still offer the barnstorming teams 60–70 percent of the gate receipts. The barnstormers would put up advertising posters when they entered a new town the evening before a scheduled game; early on game day, the players would put on their uniforms and practice so as to further entice spectators to purchase a ticket. There were often parades led by the local municipal band to drum up even more interest and add to the pageantry of the game.

In order to avoid possible hurt or angry feelings by spectators, the players would ask the locals if they'd like to have the comic doings or if they'd prefer a more serious game. The barnstormers recognized that they were professionals who were playing against amateurs and the African American players went to great lengths to avoid creating feelings of resentment.

The comic routines themselves were often quite mild. For example, if the umpire called a pitch that a visitor thought was too low the batter might get on his knees for the next delivery. If a batter hit a long home run, he might run the bases backward. Or if a local pitcher struck out one of the members of the traveling team, the befuddled batter might hand the hurler a bouquet of weeds. In fact, most of the humor was directed at the barnstormers themselves, who as nomads were always on the road and had to draw a fine line between fun, showmanship, and the potential for creating hurt feelings.[9]

Among baseball people, there was wide disagreement about the role of clowning within the national pastime:

> It [clowning] was often good box office, particularly for white audiences, but baseball purists frowned on it because they felt it degraded both the game and the players. Sometimes the humor was of the plantation or minstrel show variety in which the white man's stereotypes of the lovable darky were pandered to — the Deep South Negro dialect, the grinning caricature of the happy-go-lucky, last fatback-and-grits Negro with which for decades, white America deceived itself.[10]

Yet, for the most part, the African American press praised these routines for their entertainment value to the ticket-buying public and because of the subsequent financial success of the African American barnstorming clubs that performed these crowd-pleasing routines:

> The Cuban Giants is the name of the only colored professional base ball nine in the country. More solid enjoyment can be found in watching them play than can be found in a game between "Baby" Anson's kickers and the New York Giants, when the Giants are winning. There are not only a first class lot of players, but their comical coaching makes a great hit wherever they go. In a recent game here the Cubans were at bat, and a man was on first base, the following dialogue took place between the coachers on first and third bases:
>
> Coacher at third base: Say, what are you doing over there standing on that base? Are you married to that bag? Come, honey, get a move on you.
>
> Coacher at first base: For goodness, child, do move off that base. Get a divorce from it and travel down to second; there's a hunk of molasses candy on that second bag just waiting for you.
>
> Coacher at third base: Yes, and here's your supper right here on this third bag. What's that, Mr. Umpire? Did you call a strike on that ball? Oh for goodness sake come off that band wagon and give the child a chance. Look out here, Mr. Abe, if you don't smash that ball on the nose, you'll get your release this blessed evening.—*Philadelphia Press*[11]

Fowler's resolve to continue in his chosen profession was superhuman. Throughout the 1890s and well into the next decade, Bud Fowler worked with such famous black teams as the Cuban Giants (which in 1885 became the first salaried team of African American players), the Smoky City Giants, the Cuban X Giants, the All-American Black Tourists, and the Kansas City Stars.[12]

One of Bud Fowler's last major efforts to combine playing and managing as an entrepreneur in black baseball was with the independent Findlay (OH) Sluggers in 1899. In a special correspondence from Findlay in early April, Bud Fowler described in detail his ambitious plans for the upcoming season:

> Dr. Drake and I have purchased the old grounds in the heart of the city, and have signed a first-class team. The teams that represented Findlay in the past need no praise. They have always been stronger than most minor league aggregations. For the first time in its history, this city will have Sunday grounds, and clubs can be booked by communicating with the manager.
>
> The team will report April 15. [A complete roster of the players signed is then listed.] The season will open in Toledo with Stroble's Interstate League Club on Saturday and Sunday, April 22–23.

From June 12 to 17 Findlays will play under the auspices of the Elks Club. Clubs "looking for games" should write to Dr. W. H. Drake.

In the same interview, Bud Fowler also reveals the ambitious plans for his touring team the Black Tourists and reveals Fowler's desire to expand the game throughout the continent in doing so:

> The Black Tourists Colored Ball Club will leave Findlay in September for California, playing through the Western states to the coast, where they will meet all the clubs of the California League. They want to arrange games in Santa Fe, Las Vegas, and Albuquerque during the New Mexico State Fair. This will be the first colored club to cross the Rocky Mountains. The aggregation will be equal in merit in all departments as any colored club ever organized. [The piece ends with a list of seven famous Findlay ballplayers, including Dummy Hoy.][13]

Early in the season, Fowler's African American Findlay independent team took on quality teams from organized baseball: "On April 25 they [Buffalo Bisons of the Western League] will run over the state line into Ohio and cross bats with the Findlay Giants, a team of negro players and managed by Bud Fowler who was once a well-known second baseman, playing with the Toledos and other clubs."[14]

As late as August of 1899, Fowler was placing advertisements in the national sporting press about this planned tour: "The All-American Black

Atlanta Baptist College baseball team (1897). The color line was nearly impregnable by the 1890s but baseball continued to be played by African Americans on the amateur, collegiate, and black barnstorming levels (National Baseball Hall of Fame Library, Cooperstown, New York).

Tourist Club is to start from Chicago on Spt. 20 for a trip to California. This will be the first colored team to cross the Rockies. The team's route will be Rock Island from Chicago to St. Louis; Union Pacific to Kansas City, Denver, and Salt Lake; Northern Pacific to San Francisco. For dates apply to manager Bud Fowler, Findlay, O."[15]

Never one to limit his options, Bud Fowler at the same time was also attempting to organize a league in the midwest: "Manager M. J. Cleary of the [Fort Wayne (IN)] Shamrocks is in receipt of a letter from Bud Fowler, manager of the Findlay team regarding a meeting Thursday [set for the] purpose of organizing an Oil League." Fowler suggested that the Shamrocks should relocate to North Baltimore "where a wealthy citizen expresses a willingness to back a good baseball club."[16]

While the Oil League didn't pan out, Bud Fowler was in at the formation of an 1899 Ohio League, which was spearheaded by the veteran ballplayer's Findlay business partner, W.H. Drake:

> The Ohio Base Ball League was organized in this city [Findlay] on the 11th last [May of 1899] by representatives from Bowling Green, Cygnet, Fostoria and this city. F. W. Parmalee, of Cygnet, was elected president, and W. H. Drake, of this city, secretary-treasurer. Bud Fowler, of this city; B. Thomas, of Fostoria; F. D. Adams, of Bowling Green; and G. L. Carmack, of Cygnet, were elected directors. A salary limit of $600 was established. Lima and either Wapakoneta or Piqua, will also join the league, making it a six-club race. The Cygnet and Bowling Green Clubs will be strengthened by the addition of new players.[17]

There is evidence that Bud Fowler did more in 1899 than organizational wheeling-and-dealing from his base in Findlay. He was in Missouri in May of 1899 to play games against the black state champion: "The Bradburys, the champion colored team of Missouri, will meet Bud Fowler's St. Joseph Beauties in St. Joseph on Thursday, and the Schmeizers at Exposition Park [in Kansas City] on Sunday."[18] It is unclear whether the St. Joseph Beauties were a local Missouri team that Fowler lent his name and expertise to or whether they were some variation of that year's Findlay All-American Black Tourists. In any case, the game resulted in a rout for the visiting team: "The Bradburys made Bud Fowler's Black Wonders look like selling platters last Wednesday at St. Joseph by trouncing them by a score of 21 to 7."[19]

This meeting of all-black clubs must have been at least a modest economic success because a rematch between the Missouri teams was quickly scheduled for Kansas City, with the added attraction of competitive baseball field events to stimulate potential fan interest: "The Bradburys and Bud Fowler's Black Wonders, of St. Joseph, will play a game of baseball this afternoon [June 25, 1899] at Exposition Park. There will be foot races, jumping, and throwing contests."[20]

1900s

The year 1900, the color line was firmly and unequivocally entrenched with no African American players participating in organized baseball at any level. However, such unfair and humiliating treatment did not dampen black Americans' love of the national pastime nor did it prevent African Americans from attempting to establish professional competition for players, leisure entertainment for spectators, and viable business opportunities for investors. In New Mexico, which had a minuscule black population in 1900, African Americans were playing baseball throughout the territory and their games were being reported in the local media: "The Carlsbad Irrigators and Roswell Red Caps, colored teams, played a game of base ball at Roswell, Tuesday. The Irrigators lost by a score of 15 to 16."[21] Local black communities were encouraging local African American businessmen to invest in baseball clubs as a means to increase civic pride and improve attendance: "We encourage merchants to support a local colored base ball association to draw the country folks to town."[22]

The Bud Fowler publicity machine was in full gear by 1900. To keep the turnstile spinning for another Ohio-based version of the Black Tourists, the African American veteran's continued presence in the sport was duly noted and his longevity was grossly exaggerated: "Bud Fowler is still in the business — playing second base and managing the Black Tourists. Bid McPhee and A.C. Anson are spry young lads compared to Fowler."[23]

The white press of the day continued to denigrate the black game by stressing its novelty and non-serious nature: "the colored teams are clever ... colored teams are not seen every day except in comic papers."[24] Bud Fowler's 1901 travels clearly underscored the precarious nature of black touring baseball: He had a hand in organizing Pittsburgh's Smoky City Giants, toured with the all-black Barnes American Giants, and ended the season by organizing and managing a black club in Monrovia

(IN).[25] This year also revealed that Fowler was engaging in another post-playing baseball activity that was aided by his vast experience in the national pastime—scouting: "Graffius and Clarke will do the backstop work. Clarke is a youngster who has been recommended by Bud Fowler, the colored ballplayer."[26]

The 1901 season also marked the beginning of an attempt to cross the color line in somewhat of a final frontier: interscholastic collegiate baseball. The career of African American William Clarence Matthews is instructive in this matter. After being educated at Tuskegee Institute in his home state of Alabama and attending Phillips Andover Academy, Matthews played baseball at Harvard for four years, serving as the captain of the team in 1905 while hitting .400 and stealing 22 bases in 25 games. During his tenure, Matthews played shortstop on one of the best amateur teams in the country with the club, going 75–18 in his four years. However, he experienced threatened and actual boycotts (versus Navy and Virginia) and racial abuse during each year of his college career, despite behaving as a gentleman throughout his career. Upon graduation, Matthews signed on with Burlington (VT) for what proved to be his only year of professional baseball: "William C. Matthews, the colored shortstop of the Harvard baseball team, has signed to play with the Burlington team, of the Vermont League. He will leave today [June 29, 1905] for Burlington."[27] However, the African American player experienced the same threats and verbal and physical abuse as he had at Harvard. He left the national pastime for a highly successful career as a lawyer, including serving as legal counsel for Marcus Garvey from 1909 to 1923, and as a politician in the Republican Party during Coolidge's election in 1924, which resulted in an appointment to the U.S. Justice Department.[28] While they came from different universes with regard to upbringing and privilege, William C. Matthews and Bud Fowler faced the same intransigence in pursuing a professional baseball career once the color line was definitively established in the 1890s. What further links these African American pioneers is their fierce independence and confidence. Matthews' words as a college junior suffice for both men: "I have to depend on my own merit."[29]

Bud Fowler continued to make Monrovia his home base in 1902, a year in which he again managed the local black team. He also helped to establish a black baseball league on June 30, 1902, in Indianapolis (IN): "'Bud' Fowler of Monrovia, Ind. was in the city [Indianapolis] this week.

Mr. Fowler is the manager of the All-American colored base-ball team which will meet the Indiana Reserves in this city next September. They will leave here for a western tour ending in Pueblo, Colorado. The colored All-Americans are composed of members of the Cuban Giants, the Chicago Unions, and the Page Fence Giants."[30] The next month the Indianapolis newspapers were reporting that Fowler had a major hand in organizing a colored league based in the capital city:

> A colored baseball league was organized last night. The Vendomes, the ABC's and the Herculeans were represented. The Unions [the best among the city black clubs] did not send a representative to the meeting, though this team is anxious to join the league. Bud Fowler, the manager of the Colored All-American team, that is to attempt a trip to California, said that the Unions would not be taken into the league, and that another team was ready to make the fourth team in the league [probably Fowler's Eastern Colored-Stars].
>
> The officers of the league are: Charles Stewart of the *Recorder*, President; Bud Fowler Secretary and Ran Butler Treasurer. The Board of Directors is made up of Thomas Haskins of the Vendomes; George Adams of the ABCs and Ervin Hardy of the Herculeans. The schedule will begin next week.[31]

Often composing his own promotional copy and acting as his own press agent, Bud Fowler continued to inflate his age by 11 years: "Bud Fowler, the veteran ballplayer, is now 55 years old, and still plays ball."[32] Equally important, Fowler continued to promote national tours based on the talent and "novelty" of black baseball:

> Bud Fowler, the most famous colored player in balldom [sic], wants [Cincinnati first baseman] Jacob Beckley to manage a trip of the All-Colored Professionals to the Pacific coast next fall. He has written "Eagle Eye" from Monrovia, Ind., and outlived his plans, which are exhaustive and on a business basis. The veteran black expects to pick his team from the Page Fence Giants, Cuban Giants and Chicago Unions. The expedition would be a novelty, for no colored team has ever gone touring west of the Mississippi. Fowler managed and played with a colored team here [Indiana] last year.[33]

The 1903 and 1904 seasons found Bud Fowler firmly ensconced in the midwest world of African American baseball. The Columbus (OH) Black Tourists club was a strong entry that was representative of local black entries in the decade's numerous attempts at stimulating fan interest and promoting African American baseball interests. The Ohio State Colored League was one such attempt of black entrepreneurship, as were the Missouri-Illinois League, the Presbyterian Base Ball League of Chicago, the Greater Boston Colored League, the New England Colored League, the Colored Texas League, and the District of Columbia League.[34]

The following year Bud Fowler began the year in his birth area in upstate New York, where his extended family lived. However, he was part of a large contingent of players who were let go by the Utica club in early May: "The Utica club has released pitchers Ross and Dekin, catcher Peterson, third baseman Fowler and outfielder Martin."[35]

For the bulk of the year, Fowler was at the helm of the all-black Kansas City Stars and still perpetuating the myth of his Methuselahean age: "Bud Fowler, patriarch among the black sons of swat, is in Redland (OH) after a season of success in Missouri, where he managed the Kansas City Stars, a team of colored ballplayers ... [Bud Fowler] is in his 57th year and has put 32 years of active life on the ball field." His stated goal for the upcoming 1905 season, which he did achieve, was to organize an all-black team in the Cincinnati area: "I expect to remain here and have a team of black boys to play in Ohio and Indiana cities next season."[36]

By the end of the 1904 season, during which he tried to organize another national black baseball league, the wily African American veteran expressed a note of exasperation that could stand as a mantra for his entire career in the national pastime: "One of these days a few people with enough nerve to take a chance will form a colored league of about eight cities and pull off a barrel of money."[37]

In one of the longest printed interviews of his career, Bud Fowler, while in Cincinnati, reminisced about his career and other great African American ballplayers and how the national pastime had developed. After a brief prologue in which he summed up the 1904 baseball season as "the greatest year in baseball's history for the independent clubs. My Kansas City Stars did splendidly in a tour of Kansas and Nebraska," Fowler began to look back over his very long career in the game:

> I haven't pitched a ball for three years.... The old whip went back on me and I've gone to the bench to stay. I began my professional career with the Old Live Oaks, in 1875, at Lynn, Mass., and Arlie Latham was my catcher. I played in a good many states in my time and played in nearly every circuit, from New England to the Pacific coast. When I began play the nine-ball three-strike rule was in force. I've helped win several pennants, and one of them was hoisted by Topeka in the old Western. The

> proscription against the negro players was not in force in those days, and I played with the Maple Leafs in Guelph, Ont., at Binghamton, Grand Rapids, Stillwater and Crawfordsville. There were four colored stars at that time — Fleet Walker, the catcher with Newark, who afterward went with Toledo; George Stovey, the left-handed pitcher with Newark, and Fred [sic] Grant, Buffalo's second baseman.
>
> I know of at least half a dozen other players with a strain of colored blood in them, but they were light fellows and were never disturbed. The long circulated story that Treadway of the Brooklyns, was colored did him an injustice. He was pure white. Cincinnati turned out the Napoleon Lajoie of the black players in Charley Grant, the second baseman with the Cuban Giants, who was once picked up by [Hall of Fame manager John] McGraw for Baltimore and heralded as an Indian infielder. Grant is one of the greatest ballplayers still in commission today, and his color is all that keeps him out of the fastest company.[38]

One of most underrated of all of Bud Fowler's talents connected to the national pastime was his ability to discern young talent. His abilities as a scout and assessment of major trends and developments in the game made him an invaluable addition to teams with small rosters and limited coaching personnel. In his long interview during the 1904 winter Hot Stove League, Bud Fowler revealed these qualities:

> Cincinnati has rounded up some good ones [players] for next season. I can vouch for two of them. In Charley Chech the Reds have a pitcher with a head. I knew Harry Arndt when he was a South Bend Green Stocking, and his team always gave my Page Fence Giants about as stiff an argument as they ever encountered. That spit ball isn't new. Nat Hudson, Bob Carruthers, and John Clarkson, as well as myself all had it, and worked during the old days in the Northwestern league. We didn't call it the "spit ball," but an "overhand drop." It was a ball of most uncertain destination and slipped off two wet fingers toward the plate. All that the pitcher knew was that it was sure to drop, but where and how much was a mystery. I could never tell whether it would be four inches or a foot. I don't believe the modern pitchers are one bit more effective than the old-timers. The fielding has improved — that's all. There was no team work in days gone by, and it was a case of every fellow for himself until Capt. Comiskey introduced the new school of play, and team work became absolutely essential to success. There is no demand for rule changes — no public demand I mean. In all my years, covering a third of a century, I never saw the enthusiasm that marked the players of the game in the West this year.[39]

In the following few years, Bud Fowler was following the tonsorial trade in two old haunts where he had enjoyed his greatest playing successes: Cincinnati in 1905 and Binghamton in 1906.[40] While working at his barber shop in 1905, Fowler still was conjuring large dreams of further baseball endeavors: "Bud Fowler, organizer of the famous Page Fence Giants, a negro baseball club, has organized in Cincinnati one of the strongest colored clubs in the country. He would like to hear from any first-class negro player wishing a position. Address all communications to Bud Fowler, no. 528 Plum Street, Cincinnati." In 1906, Fowler, back in his home state of New York, had a connection with the Brooklyn Royal Giants, who, in an advertisement for a game in Harlem against the Murray Hills, were lauded as follows: "The Royal Giants are made up of the pick of colored baseball talent in the East."[41]

Strong circumstantial evidence and the repeating pattern of Bud Fowler's returning to people and places of past successes suggest that in 1907–1908 he served in significant advisory roles on the playing field and in the business sectors of black baseball. Grant Johnson, Fowler's former teammate, captain, protégé, and business partner on the Findlay Sluggers, played 11 games for the 1907 Philadelphia Giants in the Cuban Fall League. It would make perfect sense for Fowler to have accompanied his friend and protégé to Cuba for the five weeks Johnson played there in October-November 1907.

During the 1907 and 1908 seasons, Fowler was said to have worked with Watkins's All-Stars. The veteran African American manager-promoter would have been a valued and logical source of expertise for Pop Watkins, who in many substantial ways was a next-generation Bud Fowler. John "Pop" Watkins caught and eventually manned first base for over two decades for the Cuban Giants, with whom Bud Fowler had many dealings over that same period. Watkins began his own team — the Havana Red Sox (frequently referred to as Watkins's "Colored Giants") — in 1907, which he based in upstate New York, Fowler's old stomping grounds.[42] Using the tactics of the elder jack-of-all trades, Watkins inflated his age by at least a decade to be able to wear the mantle of the experienced veteran whose experience and professional expertise would be unquestioned. His reputation as a great scout and judge of young talent in the African American baseball world would have further drawn him to Fowler.[43] During these somewhat fallow years of the later part of the decade, Fowler made a number of unsuccessful attempts to revive the Black Tourists[44] before returning to his birth area in upstate New York to live on a permanent basis.

The year 1908 was a significant one black baseball in New York City. On Decoration Day, the Brooklyn Royal Giants and the Cuban Giants faced off in "a double-header in the opening game of the National Association of Colored Professional Clubs at the famous Polo Grounds, located at 15th Street and 8th Avenue." A local reporter saw this event as "a step nearer to the playing of games with the clubs of National and American League clubs in the future of this city. The event was to be both historic—"the first time in the history of colored baseball that a colored team has played on this famous ball park with its bleachers and commodious grandstand." The price of admission and service "including to the ladies" was to be the same as at a National League game. Dignitaries were to attend the contest, with Booker T. Washington heading the august list. The pleasantries would consist of "a band concert [that] will be given both before and during the games as well as the usual parade from the clubhouse."[45]

This 1908 series had a very personal impact on Bud Fowler. Home Run Johnson and showman Monroe had comprised the left side of the infield on the 1905–1906 African American champion Philadelphia Giants on a team with Fowler and were holding down the same positions on the 1908–1909 Brooklyn Royal Giants, who were captained by Johnson. In April of 1909, Bud Fowler wrote a song entitled "The Royal Giants" that was published in his hometown of Frankfort (NY) and dedicated to Monroe and his old friend Johnson![46]

In all probability Fowler's song was a form of thanks to the players who were responding to the elder statesman of black baseball's financial need in 1908. Fowler appeared to be at death's door in a report that seems to be a trial obituary emanating from Frankfort (NY):

"A Veteran's Distress—'Bud' Fowler Is Dying with Consumption in Destitution"

Bud Fowler, probably the greatest colored ballplayer who ever lived, and a man well-known in the professional base ball world for thirty years, is dying here of slow consumption. Fowler is in destitute circumstances and deserving, on the strength of his long and clean record, of some recognition of his many acquaintances in the base ball world. Fowler, whose real name is John Jackson, was born at Cooperstown, N.Y., in 1854. In 1871 Fowler began his professional career [note the incorrect dates in Fowler's personal history] and it carried him to all sections of the country. Every manager and player of a few years' experience knows and has seen Bud Fowler in action during his 31 years of his playing career. He was a fine all-around player, good batter and fine fielder, and owing to his careful habits remained long in the game.[47]

Yet within six months, Fowler was recovering from both a surgery and a major misdiagnosis:

> "Has Not Consumption — Bud Fowler's Trouble
> at Last Revealed by X-Ray Examination"
>
> "Bud" Fowler, the veteran colored player, who was supposed to be dying of consumption, writes us from his home in Frankfort, N.Y, that he has not consumption at all. An x-ray examination has revealed that he has for six years been suffering from an injury sustained while stealing a base at Indianapolis [in 1902]. He broke the lower left rib, which bent inward, growing on the end hard flesh which pierced a kidney. Fowler has had the rib removed by an operation and is now rapidly recovering his health and strength. He has just composed a ball song which he had dedicated to the National Commission. It deals with Cooperstown, N.Y., where the game was first named and the first diamond was laid out by General Doubleday. This is also Fowler's birthplace.[48]

An ironic "wise saying" attributed to Bud Fowler during this difficult period summarizes the African American player's plight: "Fewer flowers to the dead and a little more charity to the living would help some — 'Bud' Fowler."[49]

However, physical problems could not stop Fowler's scheming and planning in late winter of 1908 for ever more ambitious grand tours of the national pastime:

> "Bud" Fowler of this city [Binghamton], business manager of the Black Tourist club, announces that the club will make one of the longest trips on record this Fall. The first game will be played in New York on Sept. 19 and on Sept. 21 will play in Binghamton. Other games will be played in Chicago, Omaha, Kansas City, Denver, Reno, Sacramento, San Francisco and El Paso. Among the games to be played in California will be two with each of the California League teams and with the Leland Stanford University and University of California. In the City of Mexico a number of games will be played. The trip Mr. Fowler says will be made in the club's palace, dining, and sleeping cars....
>
> [A reliable and beloved source from the *Los Angeles Examiner* then discussed the veteran African American infielder:] "Bud's skin is as black as a March night in Kansas, but his heart is white, and he was one of the greatest ballplayers in his time that ever huddled around second base."
>
> [He revealed that the Tourists would be traveling twelve thousand six hundred miles during the tour and that Fowler had provided "about one thousand words of press agent dope" on the greatness of his team.]

"Fowler's best days were a little before my time, but I remember the old boy well, when he was playing, with that Grant Johnson, in that dear old Findlay, O.

"These two black boys, one at second and the other at short, formed a combination that was the pride of the gas belt at that time.

"Ask any old-timer about that Findlay team and they will tell you that it was one of the greatest independent teams ever organized.

"How those boys in gray did love to get a pampered National League team on the old town lot and tan the visitors until the game became a farce.

"Their team work was like a perfect bit of mechanism with Fowler as one of the jewels. It appears ... that the old boy is still playing the game and, to use Danny Webster's favorite saying, 'living soft.'"[50]

The plans for a benefit game to defray the medical (and expected burial) expenses of Bud Fowler began in early 1909 by presenting the ill veteran's dire circumstances to both the African American baseball community and the nation at large. As usual, Fowler's story was a mixture of fact, myth, tall tale, press agent exaggeration, and outright fiction: the medical problem was correctly presented — a growth based on an old playing injury — not consumption — that might be helped by surgery. But many of the "facts" reported about his career, including having started his professional career in 1873 in Binghamton, are pure fabrication. However, the final assessment of Fowler as a player — "the equal of any second baseman" who was a "fairly good sticker and excellent base runner" and "was popular everywhere" — does capture the essence of his greatness.[51] The following month, the story of the upcoming Fowler benefit game was repeated with the now tired comments about his connection to Cooperstown and how he received his nickname. However, a few more specifics were added: "With F. D. Ellis, Sol [White] hopes to work up a big benefit for the veteran Bud Fowler in the spring at Meyer Rose Park in Brooklyn."[52]

That spring benefit game never was played but instead a fall benefit was re-scheduled for late October. It was to take place at the Marquette Oval at Second Avenue and 10th Street in Brooklyn and to feature the Brooklyn Royal Giants (with friends and former Fowler teammates Johnson and Monroe on the roster) and Joe Wall's All-Leaguers.[53] In the intervening months between the planned benefits, Fowler had his surgery and returned in full force with a local touring all-black club. There is no record that the October benefit for the recovering African American entrepreneur was ever played.

By April of 1909, Bud Fowler had organized another club with the aid of Tead Pell of the Deerfields—the Buffalo Black Tourists, which was headquartered in Frankfort (NY). The structure of the organization was the familiar one that had now been employed for decades by the former star: Fowler managed the club and served as club secretary and chief publicist. Some of the comments in the press were tried-and-true expressions Fowler had used over the years: "Contact Bud Fowler for games"; "[One] knows what the colored boys can do when it comes to the national game"; "the colored boys are clean players"; "The Black Tourists are a strong combination—the best Negro players in the state [who are now] touring Western New York."

The level of competition with this incarnation of the Black Tourists was not overly strong with games against local amateur and semipro clubs, such as the Stars and Stripes AC (Niagara Falls), the Black Rocks (Buffalo), and the Remington Arms (Ilion). Nor did Fowler's team dominate this opposition as demonstrated by a 12–0 loss with only two hits to Remington Arms pitcher Brown in early June of 1909.[54] There is also an intriguing report in the (frequently unreliable) newspapers that Fowler was also managing the Barnes' American Colored Giants during a swing through Ohio and Pennsylvania in late May of 1909: "Barnes' American Colored Giants will play three games at Norwood next week.... The club is under the management of the celebrated Bud Fowler, late of Cuban X-Giants. The club left Pittsburgh last week, playing Ashtabula, Ohio, Friday, Alliance Saturday and Warren, Ohio, Monday. The Weedsport club, under the management of Lew Paul, will meet the colored club."[55]

Now working from Newark (NJ), Fowler in 1910 was organizing a cross-country tour for July that would be memorable for all involved. The "Colored All-Stars Baseball Team" would have an imposing lineup and schedule of:

> such players of national fame as Johnson, Monroe and Harrison, not to mention numerous colored stars who made enviable reputations playing on the big eastern negro teams. It is the intention of the manager of the team to procure playing dates in New York, Ohio, Michigan, Illinois, Iowa, Nebraska, Kansas, Colorado, Utah, Montana, Washington, Oregon, California, Arizona, Old Mexico, and New Mexico and the tour will probably not be completed until much later than the finish of the world's series between the winners in the National and American leagues.[56]

This tour went up in smoke as did all his ambitious tour plans, yet Bud Fowler was back swinging for the fences the following year. Now in Amsterdam (NY), the African American owner was looking for an investment to fund another black ball club on an inter-continental tour: "Henry B, Jones of St. Louis, a western promoter in amusements, has purchased a one-third interest in the all-star colored team 'Bud' Fowler of this city [Amsterdam], and at one time one of the best players in the country, is going to take with him on a tour of the Pacific coast. The deal was closed recently in New York."[57] This project was apparently Bud Fowler's last attempt at successful black baseball ownership and effectively ended his involvement with the national pastime.

A May 1911 article published in the Sandwich Islands appears to have been the final example of the promotional and scheduling strategies that Bud Fowler had employed for three decades. Fowler's formula remained simple: send a letter to baseball and media organizations in a particular area, praise his touring club to build local interest, include a schedule of previously booked games to suggest the need to act quickly to ensure inclusion on Fowler's proposed tour, and, for areas new to the African American entrepreneur, inquire about the popularity of the game and the opportunities for a financially successful game with his all-black club:

Bud Fowler Tells of What the Colored Nine Has Done and Can Do Here

Writing to the sporting editor, Bud Fowler, business manager of the All-Star Colored Baseball Club of Amsterdam, N.Y., wants some information in regard to coming to Hawaii with his aggregation of ball tossers in November...

The All-Stars Colored are some team according to the news from the mainland, and they have beaten several teams of national fame.

Bud says the club is equal to any National or American League club when it comes to the science of the diamond; they have defeated the champion Athletics and the Detroits — ex-champions of the world — and have made the trip to Cuba for play there.

The tour planned for the coast will start after the regular season in the East is over and when the bunch arrives in San Francisco they think a trip to Hawaii would be just about the right thing to put the finishing touch on their wanderings.

It is now up to the baseball men here to get busy if they want to see these star performers perform on the diamond, and a letter to Bud Fowler, 49 Wall Street, Amsterdam, N.Y., will do the business.

Bud sends out the regular printed letter which he has used to make arrangements for the tour, in inquiry to Hawaii, but at the end he has written more explicitly of what the Stars are.

He says: "Can you give me any information in regard to baseball in Honolulu? Who is the president of the league, and what is your idea of this great colored club coming to your city when it is on the California trip? Could we get a reasonable guarantee in November? What kind of crowds does baseball draw at the games and will you turn this letter over to the proper parties and have them write me in regard to the trip..."

Now it is up to some good baseball fan to get busy if the colored outfit is to come here.[58]

To the very end of his life, Bud Fowler was still angling to share in the financial rewards of professional baseball and trying to remain directly engaged with the national pastime that was his abiding passion for 35 years.

— Eight —

Bud Fowler's Legacy

At the turn of the 20th century, America was in the middle of its second industrial revolution which was transforming the country into large urban centers. There local economies were being subsumed into a national one with goods and services that were made available both nationally and internationally. The need to fill these urban centers with workers to run this newly created national economy led directly to an internal migration of millions of workers in search of a more prosperous life.

Baseball profited from these geographical and economic shifts both financially and psychologically: "The onslaught of urbanization brought higher standards of living and increased leisure time for some and provided a new market of middle- and upper-class individuals with discretionary time and spending money for the newly formed professional baseball league(s)."[1] Baseball emerged as a successful enterprise that provided its supporters with a new diversion that relieved psychological stress and created a new set of role models for an American facing not only a new century but a new set of social structures: "It was as if American needed new rituals to unify and sustain themselves in a new world of city and factory … baseball met both challenges by providing fans with a tension-relieving spectacle … played by skilled new heroes. Beyond this, hope of becoming a player offered poor boys a bit of the American dream of cash and glory."[2]

On the diamond as the United States was entering the 20th century, baseball underwent a major growth spurt that cemented its place as America's national pastime. There was also a new challenge to the National League's monopoly on professional baseball, a circuit led by Ban Johnson and named the American League (which was more suitable than the previous moniker of the "Western League" because the ambitions judgment of such men as Boss McGraw, Boss Lynch and Boss Johnson, and the whole plutocracy of magnates.

I am with the underdog. When I have my way the bleacherites shall sit in the grandstand. In the Southern cities, where there are special stands reserved for our colored brethren, I shall follow the example of Abraham Lincoln and abolish the color line in baseball and I want right here to thank the colored fans for their support in the great work to which I have dedicated my life.... Down with the bosses, down with organized baseball, kill the umpire, and let the people rule![17]

A more conventional response regarding the early 1900s love affair with baseball is succinctly articulated in the following observation by Allen Sangre in a piece called "Love of the Game": "In baseball we have the only forum where an American citizen feels free to take off his coat and cut loose."[18] Even today for the fan disenchanted with baseball excesses, the "gift" of the partial rebirth of the minor leagues by independent ownership may lead to a return to the game's inherent virtues. As one observer put it: "In the smaller towns, beyond the networks and the metropolitan dailies, baseball is enriching America, and the country is again celebrating its good fortune."[19] The fears that baseball is not in tune with contemporary society appear to be receding — instead the game's supposed deficiencies make it attractive to those seeking a respite from the culture's breakneck pace.[20]

Bud Fowler's Impact on the National Pastime

Bud Fowler died of pernicious anemia in Frankfort, New York, on February 26, 1913, at the home of his sister Mrs. Harriet Odom, who also had her maternal aunt, Carrie Lansing, living in the household. Fowler had another sister in the area — Mrs. Edward (Mary) Skinner of Fort Plain — whose husband, as were many males in his extended family, was a barber.[21]

Bud Fowler's obituaries were accurate with regard to his later situation: "John W. Jackson, the one-time famous baseball player known as 'Bud' Fowler, died a few days ago at the home of his sister Mrs. John Odom at Frankfort. For about a year Mr. Jackson conducted a barber shop in the Flatiron building at the corner of Market and Shuler streets in this city [Amsterdam] and was well known here. He was born in Fort Plain...." However, when it came to discussing his longevity and accomplishments on the diamond, the writers got nothing correct: "He played at various times with the Chicago White Sox [this was a persistent rumor], the Boston Americans, in the New York State league, and with Mexican, Cuban and Australian teams."[22]

Perhaps Fowler's time in New Mexico provides the best synopsis of his legacy. His presence in a community that was seeking to solidify its self-worth by embracing the American game often had an unacknowledged positive impact that went beyond the dazzling plays he contributed in the field or at bat on the baseball diamond. His brief stay in the Land of Enchantment, for example, helped to introduce the national pastime in a dignified and professional manner to a rather unsettled territory in search of its American identity. His focused attention on the matters at hand and his perseverance in pursuit of his personal goals and dreams provided an example for New Mexico's polyglot peoples in their drive to statehood, which, ironically, occurred almost simultaneously as Bud Fowler was absenting himself from the national pastime.

Furthermore, Bud Fowler's four-month stay in Santa Fe also helped to reveal the rather tolerant nature, at least by the standards of the day, of its inhabitants toward the "other." In fact, when African American ballplayers had been banned from playing on white teams in organized baseball for a decade, the Santa Fe Mechanics of 1909 had a team that was one-third African American.[23] New Mexico was a (small) step ahead of many of its fellow states in race relations when it entered the union in 1912. Baseball functioned as a pleasing civic diversion and helpful tool in creating such an atmosphere. An editorial by J.F.W. in late September of 1888 can stand as the last word on the importance of baseball to Territorial New Mexico, and the country at large, both of which were on the cusp of a new and challenging future:

> There were also the never-failing exhibitions of the noble base ball game, compared with which the Olympic games of the Greeks, or the bull fights of the Spaniards were and are as nothing. The remarkable physical development and the refinement and ethical culture of the present American generation are in my opinion due to the base ball game. When the base ball matches once cease, and the small boy or girl no longer stops you on the street to ask who has won, then shall the eagle scream his last scream and American liberty perish? The development and progress of New Mexico seem to me intimately interwoven with the grand, the noble, game of base ball. At least I have heard base ball discussed far more earnestly and frequently by old and young in New Mexico, this

summer than mining, grazing, farming, or even politics; from which I have inferred that the game of base ball must be more important than any of these great interests or probably than all of them put together.[24]

In this larger picture of what constitutes the American experience, Bud Fowler's life was both triumph and tragedy. His professional involvement in baseball tracked the rise and fall of the treatment of African Americans in America's national pastime.

Yet baseball was not everyone's national pastime. In 1887, the all-black Cuban Giants lost a close game, 6–4, to the champion Detroit Wolverines. Historians have speculated on how strong the Giants could have been in the 1880s if they had been allowed access to all the top African American baseballists then playing in organized baseball.[25]

By 1913, Bud Fowler was living in obscurity in upstate New York after years of pioneering for black baseball. What exactly had he accomplished? The claims that the African American baseball pioneer revolutionized the national pastime by inventing shin guards and initiating the feet-first slide and became a "King Globe Troter [sic]" are defeatable. Yet Bud Fowler unquestionably made a direct contribution to black baseball's athletic, no-holds-barred style with his flashy fielding, his aggressiveness on the base paths, and his "brainy" strategy. As well as helping to revolutionize the game on the field, Fowler aided African American economic and social development with his career in organizational management.[26]

Perhaps Bud Fowler's greatest contribution to the sport was his sheer longevity and perseverance in light of the many contributing factors that forced 19th-century African American ballplayers to be constantly on the move "lack of money, heckling and antagonism from teammates, managements' fears of losing games by forfeit if they kept their black players, and white teams' often letting black players go after a season regardless of their contributions."[27] Such doggedness in pursuit of a professional career in baseball led the African American pioneer to a truncated ten-year career in organized baseball, a 20-plus career of playing the sport at the highest levels in which he was allowed to participate, and 30 years of trying to use his entrepreneurial skills to carve out a place for all-black baseball within the national pastime.

Always a gamer, Bud Fowler never wavered in his passion for the national pastime and held on to the ever-receding dream that there was a future for African Americans in the national pastime, if not on integrated teams at the highest level of the game at least as owners and managers of all-black clubs:

> In the years after 1895, when daunting obstacles of racism and insufficient capital thwarted his attempts to promote baseball clubs and barnstorming tours, he turned increasingly to the idealistic notion of the far west as a land of equality of opportunity. Despite the treatment he received, Bud Fowler never lost his passion for baseball and never gave up hope that the day would come when ballplayers would be judged on their merits rather than the color of their skin.[28]

In times of great stress, sameness brings security while otherness signals threat. Such was the social and economic temper of Fowler's time. Similar social and cultural battles are being fought today in our local and national elections. The battle of minority groups to attain equal opportunity within professional sports is a conflict not yet finally won.

At bottom, American democracy is a messy business with unresolved feelings and ambivalences and its institutions and mores are always in the process of development. If it were a ballgame, America would be a tied game in the bottom of the ninth with the pennant on the line and two sets of crazed fans with lungs bursting would be cheering on their favorites as the clean-up hitter steps into the box and the relief specialist rubs up the ball and toes the rubber as the umpire crouches in readiness as the players in the field lean forward on their toes in anticipation of the pitch and ... it would go into extra innings and Casey would get another crack at bat. And if Casey again went down swinging, there would still be the realization that there is another game tomorrow. And it is these tomorrows that sustain baseball fans from their infancy to their dotage and all the years between. As John Thorn, the Official Historian of Major League Baseball, put it:

> For this old boy, with more years behind than ahead, baseball is still at life's core. Not in the same dizzying way as when I was ten years old and my beloved Brooklyn Dodgers left town and, more pointedly, me; not in the same way that the Mets swept in implausible glory in 1969, filling my heart with joy and my mind with the certainty that anything, yes, anything could happen. No longer in the same warming way as seeing my sons become first players and then fans for life. They are grown now, scattered, yet baseball remains a link for all of us. The game is what we talk about when we want to connect not only with each other but with our shared past.
> Sport replaces faith for some while enhancing it for others. More

importantly for Americans, and more specifically when it comes to baseball, sport constitutes family for the lonely among us ... ballgames of days gone by are stored like holiday snapshots.
Still baseball, after all these years.[29]

In his research and writings, Thorn goes beyond how the sport of baseball enriches individual lives and posits why baseball is America's national pastime: Baseball is "our game" not only because it connects us to our youth and remains a relative constant in an ever-changing world, but because it has "infinite variety" and a form of "national theater" with the outcome never resolved until the last out. Baseball also possesses a dual nature in which it is both "democratic" (and a "*de facto*" religion for many) and "romantic" (tying us to an "Edenic" past that never was). Thus our national pastime is rooted in history (what has happened) and in what is past (that which "sustains" us as myth). As with American society as a whole, baseball is built on these pillars and in its best moments "equips us to have dreams, to take risks, and to be good Americans."[30] Bud Fowler's career in all phases of professional baseball in the late 19th and early 20th centuries is a matter of historical record and, equally important, a useful symbol of perseverance and dignity in a young post–Civil War society searching for the answers to questions that haunt Americans to this day: What is our best self? and What, finally, does it mean to be American?

Epilogue
*Frankfort, New York,
July 1987 — Bud Fowler Day*

On July 25, 1987, a crowd of nearly 100 people including members of the Society for American Baseball Research (SABR) and African American Hall of Fame member Monte Irvin attended a memorial service for Bud Fowler at the Oak View Cemetery in Frankfort (NY). Fowler was honored as baseball's first African American professional player and the day was named in his honor by Frankfort Mayor Frank Grates. SABR co-founder L. Robert Davids was the master of ceremonies and opening speaker; he dedicated a plaque from the organization to honor a baseball pioneer. The keynote speaker was Irvin, who spoke of the importance of the day: "It [the memorial service] is a great tribute to Bud, and it makes me proud just to be a part of it." Equally important, Irvin also understood the tribute to be a partial correcting of a past injustice: "When asked if the ceremony should be taken as a symbol of the movement to integrate blacks into executive management positions in baseball, Irvin said 'yes, and it is a situation that needs to be rectified.'"[1]

Bud Fowler is finally starting to receive the acclaim he has earned as a superb player, experienced teacher and talent evaluator, effective organizer, and tireless promoter of the national pastime during an age that established unprecedented social, political, and legal obstacles to hinder his full participation in his chosen profession. The only more fitting tribute for Cooperstown's favorite son Bud Fowler would be a much deserved plaque in the Baseball Hall of Fame.

Chapter Notes

Prologue

1. *Sporting Life (SL)*, 19, 3; 16 April 1892, 15.
2. *The Sporting News (TSN)*, 9 April, 1892, 5. The Nebraska newspapers typically stressed Fowler's experience as a key element in his signing before the season began: "Bud Fowler, the old Leadville, Colo. [sic] second baseman, will shake off the barnacles off his frame around second base for Lincoln" (*Omaha Daily Bee [ODB]*, 37 March 1892, 15).
3. After Fowler resigned under pressure from the International Association's Binghamton (NY) franchise in 1887, he signed in August with Montpelier of the Vermont State League and was named the team's co-captain, thus making him the first and only African American to serve in such a position on an integrated team in organized baseball in the nineteenth century and the last until after World War II (Gregory Bond, "'Too Much Dirty Work': Race, Manliness, and Baseball in Gilded Age Nebraska," *Nebraska History*, 85 [2004]: 177–178).
4. *TSN*, 9 April 1892, 5.
5. *TSN*, 25 June 1892, 6.
6. "Baseball for Nebraska," *Nebraska State Journal (NSJ)*, 24 Apr. 1892, 6 quoted in Bond, 177.
7. *SL*, 18, 25; 19 March 1892, 14. 26 March 1892, 13.
8. *SL*, 18, 26; 26 March 1892, 13.
9. *TSN*, 30 April 1892, 1.
10. One other African American casualty of the Nebraska Baseball League was William Castone, a legendary figure in Nebraska baseball from 1889 to 1892 and a teammate of Bud Fowler on the Lincoln-Kearney Cotton Pickers of 1892: "[Castone] was a pitcher, batter, captain, manager, promoter, sportswriter and league booster." He had organized and starred on an all-black touring team — the Lincoln Giants — that garnered a national reputation until it disbanded in August of 1891 due to raids by integrated independent teams that were sick of losing to Castone's assemblage of African American ballplayers. Apparently disheartened by his 1892 experiences in organized and integrated baseball in spite of being "one of the best [players] in the association" *(ODB*, 10 April 1892, 8), Will Castone slipped into obscurity in the mid–1890s. His fate was all-too-typical for talented African American baseball players in the late nineteenth century (*TSN*, 9 April 1892, 2; Bond, 174–175).
11. *SL*, 19, 3; 16 April 1892, 4.
12. *SL*, 19, 11; 11 June 1892, 2.
13. Bond, 181.
14. *Ibid.*, 181–182.
15. Sol White, "Colored Ballplayers," *The Sporting News*, 23 March 1889 (reprinted in *Sol White's History of Colored Base Ball with Other Documents on the Early Black Game, 1886–1936* [Lincoln: University of Nebraska Press, 1995], 137–138).
16. Brian McKenna, "Bud Fowler" The Baseball Biography Project: 11 http://bioproj.sabr.org/bioproj.cfm?a=v&v=1&bid=3116&pid=19716 (accessed 10/13/10).
17. James A. Riley, *The Biographical Encyclopedia of the Negro Baseball Leagues* (New York: Carroll & Graf, 2002), 294.

Chapter One

1. Adam Gopnik, *Winter: Five Windows on the Season* (Toronto: House of Anansi Press, 2011), 150–152.
2. *Ibid.*, 166.
3. *Ibid.*, 175–176.
4. Gregory Bond, "'Too Much Dirty Work': Race, Manliness, and Baseball in Gilded Age Nebraska," *Nebraska History*, 65 (2004): 175–176.
5. *Ibid.*, 176.
6. *Ibid.*
7. Tony Judt, "The Glory of the Rails,"

New York Review of Books, 23 December 2010: 61–62.

8. Marci L. Riskin, *The Train Stops Here: New Mexico's Railway Legacy* (Albuquerque: University of New Mexico Press, 2005), 12.

9. Ibid., 12–13 and 16.

10. Lesley Poling-Kempes, *The Harvey Girls: Women Who Opened the West* (Cambridge, MA: De Capo Press, 1989), 119.

11. Victoria E. Dye, *All Aboard for Santa Fe: Railway Promotion of the Southwest, 1890s to 1930s* (Albuquerque: University of New Mexico Press, 2006), 6.

12. *Santa Fe Daily New Mexican* (SFDNM), 28 October 1987, 4.

13. David Myrick, *New Mexico Railroads: A Historical Survey* (Revised Edition) (Albuquerque: University of New Mexico Press, 1990).

14. "Baseball in the West." www.historynet.com/baseball-in-the-west.

15. A congressional act of Congress allowed African Americans to serve in the army in 1866. Buffalo Soldiers who served in the Western Territories signed on for five-year commitments at $13 a month. Official website of the City of Albuquerque. www.cabq.gov (http://cabq.gov/humanrights/hts/public-information-and-education/diversity-bookletsd/blac...) (accessed 1/15/2010)

16. Dorothy Z. and Harold Seymour, *Baseball: The People's Game*, Vol. 3 (New York: Oxford University Press, 1991), 437.

17. For example, African American soldiers took great pride in participating in the Great Bicycle Experiment of the 1890s wherein soldiers were employed to see if men and materials could be effectively transported on bicycles rather than depending on horses. Bruce Glasrud and Michael N. Searles (eds.), *Buffalo Soldiers in the West: A Black Soldiers Anthology* (College Station: Texas A & M University Press, 2007), 213–214.

18. Seymour, 567.

19. *Santa Fe New Mexico Review* (SFNMR), 23 July 1898, 4.

20. Monroe Lee Billington. *New Mexico's Buffalo Soldiers* (Niwot: University Press of Colorado, 1991), 201.

21. In a conversation with American poet Walt Whitman on April 7, 1889, Horace Traubel quotes the bard and baseball enthusiast on the American quality of the game: "That's beautiful: the hurrah game! Well — it's our game: that's the chief fact in connection with it: America's game: has the snap, go fling, of the American atmosphere — belongs as much to our institutions, fits into them as significantly, as our constitutions, laws: is just as important in the sum total of our historic life" (*With Walt Whitman in Camden*, vol. IV [1906]).

22. William J. Ryczek, *When Johnny Came Sliding Home: The Post-Civil War Baseball Boom, 1865–1870* (Jefferson, NC: McFarland, 1998), 16.

23. George B. Kirsch, *Baseball in Blue and Gray: The National Pastime during the Civil War* (Princeton, NJ: Princeton University Press, 2003), 16.

24. Ryczek, 19.

25. Jules Tygiel, *Past Time: Baseball as History* (New York: Oxford University Press, 2000), 6–7.

26. Peter Morris, *But Didn't We Have Fun? An Informal History of Baseball's Pioneer Era, 1843–1870* (Chicago: Ivan R. Dee, 2008), 111.

27. Melvin L. Adelman, *A Sporting Time: New York City and the Rise of Modern Athletics, 1820–1870* (Champaign: University of Illinois Press, 1990), 107–108, 113–114, 116

28. Warren Goldstein, *Playing for Keeps: A History of Early Baseball* (Ithaca, NY: Cornell University Press, 1989), 2.

29. Kirsch, 12–14.

30. Adelman, 121, 138.

31. Morris, 114–115; Daniel R. Biddle and Murray Dubin, "An Early Quest for Equality on the Diamond," 2. www.philly.com... (accessed 9/16/10).

32. Kirsch, 24.

33. Adelman, 123–124, 135.

34. Ibid., 129–130, 132–133.

35. Goldstein, 4, 17–19, 101; Tom Melville, *Early Baseball and the Rise of the National League* (Jefferson, NC: McFarland, 2001), 18, 33, 68.

36. Leonard Koppett, *Koppett's Concise History of Major League Baseball* (Philadelphia: Temple University Press, 1998), 9.

37. Kirsch, 14–15.

38. Morris, *But Didn't We Have...*, 43–44.

39. With the elimination of soaking, baseballs became gradually harder to increase distance with the new emphasis on hitting. Also, the difficulty in making baseballs in mid-nineteenth century led to problems on the diamond: The scarcity of balls limited practice time and hindered the development of batting and fielding skills (*ibid.*, 80, 83).

40. Ibid., 48–49, 52, 67, 73.

41. Kirsch, x, xiv.

42. Leslie Heaphy, *The Negro Leagues, 1869–1960* (Jefferson, NC: McFarland, 2003), 10.

43. Morris, *But Didn't We Have...*, 135–144.

44. Ibid., 124–132.

45. Dorothy Z. and Harold Seymour, *Baseball: The People's Game* (New York: Oxford University Press, 1991), 537

46. Seymour, ix.
47. Morris, *But Didn't We Have...*, 146, 149, 157, 161, 165.
48. Seymour, 29–31.
49. *Ibid.*, 35.
50. *Ibid.*, 128–129.
51. Albert G. Spalding, *America's National Game* (Lincoln: University of Nebraska Press, 1992 reprint of 1914 publication), 361.
52. Goldstein, 20 and Ryczek, 27.
53. Ryczek, 29–30. The first paid attendance baseball game was in 1858 near Flushing (Queens) between all-star aggregations from Manhattan and Brooklyn. The entrance fee was fifty cents (Ryczek, 13).
54. Gunther Barth, *City People: The Rise of Modern City Culture in Nineteenth Century America* (Mew York: Oxford University Press, 1980), 149–151 and 159.
55. Kirsch, 62–63.
56. Ryczek, 30, 35.
57. *Ibid.*, 35–36.
58. John Thorn, *Baseball in the Garden of Eden: The Secret History of the Early Game* (New York: Simon & Schuster, 2011), 70, 87–88.
59. *New York Daily Tribune (NYDT)*, 7 Aug. 1865, 4; for a contrasting view on the subject of baseball as a business enterprise, SEE Adelman, 152–154, 160–162, and 174–175.
60. *Gallipolis (OH) Journal (GJ)*, 20 Sept. 1866, 3.
61. *The Philadelphia Evening Telegraph (PET)*, 18 Oct. 1866, 2.
62. *GJ*, 1 Nov. 1866, 3.
63. *PET*, 30 Nov. 1866, 5.
64. *PET*, 23 Oct. 1866, 4.
65. *PET*, 26 June 1866, 1.
66. *PET*, 1 Oct. 1866, 4.
67. *PET*, 2 Oct. 1866, 4.
68. Tygiel, "The National Game: Reflections on the Rise of Baseball in the 1850s and 1860s," *Past Time: Baseball as History*, 13–14.
69. Koppett, 15, 20, 28.
70. William J. Ryczek, *Blackguards and Red Stockings: A History of Baseball's National Association, 1871–1875* (Jefferson, NC: McFarland, 1992), 8, 19, 21; Benjamin Rader, "Introduction" in Albert G. Spalding's *America's National Game* (Lincoln: University of Nebraska Press, 1992), xi.
71. *Ibid.*, 33 and 35; Leslie Heaphy, *The Negro Leagues, 1869–1960* (Jefferson, NC: McFarland, 2003), 16.
72. *Ibid.*, 38, 213.
73. Goldstein, 21–39; Kirsch, ix, 16.
74. Melville, 81, 101, 129; Koppett, 28.
75. Morris, *But Didn't We Have...*, 176, 217.
76. Thorn, 190.
77. Tygiel, 34.
78. Goldstein, 143–145.

Chapter Two

1. Kermit Hill, Personal Interview (1), 6 September 2010.
2. Ernest M. Ormsby, "Real 'White Man's Burden,'" *Cleveland Gazette (CG)* 16, 37 (15 Apr. 1899), 2.
3. Gregory Bond, "'Too Much Dirty Work': Race, Manliness, and Baseball in Gilded Age Nebraska," *Nebraska History*, 65 (2004): 175–176.
4. *Ibid.*, 176.
5. *Ibid.*
6. Dorothy Z. and Harold Seymour, *Baseball: The People's Game*, Vol. 3 (New York: Oxford University Press), 555.
7. Sean Lehman's Archives, *Baseball Statistics Systems*. http://baseball.com/category/baseball (accessed 10 February 2007).
8. Kermit Hill, *Personal Interview* (2), 17 March 2011.
9. Janet Bruce, *The Kansas City Monarchs: Champions of Black Baseball* (Lawrence: University Press of Kansas, 1985), 3–6 and 9–10.
10. Erica Childs, "Images of the Black Athlete: Intersection of Race, Sexuality, and Sports," *Journal of African American Studies*, 4, 2 (1999): 20–22.
11. *Ibid.*, 27.
12. *Ibid.*, 28.
13. *The Kingston (NY) Daily Freeman (KDF)*, 4 Aug. 1911, 10.
14. *The New York Daily Sun (NYDS)*, 5 Aug. 1907, 1.
15. Childs, 29.
16. *Ibid.*, 30, 32.
17. Renford Reese, "The Social Political Context of the Integration of Sport in America," *Journal of African American Studies*, 3, 4 (1997), 21.
18. *Ibid.*, 9–10.
19. *Ibid.*, 15–16 and Michael E. Lomax, "Black Baseball's First Rivalry: The Cuban Giants Versus the Gorhams of New York and the Birth of the Colored Championship," *Sport History Review*, 28 (1997), 135–136.
20. Reese, 22.
21. William J. Ryczek, *When Johnny Came Sliding Home: The Post–Civil War Baseball Boom, 1865–1870* (Jefferson, NC: McFarland, 1998), 52.
22. David W. Zang, *Fleet Walker's Divided Heart: The Life of Baseball's First Black Major Leaguer* (Lincoln: University of Nebraska Press, 1995), 56–57.
23. *Sporting Life*, 19, 14; 2 July 1892, 14.

24. *Burlington (IA) Hawk-Eye*, 15 May 1885, 7.
25. *TNYDS*, 26 May 1909, 2.
26. *Cedar Rapids (IA) Evening Gazette*, 19 May 1885, 4.
27. *Cincinnati Enquirer*, 12 April 1895 cited in Dean A. Sullivan, *Early Innings: A Documentary History of Baseball, 1825–1908* (Lincoln: University of Nebraska Press, 1995), 232.
28. *CG*, 11, 3 (26 Aug. 1893), 2.
29. *CG* 1, 42 (7 June 1884), 1.
30. *CG*, 14, 43 (29 May 1897), 2.
31. *CG*, 3, 10 (24 Oct. 1885), 2.
32. Bond, 183.
33. Leslie A. Heaphy, *The Negro Leagues, 1869–1960* (Jefferson, NC: McFarland, 2003), 19–20.
34. Jules Tygiel, *Past Time: Baseball as History* (New York: Oxford University Press, 2000), 117–118.
35. Lawrence D. Hogan, *Shades of Glory: The Negro Leagues and the Glory of African-American Baseball* (Cooperstown, NY: National Baseball Hall of Fame and Museum, 2006), 41, 44–46, 57.
36. Quoting the *Burlington (IA) Free Press (BFP)* in *Hutchison (KN) Daily News (HDN)*, 16 Sept. 1887; Jeffrey Powers-Beck, *The American Indian Integration of Baseball* (Lincoln: University of Nebraska Press, 2004), 1–5, 8. (SEE also T.C. McLuhan's *Dream Tracks: The Railroad and the American Indian, 1890–1930* [New York: Harry N. Abrams, 1985], Introduction.)
37. Powers-Beck, 6–7.
38. *Ibid.*, 15–16, 18.
39. *Ibid.*, 15.
40. Michael M. Oleksak and Mary Adams Oleksak, *Beisbol: Latin Americans and the Grand Old Game* (Grand Rapids, MI: Masters Press, 1991), 5–6.
41. *Ibid.*, 8.
42. *Ibid.*, 31–33.
43. Bond, 179.
44. *Auburn (NY) Weekly News and Democrat (AWND)*, 29 Sept. 1897.
45. Patrick B. Miller, "The Anatomy of Scientific Racism: Racialist Response to Black Athletic Achievement," *We Are a People: Narrative and Multiplicity in Contrasting Ethnic Identity* (Philadelphia: Temple University Press, 2000), Paul R. Spickard and W. Jeffrey Burroughs (eds.), 125, 127 and 130.
46. "Get That Negro Off the Field!" www.negro-league-baseball.com. http://www.negro-league-baseball.com/blog/get-that-negro off-the-field.html (accessed 12/27/10).
47. Dorothy Z. and Harold Seymour, 557.
48. *CG*, 22, 13 (29 Oct. 1904), 1.
49. McKenna, 7.
50. "Get That Negro Off the Field."
51. *Sacramento Daily Record-Union (SDRU)*, 13 Sept. 1887, 1.
52. Michael E. Lomax, "'If He Were White': Portraits of Black and Cuban Players in Organized Baseball, 1880–1920," *Journal of African American Studies*, 3, 3 (1997), 36–37.
53. *Ibid.*, 38–40.
54. *Ibid.*, 42; Walker's attitude toward African American disengagement from mainstream society was affected by his own experience with the judicial system: "Syracuse, N.Y.—Moses F. Walker, an Afro-American, catcher of the Syracuse baseball club in the season of 1889, who about two months ago killed Patrick Murphy, a tough, in an encounter provoked by the dead man, was acquitted June 3. The plea was self-defense. When the verdict was announced the court house was thronged with spectators, who received it with a tremendous roar of cheers, which Justice Kennedy in vain attempted to suppress ... there was no cessation in the demonstration, and, in despair, the court was adjourned. Walker is the hero of the hour" *CG*, 8, 43 (13 June 1891), 2.
55. *SDRU*, 27 July 1887, 1.
56. *National Republican (Washington, DC) (NR)*, 10 Mar. 1887, 1.
57. *The Washington (DC) Bee (WB)*, 2 July 1887, 1.
58. *Ibid.*
59. Phil Dixon (with Patrick J. Hannigan), *The Negro Baseball Leagues: A Photographic History* (Mattituck, NY: Amereon Ltd., 1992), 244–246. Segregation based on class and language as well as race persisted throughout the concluding decade of the nineteenth century. For example, in Albuquerque (NM), there were four separate militias organized in the New Mexico Territory: African-Americans, Spanish-speakers, upper class whites, and working class whites (Kermit Hill, Personal Interview [2]).
60. Brian McKenna, "Bud Fowler," *The Baseball Biography Project*: 8. http://bioproj.sabr.org/bioproj.cfm?v=l&bib=3116&pid=19716. (accessed 12/29/11).
61. *Los Angeles Daily Herald (LADH)*, 5 Dec. 1887, 9.

Chapter Three

1. *Brooklyn Eagle (BE)*, 25 January 1909, p. 2
2. Sol White, "Sol White Remembers," *New York Age*, 20 December 1930 (reprinted in *Sol White's History of Colored Base Ball with Other Documents on the Early Black Game,*

1886–1936 [Lincoln: University of Nebraska Press, 1995], 154–155).
  3. *Sporting Life* (*SL*), 53, 3; 27 March 1909, p. 3. I have discovered that Bud Fowler has allegedly written at least one other song at about this time entitled "The Royal Giants" that was published in Frankfort (NY) and dedicated to African American baseball stars Monroe and Johnson, both of whom were scheduled to appear in a benefit game in Brooklyn to help defray the medical costs of their elder colleague. (*New York Age* [*NYA*], 8 April 1909). I am uncertain if these songs are one and the same or separate compositions. Such reports do underscore Fowler's tireless promotion of the game of baseball as entertainment for the paying customers.
  4. Sylvea Hollis, "The Dark Man Has Almost Disappeared from Our Country: African American Workers in Cooperstown, New York, 1860–1900." *New York History*, 88, 1 (Winter 2007). Cooperstown was also where a young Bud Fowler learned the burden of being an African American in a white world. A white resident reminisced about Fowler: "There played with us a little black boy, Johnnie Jackson [Fowler], who felt his color so much that he used to say if it'd make him white, he could willingly be skinned alive."
  5. In 1878, Tommy Bond had a hand in all of his team's decisions, going 40–19 with a 2.06 era in 532.2 innings. The Boston Red Caps also repeated as National League champs. www.baseball-reference.com>Encyclopediaof-Players>Blisting.
  6. *Boston Daily Globe* (*BDG*): Apr. 25, 1878, p. 3.
  7. *Ibid*.
  8. *Ibid*.
  9. *BDG*: May 16, 1878, p. 4.
  10. *BDG*: May 18, 1878, p. 4.
  11. *Boston Daily Advertiser* (*BDA*): May 18, 1878 (All the *Boston Daily Advertiser* and *Worcester Spy* references are cited in Brian McKenna http://baseballhistoryblog.com/category/black-baseball-history).
  12. *BDG*: May 18, 1878, p. 4.
  13. *Ibid*.
  14. *BDA*: May 18, 1878; The London Tecumsehs' rookie manager was Ross Barnes, who in nine years from 1871 to 1881 won five pennants in nine years in the National Association (Boston — 4) and in the National League (Chicago —1). Barnes won the first National League batting title at .429 when a ball hitting first in fair territory but then rolling foul was considered a live ball as is the case in cricket. This was a highly developed skill of the slick fielding middle infielder. He also led the senior circuit in its debut season in hits, runs, doubles, and triples while also hitting the league's first home run on May 2, 1876. However, his character was less impressive than his skill on the diamond. Barnes' disdain for playing against African American ball players was a mirror of his teammate Cap Anson of Chicago with whom Barnes played in 1876–1877. Both players could not abide losing to an "inferior" race.
  15. *BDG*: May 18, 1878, p. 4. A teammate of Bud Fowler on the Lynn Live Oaks club was Hall-of-Famer William Arthur "Candy" Cummings who it was claimed was the first to employ the curve ball. — Neil J. Sullivan's *The Minors: The Struggles and Triumph of Baseball's Poor Relation from 1876 to the Present* (New York: St. Martin's Press, 1990), 12.
  16. *BDG*: May 20, 1878, p. 4.
  17. *Ibid*.
  18. *Worcester* (MA) *Spy* (*WP*): May 20, 1878.
  19. *BDG*: May 25, 1878, p. 7.
  20. *BDG*: May 30, 1878, p. 2.
  21. *Ibid*.
  22. *Fitchburg* (MA) *Sentinel* (*FS*): May 30, 1878, p. 3.
  23. *Ibid*.
  24. *BDG*: May 31, 1878, p. 4.
  25. *BDG*: June 1, 1878, p. 1.
  26. Brian McKenna, "Bud Fowler": 3 http://bioproj.sabr.org/bioproj.cfm?a=v&v=l&bid=3116&pid=19716.
  27. *New York Clipper* (*NYC*): 20 July 1878, 133.
  28. *NYC*: 25 May 1878, 69.
  29. David L. Porter (editor) *Biographical Dictionary of American Sports, Baseball (A–F)* (New York: Greenwood Press, 2000), 62.
  30. *Lowell Sun* (*LS*), 26 July 879, 4.
  31. *New York Spirit of the Times* (*SOT*), 9 July 1874 in *SOT Almanac*, January–December, 1874, 577.
  32. *Ibid*. It seems that Canadian reporters of nineteenth century baseball were addicted to making humorous analogies with other occupations and mixing occupational jargons, e.g., in discussing a local game of amateur clubs, the reporter rhapsodized that "The butchers of Guelph taught the bakers that they should not be loafing on a ball field by the score of 18 to 3. Now they intend to make mincemeat of the printers" in *The Toronto World*, 5 Sept. 1881, 3.
  33. "Canadians in Baseball: The 'Lost Tribe.'" *The Canadian Encyclopedia*: 1–2 http://thecanadianencyclopedia.com/PrinterFriendly.cfm?Params=A1ARTFET_E16 (Accessed 12/13/10).
  34. *Boston Herald* (*BH*) (1881) cited by David McDonald, "Jim Crow Comes North," *Dominionball: Baseball above the 49th* (Cleve-

land, OH: Society of American Baseball Research, 2005), 76.
35. *Ibid.*; Brain McKenna, "Bud Fowler," *The Baseball Biography Project*: 3 http://bioproj.sabr.org/bioproj.cfm?a=v&v=l&bid=3116&pid=19716 (Accessed 10/13/10).
36. Mark Ribowsky, *A Complete History of the Negro Leagues, 1884 to 1955* (New York: Citadel Press, 2002), 16.
37. *The New York Clipper Almanac* (1880), 41.
38. *The New York Clipper (NYC)* 18 June 1881.
39. http://medianola.tulane.edu/index.php/Pickwick_Club (accessed 10/15/11); Dale A. Somers, *The Rise of Sports in New Orleans, 1850–1900* (Baton Rouge: Louisiana State Press, 1972).
40. McKenna, 3. Actually, the founding date of the Swans is somewhat in doubt since an advertisement for an "1880 series between the team and the Peabodys at Richmond Base-Ball Park at the head of Clay Street" appeared in the *Richmond Daily Dispatch*, 5 Sept. 1880, 1.
41. *The Daily (Richmond, Virginia) Dispatch (DD)*, 5 Aug. 1881, 2.
42. *DD*, 9 July 1882, 1.
43. *National (Washington D.C.) Republican (NR)*, 23 Apr.1883, 1.
44. *The Evening (Washington D.C.) Critic (EC)*, 27 Apr. 1883, 4.
45. *NR*, 28 Apr. 1883, 5.
46. James Edward Brunson (citation of *St. Louis Republican*), *The Early Image of Black Baseball: Race and Representation in the Popular Press, 1871–1890* (Jefferson, NC: McFarland, 2009), 188.
47. McKenna, 3–4; The Niles Grays along with the Reading (PA) Actives and Lancaster (PA) Ironsides were prominent eastern teams in 1884 with African American ball players on their rosters.
48. Goldstein, 62.
49. *The New York Times* (23 September 1883) cited in Dean A. Sullivan's *Early Innings: A Documentary History of Baseball, 1825–1908* (Lincoln: University of Nebraska Press, 1995), 133–135. As a report three days earlier in an Ohio newspaper indicates, women's games were treated in a standard patronizing fashion: "The seventeen young women who played at base ball at Oriole Park, Baltimore, on Saturday afternoon last, drew four thousand spectators. The nines wore comfortably fitting and dresses, cut off an inch or two below the knee. Jaunty hats, colored stockings, striped belts, and fancy base ball shoes completed the outfit. With the brunettes the trimmings were red; with the blondes, blue. The diamond was much smaller than the regulation arena, the distance between bases being sixty instead of ninety feet, and the pitcher's stand being much nearer the home plate. Few balls were caught..." (*The Elyria Republican*, 20 September 1883, 1).
50. *The Daily (Richmond, VA) Dispatch (DD)*, 15 Aug. 1882, p. 4.
51. Thorn, 193–194. Such novelty games were not limited to the Philadelphia area as was observed in the national publication *New York Clipper*: "A game was played May 30, in Castleton, Vt., in which the contestants were men ranging from forty-five to eighty years of age. The player who did the best batting was the Rev. Mr. Knappen, over seventy years of age.... A team of fat men — none weighing less than 200 lb.— played in several Canadian towns.... Several games between mercantile nines were played in Troy, N.Y., commencing at five o'clock in the morning." A play[off] took place June 29 in Albany, NY, between nines made up respectively of Democratic and Republican members of the Legislature" (*NYC Annual Almanac* [1880], 41).
52. William J. Ryczek, *When Johnny Came Sliding Home*, 55–56 and 99.
53. Thorn, 194. *Sporting Life* even discussed the failure of baseball on roller skates to catch on as a spectator sport. The major problem for the participants was standing still. Also, too many errors were made which lessened the quality of play and effort by the players who were conscious of making so many miscues (6, 4 [1885], 3).
54. Joel Zoss & John S. Bowman, *Diamonds in the Rough: The Untold Story of Baseball* (Lincoln: University of Nebraska Press, 2004), 7.
55. *Albany (NY) Journal* cited in *Lowell (MA) Sun*, 16 August 1879. Almost from its earliest days, a staple of baseball humor has been the beleaguered and universally despised umpire: "Next year they say they are going to have the game of baseball to consist of ten innings. This is designed to prolong the game till after dark and so give the umpire a chance to escape" (*Lancaster [PA] Daily Intelligencer*, 19 Oct. 1881, 4); *The Fitchburg (MA) Sentinel*, 6 Oct. 1879, 4; *Toronto (Ontario) World*, 27 July 1881, 4.
56. *The Fitchburg (MA) Sentinel (FS)*, 6 Oct. 1879, 4.
57. *Toronto (Ontario) World (TW)*, 27 July 1881, 4.
58. Zoss & Bowman, 25 and 27.
59. David Zang, *Fleet Walker's Divided Heart: The Life of Baseball's First Black Major Leaguer* (Lincoln: University of Nebraska Press, 1995), 55, 57, 59.

was fifty feet from home plate which was made either of rubber or marble. It was only in 1884 that all restrictions on a pitcher's delivery were abolished, and in 1887 that batters could no longer request a high or low ball. The pitching box was replaced with a slab and the distance to home plate was increased to the current sixty feet six inches in 1893.

40. *Santa Fe Weekly New Mexican (SFWNM)*, 17 May 1888, 3.

41. *SFWNM*, 1887.

42. Adrian Bustamante, Personal Interview (September 21, 2010). Professor Bustamante went on to explain that many people in Santa Fe were (and are) pleased that the town of Santa Fe is built on a plateau and, as a result, that the railroad actually had its main station in Lamy, approximately twenty miles away. Otherwise, the conventional wisdom believes that Santa Fe would have suffered from the same urban and industrial sprawl that is a hallmark of Albuquerque.

43. *Ibid.*

44. Chris Wilson, "The Reluctant Tourist Town," *The Myth of Santa Fe: Creating a Modern Regional Tradition*, UNM Press (1997), 82 and 84. The development of the Santa Fe style with its borrowings from Pueblo culture also owes a debt to Adolph Bandelier and his archaeological discoveries and the New Mexico State Bureau of Ethnology (1879).

45. *Ibid.*, 84.

46. *SFWNM*, 17 May 1888, 3.

47. *Santa Fe Daily Herald (SFDH)*, 4 August 1888.

48. *SFWNM*, 3 May 1888, 4.

49. *Santa Fe Daily New Mexican (SFDNM)*, 5 June 1888, 4.

50. *SFDNM*, 5–6 June 1888 and *SFWNM*, 7 June 1888, 4.

51. *SFWNM*, 7 June 1888, 4; *Albuquerque Daily Citizen (ADC)*, 6 June 1888. Hapeman had staying power throughout the 1888 season. He played for Las Vegas in June after the NMBL reformed and began a second season. Recognized as the ace pitcher of the league, Hapeman pitched a three-hit shutout of the Ancients. He was the losing pitcher three months later in Santa Fe's last game victory over Las Vegas before the Meadow City team disbanded. He also was the losing pitcher ten days after that game when Las Cruces lost, 1–4, to the Albuquerque ("Boys in Green") ball club.

52. *Santa Fe Herald (SFH)*, 16 June 1888, 4.

53. *SFH*, 28 July 1888, 4.

54. *Las Vegas Optic (LVO)*, 10 August 1888, 4.

55. *SFH*, 30 June 1888, 4.

56. *SFH*, 4 August 1888, 4.

57. *SFH*, 18 August 1888, 5.

58. *LVO*, 10 August 1888.

59. *SFH*, 25 August 1888, 3.

60. *The Daily Herald (TDH)*, 31 August 1888.

61. *SFH*, 11 September 1888, 1; *LVO*, 10 September 1888.

62. *SFDNM*, 3 October 1888; *LVO*, 10 September 1888.

63. *TDH*, 14 September 1888, 4.

64. *SFDNM*, 7 September 1888, 3.

65. *SFH*, 3 September 1888, 4.

66. *LVO*, 10 September 1888.

67. *TDH*, 25 September 1888, 4.

68. *TDH*, 18 September 1888, 4.

69. *Ibid.*

70. *TDH*, 24 September 1888, 4.

71. *SFH*, 1 October 1888, 4.

72. *TDH*, 4 October 1888, 4.

73. *Ibid.*

74. *Ibid.*

75. *SFH*, 14 September, 4.

76. *TDH*, 26 September 1888, 1.

77. *TDH*, 4 October 1888, 4.

78. *SFDNM*, 3 October 1888.

79. *SFDNM*, 19 June 1888, 4.

80. *SFWNM*, 3 May 1888, 4.

81. *Albuquerque Morning Democrat (AMD)*, 3 October 1888, 4.

82. *TDH*, 23 October 1888.

83. "Adrian C. Anson," 10 November 1888 cited in Jean-Pierre Caillaut (complier), *The Complete New York Clipper's Baseball Biographies*, Volume, I (Jefferson, NC: McFarland, 2009), 18.

84. "1888 — Charlton Baseball Chronology." http://www.baseballlibrary.com/chronology/byyear.php?year=1888 (Accessed 4/5/2011).

85. *SFDNM*, 28 September 1888, 4. The Capital Barber Shop was a few doors down from the Hotel Capital on the Northwest Corner of the Santa Fe Plaza, the current home of Santa Fe's First National Bank Main Branch.

86. *SFH*, 6 October 1888, 4.

87. SFDH, 25 September 1888, 4.

88. *SFDH*, 6 October 1888, 4.

89. *The Sporting Life (SL)*, 12, 11 (December 19, 1888), 3.

90. "Southern California League" www.baseball-reference.com: 1–2. http://www.baseball-reference.com/minors/league.cgi?code=SCAL&class=N/A (accessed 4/5/11).

91. *SL*, 12, 16 , 12 January 1889, 5.

92. *SL*, 12, 24, 7 March 1889, 5.

93. Eric Enders, "Buck Freeman": 1. http://sabr.org/bioproj/person/46f0454e (accessed 5/24/2012).

94. *Sporting Life (SL)*, 13, 7, 1889, 4.

95. *The Grand Rapids (MI) Democrat*

(GRD) cited in Phil Dixon's *The Negro Baseball Leagues: A Photographic History* (Ameron House, 1992), 52.
 96. Brian B. Holway, *The Complete Book of Baseball's Negro League: The Other Half of Baseball History* (Mattituck, NY: Hastings House Publishers, 2001), 26–27; Hoffbeck, 27.
 97. "1889–1890 Michigan State League" www.baseball-reference.com/bullpen.
 98. *SL*, 13, 20; 21 August 1889, 4.
 99. *SL*, 15, 1; 15 April 1890, 11.
 100. *Pittsburgh Dispatch (PD)*, 7 Mar. 1890, 6.
 101. Brian McKenna, "Bud Fowler" *The Baseball Biography Project*: 9. http://bioproj.sabr.org/bioproj.cfm?a=v&v=l&bid=3116&pid=19716 (accessed 10/13/10).
 102. John Thorn, *Baseball in the Garden of Eden: The Secret History of the Early Game* (New York: Simon and Schuster, 2011), 241, 260.
 103. *SL*, 28 May, 1910 (Thorn [citation], 286).
 104. O. P. Caylor, *Harper's Weekly* (3 May 1890) cited in Dean A. Sullivan's *Early Innings: A Documentary History of Baseball, 1825–1908* (Lincoln: University of Nebraska Press, 1995), 204–205.
 105. Jacob Morse, "Introduction" in *Sphere and Ash: History of Base Ball* (1888) cited in Sullivan, 156–157.
 106. William Anderson, "Creating the National Pastime: The Antecedents of Major League Baseball Public Relations," *Media History Monographs:* 22. http://facstaff.elon.edu/dcopeland/mhm/mhmjoufr4-2.htm (accessed 10/26/11).
 107. *SL*, 21, 25; 16 September, 1883, 12; George B. Kirsch *Baseball in Blue and Gray: The National Pastime during the Civil War* (Princeton, NJ: Princeton University Press, 2003), 134.

Chapter Five

 1. Bud Fowler's days as a pitcher except in the cases of extreme emergency were over by 1890. Evansville signed him as a catcher and a second base man (*Sporting Life*, 14, 15; 15 January 1890, 3).
 2. *SL*, 15, 1; 5 May 1890, 6.
 3. *SL*, 15, 9; 31 May 1890, 11.
 4. *SL*, 15, 6; 10 May 1890, 12; 15, 8; 24 May 1890, 11; and 15, 9; 31 May 1890, 11.
 5. *SL*, 15, 8; 24 May 1890, 1
 6. McKenna, 10.
 7. *(Sterling) Evening Gazette (EG)*, 3 July 1890, 3.
 8. *EG*, 12 July 1890, 2.
 9. *Cedar Rapids (IA) Evening Gazette (CREG)*, 26 July, 1890, 4.
 10. *EG*, 10 July 1890, 3.
 11. *EG*, 21 July 1890, 3.
 12. *EG*, 10 July 1890, 3.
 13. *CREG*, 2 August 1890, 1.
 14. *EG*, 9 July 1890, 3.
 15. *CREG*, 30 July 1890, 4.
 16. *The Dubuque (IA) Daily Times (DDT)* cited in Phil Dixon's *The Negro Baseball Leagues: A Photographic History* (Mattituck, NY: Amereon House, 1992), 52.
 17. *Burlington (IA) Hawk-Eye (BHE)*, 29 August 1890, 4.
 18. *CREG*, 29 August 1890, 3.
 19. Holway, 29 and McKenna, 10.
 20. *Cleveland Gazette (CG)*, 2 August 1890: 2. http://powellsplace.blogspot.com/2010/10/19th-century-baseball-pioneer-bud.html (accessed 11/21/11).
 21. Leonard Koppett, *Koppett's Concise History of Major League Baseball* (Philadelphia: Temple University Press, 1998), 34.
 22. Neil J. Sullivan, *The Minors: The Struggles and the Triumph of Baseball's Poor Relation from 1876 to the Present* (New York: St. Martin's Press, 1990), 202, 7, and 9–10.
 23. *Ibid.*, 11–12.
 24. *Ibid.*, 45.
 25. "Bud Fowler," *Minor League History & Statistics*: 1–2. http://www.baseball-reference.com/minors/players.cgi?id=fowler004joh (accessed 8/12/10).
 26. *Omaha Daily Bee (ODB)*, 1 Feb. 1891 16.
 27. McKenna, 10.
 28. *Omaha Daily Bee (ODB)*, 1 Feb. 1891, 16.
 29. *ODB*, 27 Mar, 1892, 15.
 30. *ODB*, 10 Apr. 1892, 8.
 31. *Capital City (Lincoln, NB) Courier (CCC)*, 21 May 1892, 1.
 32. *The McCook (McCook, NB) Tribune (TMT)*, 27 May 1892, 5.
 33. *ODB*, 15 July 1892, 2.
 34. Hoffbeck, 26.
 35. *Ibid.*, 29.
 36. Merl Kleinknecht, "Blacks in 19th Century Black Baseball," *SABR Research Archives*: 1–2. http://research.sabr.org/journal/blacks-in-19th-c-baseball?tmpl=component&print=1&page (accessed 11/16/11).
 37. *SL*, 25, 4; 5 November 1892, 13.
 38. "Homerun Johnson," *Pitch Black: Negro Player of the Month*: 1–2. http://www.pitchblackbaseball.com/nlothomerunjohnson.html (accessed 11/11/2010); McKenna, 11. Fowler's participation on the 1894 Findlay Sluggers had one of those delicious conver-

gences of fate in which teammate Reddy Grey's brother — Western author-to-be Zane Grey — played with the team that summer under the assumed name "Pearl Zane" (which were his surnames) in order to avoid jeopardizing his baseball scholarship to UPenn where he was studying dentistry.

39. *Lima (OH) Times Democrat (LTD)*, 27 Aug. 1894, 3.
40. *SL*, 18 September 1894, 4.
41. *Adrian Daily Telegram (ADT)*, 30 August 1894 (All the following references to the ADT are cited in Brian McKenna's "Genesis of the Page Fence Giants, August–September 1894," *Baseball History Blog*: 5–8). http://baseballhistoryblog.com/2291/genesis-of-the-page-fence-giants-aug-sept-1894/ (accessed 11/23/11).
42. *ADT*, 31 August 1894.
43. *ADT*, 21 September 1894.
44. *ADT*, 20 September 1894 and 5 November 1894.
45. *SL*, 24, 11 and 24, 9; November 1894, 2.
46. *SL*, 24, 2; 20 Oct. 1894, 2.
47. *SL*, 24, 11; 8 Dec. 1894, 2.
48. *SL*, 24, 22; 23 Feb. 1895, 6.
49. *SL*, 25, 17; 20 July 1895, 11.
50. *Ibid.*
51. *SL*, 25, 21; 17 Aug. 1895, 3.
52. *Cincinnati Enquirer*, 12 April 1895 cited in Dean A. Sullivan (editor) *Early Innings: A Documentary History of Baseball, 1825–1908* (Lincoln: University of Nebraska Press, 1995), 232; 234.
53. Hogan, 76.
54. *SL*, 25, 4; 20 Apr. 1895, 13; *SL* 35, 12; 9 June 1900, 3; *SL*, 39, 6; 26 Apr. 1902, 11.
55. Riley, 294–295 and McKenna, 11–12
56. "1895 Michigan State League." www.baseball-reference.com/minors.
57. *SL*, 25, 7, 1895, 4.
58. Holoway, 31–32.
59. *SL*, 28, 10; 14 May 1896, 7.
60. *Delphos (OH) Daily Herald (DDH)*, 15 May, 1896, 8; McKenna, 12.
61. *Sporting News*, 31 Oct. 1896.
62. Peter Morris, "Bud Fowler's Lost Years," *Black Ball: A Negro League Journal*. 2, 2 (Fall 2009): 13; *SL*, 28, 26; 1896.
63. *Galveston Daily News (GDN)*, 25 Jan. 1897, 5; Morris, 14.
64. *DDH*, 16, Sept. 1897, 3; *Lima (OH) Times Democrat (LTD)*, 16 Sept. 1897, 8; McKenna, 12.
65. *Utica Daily Press (UDP)*, 11 May 1898, 5.
66. *The Hudson Evening Register (THER)*, 20 June 1914, 3.
67. Morris, 15. Morris speculates that this beating had a bearing on Fowler's health problems more than a decade later and is a more reasonable explanation than a hard slide as being the precipitating event for his eventual surgery in 1909.
68. *SL*, 39, 9; 1898, 5.
69. *Fort Wayne (IN) News (FWN)*, 8 Dec. 1898, 5.
70. *Mansfield (OH) News (MN)*, 7 Jan. 1899, 4.
71. *SL*, 32, 17; 7 January 1899, 7.
72. *TSN*, 22 July 1899, 5.
73. *SL*, 33, 21; 7 August 1899, 6.
74. *DDH*, 30 Sept. 1899, 8.
75. *Capital City (Lincoln, NB) Courier (CCC)*, 16 Apr. 1892, 4.
76. *Belmont (St. Clairsville, Ohio) Chronicle (BC)*, 11 June 1891, 4.
77. *BC*, 27 Aug. 1891, 1.
78. *Deming (NM) Headlight (DH)*, 14 Feb. 1891, 4.
79. *The Eddy (Carlsbad (NM)) Current (EC)*, 4 Sept. 1897, 2.
80. Leonard Koppett, *Koppett's Concise History of Major League Baseball* (Philadelphia: Temple University Press, 1998), 77–78.

Chapter Six

1. *Santa Fe Weekly New Mexican (SFWNM)*, 7 June 1888, 1.
2. *Santa Fe Herald (SFH)*, 7 July 1888, 4; *The Weekly (Windsor, Ontario) Sentinel Review*, 25, Mar. 1881, 3. It seems that in the late nineteenth century, no matter how serious a sermon topic might be, clergymen were quite practical in realizing what was truly on the minds of their parishioners: "'My sermon today,' said a Nebraska clergyman, looking placidly over his congregation 'will treat of Sabbath desecration and I trust that I might be able to point out its wickedness to good effect. Before opening my discussion, however; I will announce that there is a baseball game in progress south of the church and for the convenience of the worshipers the score by innings will be posted on the blackboard by Brother Johnson. My text is: "Remember the Sabbath Day keep it holy"'" in *The Fort Wayne (IN) Daily Gazette*, 2 September 1888, 6.
3. *SFWNM*, 24 November 1887. This driving force of capitalism and individual entrepreneurial endeavor is embodied in Eastern Anglo culture which is "characterized by commercial agriculture, land speculation, mineral exploitation and the veneration of 'free' white labor and private property" in Colin D. How-

ell's "Baseball and Borders: The Diffusion of Baseball into Canadian and Mexican-American Borderland Regions, 1885–1911," *Nine*, 11, 2 (Spring, 2003): 17.
4. *The Herald* (Syracuse), 13 February 1887, 5.
5. *SFH*, 28 July 1888.
6. Howard Burman, *Gentlemen at the Bat* (Jefferson City, NC: McFarland and Company, 2010), 3–14. The newspapers in this era frequently punned on the jargon of the game to underscore its boyish nature: "Some boys undertook to play base ball in a field where a ram was feeding recently. He butted the shortstop through a picket fence, and forced all the rest to make a home run. The boy who was batted through the fence was the only one who scored, and he carried his score with him" (*The Fitchburg Sentinel*, 6 October 1879, 4).
7. Dorothy W. Hartman, "Play Ball! Baseball in the Nineteenth Century: From Gentlemen's Sport to Professional Play." http://www.cornerprairie.org/Learn-and-Do/Indiana-History/American-1860-1900 (accessed 1/23/10); Gregory Bond, "'Too Much Dirty Work': Race, Manliness, and Baseball in Gilded Age Nebraska," *Nebraska History*, 85 (2004): 174.
8. *Santa Fe Daily New Mexican* (*SFDNM*), 19 September 1887.
9. *SFH*, 6 August 1888.
10. *Las Vegas Optic* (*LVO*), 10 September 1888.
11. *SFH*, 16 June 1888.
12. Marc Simmons, "Play Ball!" in *Santa Fe Reporter*, 18 July 19.
13. Hartman, 5.
14. *Burlington (IA) Hawk-Eye*, 17 June 1885, 7.
15. *The New York Evening World (TNYEW)*, 14 July 1903, 8.
16. *Waterloo (IA) Courier*, 27 May 1885, 6.
17. *Iowa State Review*, 15 June 1885, 2.
18. *The Weekly Fort Wayne (IN) Sentinel*, 12 September 1888, 1.
19. *SFH*, 23 June 1888, 4.
20. *Ibid.*, 2.
21. *SFH*, 25 June 1888, 4.
22. *SFH*, 7 July 1888, 1.
23. Youth baseball games in Santa Fe were well-attended and fans were charged fifteen cents admission (*SFDNM*, 26 June 1888, 4). The games were hard-fought and could result in as petulant and acrimonious behavior as the adult teams: "The game between the town boys and the Indian team played yesterday at the College grounds resulted in the umpire rendering a decision of 9–0 in favor of the town boys, due to the effect that the Indians threw up the game and refused to play any more than seven innings. The Indian boys, however, refused to give up the league [pennant] they justly lost" (*SFDNM*, 26 July 1888, 4).
24. *SFH*, 4 August 1888, 1 and 7 July 1888.
25. *The New York Sun (NYS)*, 7 July 1908, 5.
26. Thorn, 86, 178–79, and 195.
27. *Atchison (KN) Daily Globe (ADG)*, 12 Sept. 1887, 2.
28. Albert G. Spalding, *America's National Game* (Lincoln: University of Nebraska Press, 1992 reprint), 368, xiv.
29. *SFDNM*, 15 March 1888.
30. *SFDNM*, 25 April 1888.
31. *The Daily Herald* (*TDH*), 24 September 1888, 4.
32. William C. Ryczek, *When Johnny Came Sliding Home: The Post–Civil War Baseball Boom, 1865–1870* (Jefferson, NC: McFarland, 1998), 37–40.
33. *SFWNM*, 28 November 1887, 3.
34. Warren Goldstein, *Playing for Keeps: A History of Early Baseball* (Cornell University Press, 1989), 149, 151; Tom Melville, *Early Baseball and the Rise of the National League* (Jefferson, NC: McFarland, 2001).
35. *SFWNM*, 17 May 1888, 3. As soon as owners gained control of the sport via the implementation of the reserve clause, they instituted a series of fineable offenses for players who "lost self-control," including "swearing, disputing a ump's decision, fighting with the team captain, and offering advice before an umpire made a decision on a call" (Goldstein, 35).
36. *SFH*, 5 August 1888.
37. *SFDNM*, 19 June 1888.
38. *The Cedar Rapids (IA) Evening Gazette*, 13 January 1890, 3.
39. Goldstein, 75–77 and 79.
40. *SL*, 21, 24; 30 August 1893, 3.
41. Sherry Monahan, *The Wicked West: Boozers, Cruisers, Gamblers, and More* (Tucson, AZ: Rio Nuevo, 2005), 129.
42. *SFH*, 28 April 1888.
43. William Anderson, "Creating the National Pastime: The Antecedents of Major League Baseball Public Relations," *Media History Monographs*: 21. http://facstaff.elon.edu/dcopeland/mhm/mhmjoufr4-2.htm (accessed 10/26/11); Monahan, 137.
44. Monahan, 138 and 152–153. In a crass note of political hypocrisy, localities in the guise of improving treatment of women would pass ordinances that ran the gamut from the outlawing of legal prostitution to banning drunk women from thoroughfares and from entering saloons for the purposes of "drinking, singing, playing cards, playing musical instru-

ments, dealing cards or playing other games...." These vice ordinances were often winked at, and the result was more of a pro forma civic stance that would fill city coffers with monetary fines and keep the dens of iniquity available but out of sight. Robert L. Spude, "Progressive Santa Fe, 1880–1912" in *All Trails Lead to Santa Fe* (Santa Fe: Sunstone Press, 2010), 347.

45. James Edward Brunson, *The Early Image of Black Baseball: Race and Representation in the Popular Press, 1871–1890* (Jefferson, NC: McFarland, 2009), 162–163. Professor Brunson also notes that gambling was among a list of the most popular sports in the American West.

46. Ryczek, 37 and 41.
47. Thorn, 168–169.
48. *SL*, 59, 19; 13 July 1912, 4.
49. *The Daily (Richmond, Virginia) Dispatch*, 2 Aug. 1883, 1.
50. Thorn, 260.
51. Patrick B. Miller, "The Anatomy of Scientific Racism: Racialist Responses to Black Athletic Achievement" in Paul R. Spickard and W. Jeffrey Burroughs (eds.), *We Are a People: Narrative and Multiplicity in Constructing Ethnic Identity* (Philadelphia: Temple University Press, 2000), 127.
52. T. J. Jackson Lears, *No Place of Grace: Anti-Modernism and the Transformation of American Culture, 1880–1920* (Chicago: University of Chicago Press, 1994), 108.
53. Miller, 127.
54. *Hutchison (KN) Daily News (HDN)*, 20 September 1887.
55. Lears, 111–114 and 117; Miller, 130.

Chapter Seven

1. Neil Lanctot, *Fair Dealing and Clean Playing: The Hilldale Club and the Development of Black Professional Baseball, 1910–1932* (Syracuse, NY: Syracuse University Press, 2007), 79; McKenna, 6.
2. McKenna, 8.
3. *Brooklyn Eagle (BE)*, 8 Aug. 1888, 1.
4. *BE*, 11 Aug. 1888, 2.
5. Michael E. Lomax, "Black Baseball's First Rivalry: The Cuban Giants Versus the Gorhamns of New York and the Birth of the Colored Championship," *Sports History Review*, 28 (1997), 40.
6. Leslie Heaphy, *The Negro Leagues, 1869–1960* (Jefferson, NC: McFarland, 2003), 24–25 and 5.
7. The discussion of the first decade of black professional baseball is distilled from the following text: Solomon White, *History of Colored Base Ball* (1907) (reprinted by University of Nebraska Press, 1995), 8–24.

8. Michael E. Lomax, "Black Baseball's First Rivalry; The Cuban Giants Versus the Gorhams of New York and the Birth of the Colored Championship," *Sport History Review*, 28 (1997), 141–142.
9. Robert Peterson, *Only the Baseball Was White: A History of Legendary Black Players and All Black Professional Teams* (New York: Oxford University Press, 1970), 147–150.
10. *Ibid.*, 151.
11. "How They Play Baseball," *Cleveland Gazette (CG)*, 5, 49 (21 July 1888), 1.
12. McKenna, 14–15 and Riley, 294.
13. *TSN*, 4 April 1899 (cited in Carlos Bauer, *Minor League Researcher*, 22 October 2005).
14. *The Saint Paul (MN) Globe (SPG)*, 9 April 1899, 10.
15. *SL*, 33, 19; 29 July 1899, 5.
16. *The Fort Wayne (IA) Sentinel*, 9 May 1899, 2.
17. *SL*, 33, 9; 20 May 1899.
18. *Kansas City Journal (KCJ)*, 9 May 1899, 5.
19. *KCJ*, 13 May 1899, 5.
20. *KCJ*, 25 June 1899, 5.
21. *Carlsbad (NM) Current (CC)*, 23 June 1900, 7.
22. *The Banner-Democrat (Lake Providence [LA])*, 24 Mar. 1900, 3.
23. *SL*, 35, 12; 9 June 1900, 3.
24. *Syracuse Evening Telegram (SET)*, 27 August 1901.
25. McKenna, 13 and Morris, 17. It is unclear how much involvement with the 1901 Smokey City Giants Bud Fowler actually had though his intention was clearly to manage the team: "Bud Fowler is going to run a colored club in Pittsburgh this season," *New Castle (PA) News (NCN)*, 17 Apr. 1901, 7.
26. *SL*, 37, 3; 2 April 1901, 7.
27. *The New York Evening World (TNYEW)*, 29 June 1905, 2.
28. Karl Lindholm, "William Clarence Matthews: Brief Life of a Baseball Pioneer, 1877–1928": 1–2. http://harvardmagazine.com/1998/09/vita.html (Accessed 6/15/12).
29. *The New York Sun (TNYS)*, 3 Jan. 1904, 8.
30. *Indianapolis Recorder (IR)*, 10 May 1902.
31. *Indianapolis News (IN)* (citation) in Debono, 16.
32. *SL*, 39, 6; 26 April 1902. Bud Fowler "never shyed [sic] away" from tough competition if a large gate was in the offing. His 1902 touring All-Americans faced the ultimate African American opposition on November 23, 1902: "The All American will meet the Cuban Giants who are beyond question the

strongest semi-professional team playing ball" *Brooklyn Daily Eagle (BDE)*, 18 Nov. 1902, 13.

33. *SL*, 39, 9; 10 May 1902. Though the color line was firmly drawn in the Midwest by the first decade of the twentieth century, Bud Fowler's exploits on the famed integrated Galesburg teams of the 1890s were not forgotten and were explicitly noted in a homage to Galesburg star player and manager Belden Hill (*Cedar Rapids [IA] Evening Gazette [CREG]*, 3 June 1903, 8.)

34. Neil Lanctot, *Fair Dealing and Clean Playing: The Hillsdale Club and the Development of Black Professional Baseball, 1910–1932* (Syracuse, NY: Syracuse University Press, 2007), 80.

35. *SL*, 43, 9; 14 May 1904, 5.

36. McKenna, 13; *The St. Paul (MN) Globe (SPG)*, 14 Nov. 1904, 5.

37. *Cincinnati Enquirer (CE)*, 10 November 1904 (cited in DeBono, 16).

38. *SPG*, 14 Nov. 1904, 5.

39. *Ibid*.

40. Morris, 18; "Between seasons, Fowler is a knight of the razor, and he is at Charles Morrison's, 528 Plum street [Cincinnati], for the winter" (*SPG*, 14 Nov. 1904, 5).

41. *SL*, 44, 18; 10 January 1905, 7; *The New York Evening World (TNYEW)*, 31 Mar. 1906, 6.

42. Pop Watkins's Havana Red Sox were playing in Watertown (NY)'s Garland City Park as early as 1910 and playing such stiff competition as the New York State League's Syracuse Stars (*Watertown Re-Union*). His club was "representing the city [of Watertown]" by 1913 and playing such well-attended games as one against the Onondaga Redskins Base Ball club (*Watertown Herald*).

43. For a thoughtful discussion of Pop Watkins's playing and business careers in African American baseball, go to Gary Ashwill's blog. http://agate type/typepad.com.

44. McKenna, 13–14.

45. *New York Age (NYA)*, 28 May 1908.

46. *NYA*, 8 April 1909.

47. *SL*, 52, 2; 19 September 1908.

48. *SL*, 53, 3; 27 March 1909, 3.

49. *SL*, 52, 3; 26 September 1908.

50. *Binghamton* (NY) *Press (BP)*, 7 March 1908.

51. *Brooklyn Daily Eagle (BDE)*, 25 January 1909.

52. *BDE*, 11 February 1909; *NYA*, 25 February 1909.

53. *BDE*, 20 October 1909.

54. *Utica Herald Dispatch (UHD)*, 19 April 1909; *Niagara Falls Gazette (NFG)*, 27 April 1909 and 6 May 1909; *Buffalo Daily Express (BDE)*, 3 May 1909; *Buffalo Morning Express (BME)*, 5 May 1909; and *Utica Observer (UO)*, 8 June 1909.

55. *Auburn* (NY) *Bulletin (AB)*, May 1909.

56. *Ogden* (UT) *Standard (US)*, 16 March 1910, 8 (cited in Morris, 20).

57. *Amsterdam* (NY) *Evening Recorder (AER)*, 8 August 1911.

58. *Honolulu Evening Bulletin (HEB)*, 21 May 1911, 6.

Chapter Eight

1. Amber Roessner, "Hero Crafting in *Sporting Life*, an Early Baseball Journal," *American Journalism*, 26:2 (Spring 2009), 40.

2. David Voigt, *American Baseball*: 35 quoted in Roessner, 40.

3. Leonard Koppett, *Koppett's Concise History of Major League Baseball* (Philadelphia: Temple University Press, 1998), 88–92.

4. *Ibid.*, 97; One very beneficial and lasting aspect of Ban Johnson's campaign to clean up the game that had the whole-hearted supported of both the fans and the press was his support of the authority of umpires. Hall of Fame arbiter Tommy Connolly summarized his feelings about the differences between the American and National Leagues in 1901 as follows: "I am glad to have the opportunity to be with Johnson.... I'll get a chance to get backed up. In my last venture in the National League, I fined 14 men in two weeks and not a fine went. All the rules in the world will not help the game if the umpires are not supported" (Rich Eldred's "Umpiring in the 1890's": 5. http://research.sabr.org/journals/umpiring-in-the-1890s (Accessed 5/24/12).

5. Edward Marshall Interview with Albert Spalding in *New York Times*, 13 Nov. 1910 reprinted in Spalding's *America's National Game* (Lincoln: University of Nebraska Press, 1992), 533.

6. Benjamin G. Rader, "Introduction" to Albert G. Spalding's *America's National Game* (University of Nebraska Press, 1992), ix–x.

7. Mark Twain 1889 quotation cited in Jules Tygiel's *Past Time: Baseball as History* (New York: Oxford University Press, 2000), 9.

8. Harold Seymour and Dorothy Z. Seymour Mills, *Baseball: The Early Years,* Volume 1 (New York: Oxford University Press, 1989), 347.

9. Joel Zoss and John S. Bowman, *Diamonds in the Rough: The Untold Story of Baseball* (Lincoln: University of Nebraska Press, 2004), xi.

10. *Ibid.*

11. Warren Goldstein, *Playing for Keeps: A*

History of Early Baseball (Ithaca, NY: Cornell University Press, 1989), 139.

12. Tom Melville, *Early Baseball and the Rise of the National League* (Jefferson, NC: McFarland, 2001), 46.

13. Neil J. Sullivan, *The Minors: The Struggles and the Triumph of Baseball's Poor Relation from 1876 to the Present* (New York: St. Martin's Press, 1990), 58–59.

14. Albert G. Spalding, *America's National Game* (Lincoln: University of Nebraska Press, 1992), 538.

15. Goldstein, 44.

16. Seymour, 348, 350.

17. *The New York Daily Sun (TNYDS)*, 17 June 1912, 8.

18. *New York Tribune (NYT)*, 30 June 1907, 7.

19. Sullivan, 282.

20. *Ibid.*, 279.

21. Peter Morris, "Bud Fowler's Lost Years," *Black Ball: A Negro League Journal*, 2, 2 (Fall, 2009), 13. Morris has done some very persuasive historical sleuthing to uncover Fowler's upstate New York family relationships.

22. *Amsterdam* (NY) *Evening Recorder and Daily Democrat (AERDD)* and *Watertown* (NY) *Daily Times* (WDT), March 1913.

23. "1909 Santa Fe Mechanics."

24. *The Daily Herald (TDH)*, 26 September 1888, 1.

25. *New York Age (NYA)*, 27 May 1939, 8.

26. *Buffalo Morning Express (BME)*, 16 February 1916; *The California Eagle (CE)*, 8 November 1931; Leslie Heaphy, *The Negro Leagues, 1869–1960* (McFarland and Company, 2003), 4, 21.

27. Leslie Heaphy, *The Negro Leagues, 1869–1960* (Jefferson, NC: McFarland, 2003), 18. The author also quotes star pitcher Tony Mullane on his relationship with African American catcher Moses Fleetwood Walker to underscore the difficulty of blacks who played on an integrated team in the 1880s: "He was the best catcher I ever worked with, but I disliked a Negro and whenever I had to pitch to him I used to pitch anything I wanted without looking at his signals," 14.

28. Morris, 20.

29. John Thorn, "Ya Gotta Believe": 3. http://ourgame.mlblogs.com/2011/o6/16/ya-gotta-believe/ (accessed 6/24/11).

30. John Thorn, "Baseball's Unchanging Past: A Necessary Illusion": 1–8. http://ourgame.mlblogs.com/2012/05/30/baseballs-unchanging-past-a-necessary-illusion/ (Accessed 6/1/12).

Epilogue

1. *Utica* (NY) *Sunday Observer Dispatch (USOD)*, 26 July 1987.

Bibliography

Books

Adelman, Melvin L. *A Sporting Time: New York City and the Rise of Modern Athletics, 1820–1870*. Champaign: University of Illinois Press, 1990.

Alexander, Charles C. *Our Game: An American Baseball History*. New York: Fine Communications, 1997.

Appel, Marty. *Slide, Kelly, Slide: The Wild Life and Times of Mike "King" Kelly*. Lanham, MD: Scarecrow Press, 1999.

Ashe, Arthur R. *A Hard Road to Glory: A History of the African-American Athlete, 1619–1918*. New York: Amistad Press, 1993.

Barth, Gunther. *City People: The Rise of Modern City Culture in Nineteenth Century America*. New York: Oxford University Press, 1980.

Bauer, Carlos, and Bob McConnell, eds. *The New SABR Guide to Minor League Statistics*. San Diego: Baseball Press Books, 2007.

Bond, Gregory. *Jim Crow at Play: Race, Manliness, and the Color Line in American Sports*. Ann Arbor, MI: Proquest, 2008.

Bruce, Janet. *The Kansas City Monarchs: Champions of Black Baseball*. Lawrence: University Press of Kansas, 1985.

Brunson, James Edward. *The Early Image of Black Baseball: Race and Representation in the Popular Press, 1871–1890*. Jefferson, NC: McFarland, 2009.

Burgos, Adrian. *Playing America's Game: Baseball, Latinos, and the Color Line*. Berkeley: University of California Press, 2007

Caillault, Jean-Pierre (compiler). *The Complete "New York Clipper" Baseball Biographies*. Jefferson, NC: McFarland, 2009.

Cohen, Marvin A. and Michael J. McCann. *Baseball in Broome County*. Portsmouth, NH: Arcadia, 2003.

Daniel, W. Harrison and Scott P. Mayer. *Baseball and Richmond: A History of the Professional Game, 1884–2000*. Jefferson, NC: McFarland, 2003.

Debono, Paul. *The Indianapolis ABCs: The History of a Premier Negro Leagues Team*. Jefferson, NC: McFarland, 1997.

Dixon, Phil with Patrick J. Hannigan. *The Negro Baseball Leagues: A Photographic History*. Mattituck, NY: Amereon Ltd., 1992.

Fleitz, David L. *The Irish in Baseball: An Early History*. Jefferson, NC: McFarland, 2009.

Gewirtz, Isaac. *Kerouac at Bat: Fantasy Sports and the King of the Beats*. New York: New York Public Library, 2009.

Goldstein, Warren. *Playing for Keeps: A History of Early Baseball*. Ithaca, NY: Cornell University Press, 1989.

Gopnik, Adam. *Winter: Five Windows on the Season*. Toronto: House of Anasi Press, 2011.

Gould, Stephen Jay. *Triumph and Tragedy in Mudville: A Lifelong Passion for Baseball*. New York: W.W. Norton and Company, 2003.

Heaphy, Leslie. *The Negro Leagues, 1869–1960*. Jefferson, NC: McFarland, 2003.

Hoffbeck, Steven R., ed. *Swinging for the Fences: Black Baseball in Minnesota*. Saint Paul: Minnesota Historical Society Press, 2005.

Hogan, Lawrence D. *Shades of Glory: The Negro Leagues and the Glory of African-American Baseball*. Cooperstown, NY: National Baseball Hall of Fame and Museum, 2006.

Holway, John B. *The Complete Book of Baseball's Negro League: The Other Half of Baseball History.* Fern Park, FL: Hastings House Publishers, 2001.

Humber, William. *A Sporting Chance: Achievement of African-Canadian Athletes.* Toronto: Natural Heritage, 2004.

Johnson, W. Lloyd, ed. *The Minor League Register.* Durham, NC: Baseball America, 1994.

_____, and Miles Wolff, eds. *The Encyclopedia of Minor League Baseball.* Second edition. Durham, NC: Baseball America, 1997.

Kirsch, George B. *Baseball in Blue and Gray: The National Pastime During the Civil War.* Princeton, NJ: Princeton University Press, 2003.

Koppett, Leonard. *Koppett's Concise History of Major League Baseball.* Philadelphia: Temple University Press, 1998.

Lanctot, Neil. *Fair Dealing and Clean Playing: The Hilldale Club and the Development of Black Professional Baseball, 1910–1932.* Syracuse, NY: Syracuse University Press, 2007. Reprint.

_____. *Negro League Baseball: The Rise and Ruin of a Black Institution.* Philadelphia: University of Pennsylvania Press, 2004.

Lears, T. J. Jackson. *No Place of Grace: Anti-Modernism and the Transformation of American Culture, 1880–1920.* Chicago: University of Chicago Press, 1994.

Lomax, Michael E. *Black Baseball Entrepreneurs, 1860–1901: Operating by Any Means Necessary.* Syracuse, NY: Syracuse University Press, 2003.

Malloy, Jerry (Introduction). *Sol White's "History of Colored Baseball" with Other Documents of the Early Black Game (1886–1936).* Lincoln: University of Nebraska Press, 1995.

Mayer, Robert. *Baseball and Men's Lives: The True Confessions of a Skinny-Marink.* New York: Delta Books, 1984.

McKenna, Brian. *The Premature Endings of Baseball Careers.* Lanham, MD: Scarecrow Press, 2006.

Melville, Tom. *Early Baseball and the Rise of the National League.* Jefferson, NC: McFarland, 2001.

Morris, Peter. *Baseball Fever: Early Baseball in Michigan.* Ann Arbor: University of Michigan Press, 2003.

_____. *Catcher: How the Man behind the Plate Became an American Folk Hero.* Chicago: Ivan R. Dee, 2009.

_____. *But Didn't We Have Fun? An Informal History of Baseball's Pioneer Era, 1843–1870.* Chicago: Ivan R. Dee, 2008.

Nemec, David. *The Beer and Whisky League.* New York: The Lyons Press, 1994.

Oleksak, Michael M., and Mary Adams Oleksak. *Beisbol: Latin Americans and the Grand Old Game.* Grand Rapids, MI: Masters Press, 1991.

Perez, Louis A. *On Becoming Cuban: Identity, Nationality, and Culture.* Chapel Hill: University of North Carolina Press, 2007.

Peterson, Robert. *Only the Baseball Was White: A History of Legendary Black Players and All Black Professional Teams.* New York: Oxford University Press, 1970.

Peterson, Todd. *Early Black Baseball in Minnesota: The St. Paul Gophers, Minneapolis Keystones and Other Barnstorming Teams of the Deadball Era.* Jefferson, NC: McFarland, 2010.

Powers-Beck, Jeffrey. *The American Indian Integration of Baseball.* Lincoln: University of Nebraska Press, 2004.

Ribowsky, Mark. *A Complete History of the Negro Leagues, 1884–1955.* New York: Citadel Press, 2002.

Riley, James A. "John 'Bud' Fowler," in *The Biographical Encyclopedia of the Negro Baseball Leagues.* New York: Carroll & Graff, 1994.

Rippel, Joel A. *Minnesota Sports Almanac.* Saint Paul: Minnesota Historical Society Press, 2006.

Robinson, Marilynne. *Gilead.* New York: Farrar, Straus & Giroux, 2004.

Rogosin, Donn. *Invisible Men: Life in Baseball's Negro Leagues.* New York: Atheneum, 1983.

Ruck, Rob. *Raceball: How the Major Leagues Colonized the Black and Latin Game.* Boston: Beacon Press, 2011.

_____. *Sandlot Seasons: Sport in Black Pittsburgh.* Urbana: University of Illinois Press, 1993.

Ryczek, William J. *Baseball's First Inning: A History of the National Pastime through the Civil War.* Jefferson, NC: McFarland, 2009.

_____. *Blackguards and Red Stockings: A History of Baseball's National Association,*

1871–1875. Jefferson, NC: McFarland, 1992.

_____. *When Johnny Came Sliding Home: The Post–Civil War Baseball Boom, 1865–1870*. Jefferson, NC: McFarland, 1998.

Seymour, Harold, and Dorothy Z. Seymour Mills. *Baseball: The Early Years*. New York: Oxford University Press, 1989.

_____, and _____. *Baseball: The People's Game*. New York: Oxford University Press, 1991.

Simmons, Marc. *New Mexico: An Interpretive History*. Albuquerque: University of New Mexico Press, 1988.

Somers, Dale A. *The Rise of Sports in New Orleans, 1850–1900*. Baton Rouge: Louisiana State University Press, 1972.

Soos, Troy. *Before the Curse: The Glory Days of New England Baseball, 1858–1918*. Neptune, NJ: Parnassus Imprints, 1997.

Spalding, Albert G. *America's National Game*. Lincoln: University of Nebraska Press, 1992. Reprint.

Sullivan, Dean A. (editor and compiler). *Early Innings: A Documentary History of Baseball, 1825–1908*. Lincoln: University of Nebraska Press, 1995.

Sullivan, Neil J. *The Minors: The Struggles and the Triumph of Baseball's Poor Relation from. 1876 to the Present*. New York: St. Martin's Press, 1990.

Sutter, L. M. *New Mexico Baseball: Miners, Outlaws, Indians, and Isotopes, 1880 to the Present*. Jefferson, NC: McFarland, 2010.

Thorn, John. *Baseball in the Garden of Eden: The Secret History of the Early Game*. Simon and Schuster, 2011.

Thornley, Stew. *Baseball in Minnesota: The Definitive History*. Saint Paul: Minnesota Historical Society Press, 2006.

Tygiel, Jules. *Past Time: Baseball as History*. New York: Oxford University Press, 2000.

Ward, John Montgomery. *Base Ball: How to Become a Player*. Cleveland, OH: Society of American Baseball Research Reprint, 1993.

Wilson, Chris. *The Myth of Santa Fe: Creating a Modern Regional Tradition*. Albuquerque: University of New Mexico Press, 1997.

Zang, David. *Fleet Walker's Divided Heart: The Life of Baseball's First Black Major Leaguer*. Lincoln: University of Nebraska Press, 1995.

Zoss, Joel and John S. Bowman. *Diamonds in the Rough: The Untold Story of Baseball*. Lincoln: University of Nebraska Press, 2004.

Periodicals and Websites

Anderson, William. "Creating the National Pastime: The Antecedents of Major League Baseball Public Relations," *Media History Monographs*: 1–26. http://facstaff.elon.edu/dcopeland/mhm/mhmjour4-2.htm (Accessed 10/26/2011.)

Arango, Time. "Myth of Baseball's Creation Endures, with a Prominent Fan," *New York Times*,. 13 November 2010, Section B, 9 & 12.

Aubrecht, Michael. "Civil War Baseball: Baseball and the Blue and the Gray." *Baseball Almanac*: 1–6. http://www.baseball-almanac.com/articles/aubrecht2004b.shtml (July, 2004) (Accessed 12/14/2010).

"Baseball in the West." www.historynet.com. http://www.historynet.com/baseballin-the-west.htm (Accessed 12/28/2010).

Biddle, Daniel R. & Murray Dubin. "An Early Quest for Equality on the Diamond." www.philly.com: 1–6 http://www.printthis.clickability.com/pt/cpt?action=cpt&title=An+early+quest+for= (Accessed 9/16/10).

Bond, Gregory. "'Too Much Dirty Work': Race, Manliness, and Baseball in Gilded Age Nebraska." *Nebraska History*, 85 (2004): 172–185. http://www.nebraskahistory.org/publish/publicat/history/fulltext/3004-Dirty_Work.pdf (Accessed 1/20/10).

Brown, Randall. "Blood and Base Ball (Parts 3 & 4). *Our Game*: 1–5. http://ourgame.mlblogs.com/2011/11/30/blood-and-base-ball (Accessed 12/30/11).

"Bud Fowler." *BR Bullpen*: 1–3. http://www.baseball-reference.com/bullpen/Bud_Fowler (Accessed 3/30/09).

"Bud Fowler." *Minor League History & Statistics*: 1–2. http://www.baseball-reference.com/minors/player.cgi?id=fowler004joh (Accessed 8/12/10).

"Bud Fowler, First Professional Black Baseball Player." *Flickr:* 1–3. http://www.flickr.com/photos/22067139@N05/2487555544/ (Accessed 9/11/08).

"Canadians in Baseball: The 'Lost Tribe.'" *The Canadian Encyclopedia*: 1–2. http://thecanadianencyclopedia.com/PrinterFriendly.cfm?Params=A1ARTFET_E16 (Accessed 12/13/10).

Childs, Erica. "Images of the Black Athlete: Intersection of Race, Sexuality, and Sports." *Journal of African American Studies*, 4, 2 (1999): 19–38.

Christian, Ralph J. "Bud Fowler: Iowa's First African-American Professional and the 1885 Keokuks." *Iowa Heritage Illustrated*, 87, 1 (Spring, 2006): 28–32.

Delaney, James, Jr. "The 1887 Binghamton Bingos": 1–5. http://research.sabr.org/journals/1887-binghamton-bingos?tmpl (Accessed 11/11/11).

Echevarria, Roberto Gonzalez. "Before You Could Say Jackie Robinson" *The New York Times:* 1–3. http://www.nytimes.com/2003/05/25/books/review/25ESCHEVAT.html (Accessed 12/13/10).

Eldred, Rich. "Umpiring in the 1890's": 1–5. *SABR Research Journals Archives*. http://research.sabr.org/journals/umpiring-in-the-1890s (Accessed 5/24/12).

Enders, Eric. "Buck Freeman" *SABR Bioproject*: 1–4. http://sabr.org/bioproj/person/46f0454e (Accessed 5/24/12).

"Get That Negro Off the Field!" http://negro-baseball-league.com/blog/get-that-negro-off-the-field.html (Accessed 12/27/10).

Hartman, Dorothy W. "Play Ball! Baseball in the Nineteenth Century: From Gentlemen's Sport to Professional Play." *Corner Prairie*: 1–14. http://www.cornerprairie.org/Learn-and-Do/Indiana-History/American-1860-1900 (Accessed 11/23/10).

Hill, Benjamin. "Fowler: A Nineteenth Century Baseball Pioneer," *Minor League Baseball*: 1–4. http://www.minorleaguebaseball.com/news/article.jsp?ymd=20060208&content_id=41022&vkey=news (Accessed 2/8/08).

"Homerun Johnson." *Pitch Black Negro Player of the Month*: 1–2. http://www.pitchblackbaseball.com/nlotmhomerunjohnson.html (January 2003) (Accessed 11/11/10).

Howell, Colin D. "Baseball and Borders: The Diffusion of Baseball into Canadian and Mexican-American Borderland Regions, 1885–1911." *Nine*. 11, 2 (Spring, 2003): 16–26.

"John 'Bud' Fowler." *Negro Leagues Baseball eMuseum:* 1–4. http://www.coe.ksu.edu/nlbemuseum/history/players/fowler.html (Accessed 2/8/08).

"John W. 'Bud' Fowler." *Negro League Baseball Players Association*: 1–2. http://www.nlbpa.com/fowler__john_w__-_bud.html. (Accessed 3/30/09).

Judt, Tony. "The Glory of the Rails," *New York Review of Books*. 23 December 2010, 61–62.

Kleinknecht, Merl F. "Blacks in 19th Century Organized Baseball," *SABR Baseball Journals Archives*: 1–8. http://research.sabr.org/journals/blacks-in-19th-c-baseball (Accessed 12/21/10).

Lindholm, Karl. "William Clarence Matthews: Brief Life of a Baseball Pioneer, 1877–1928": 1–2. http://harvardmagazine.com/1998/09/vita.html (Accessed 6/15/12).

Lomax, Michael E. "Black Baseball's First Rivalry: The Cuban Giants Versus the Gorhams of New York and the Birth of the Colored Championship," *Sport History Review*, 28 (1997), 134–145.

_____. "'If He Were White': Portraits of Black and Cuban Players in Organized Baseball, 1880–1920," *Journal of African American Studies*, 3, 3 (1997): 31–44.

Malloy, Jerry. "Out at Home: Baseball Draws the Color Line, 1887," *The National Pastime* (SABR), 2 (1983): 14–28.

McDonald, David. "Jim Crow Comes North," *Dominionball: Baseball above the 49th*," edited by Jane Finnan Dorward (Society for American Baseball Research, 2005), 76–79.

McKenna, Brian. "Bud Fowler," *The Baseball Biography Project*: 1–19. http://bioproj.sabr.org/bioproj.cfm?a=v&v=l&bid=3116&pid=19716> (Accessed 10/13/10).

Miller, Patrick B. "The Anatomy of Scientific Racism: Racialist Responses to Black Athletic Achievements" in Paul R. Spickard and W. Jeffrey Burroughs (eds.). *We Are a People: Narrative and Multiplicity in Constructing Ethnic Identity* Temple University Press, 2000: 124–141.

Morris, Peter. "Bud Fowler's "Lost Years," *Black Ball: A Negro League Journal.* 2, 2 (Fall 2009): 10–23.
"Professional Black Baseball." *Josh Gibson Foundation*: 1–5. http://www.joshgibson.org/index.php?page=Negro_League_History (Accessed 11/10/10).
Reese, Renford. "The Social Political Context of the Integration of Sport in America," *Journal of African American Studies*, 3, 4 (1997): 5–22.
Riley, James A. "John 'Bud' Fowler," in *The Biographical Encyclopedia of the Negro Baseball Leagues*. Carroll & Graf, 1994.
Russell, Lauren [poem]. "Reckoning at Keystone Sack: The Peculiar Career of Bud Fowler," "The Baseball Issue," *Boog City* 37 (2006), 9.
Simmons, Marc. "Play Ball!" *Santa Fe Reporter*. 18 July 1984.
Spivey, Donald. "Black Baseball Entrepreneurs, 1860–1901: Operating by Any Means Necessary." *The Journal of African American History*. 89 (2004).
Sprague, Dana. "John Foley" *SABR Bioproject*: 1–4. http://sabr.org/bioproj/person/3328dc3f (Accessed 5/24/12).
Tholkes, Bob. "Bud Fowler, Black Pioneer, and the 1884 Stillwaters." *SABR Research Journals Archives*: 1–3. http://research.sabr.org/journals/bud-fowler-black-pioneer-and-the-1884-stillwaters (Accessed 11/10/10).
Thorn, John. "Baseball's Unchanging Past: A Necessary Illusion." http://ourgame.mlblogs.com/2012/05/30/baseballs-unchangingpast-anecessary/illusion (Accessed 6/1/11).
_____. "My 19th Century Pantheon": 1–5. http://ourgame.mlblogs.com/2011/06/23/my-19th-cdentury-pasnthron/ (Accessed 6/24/11).
_____. "The Baseball Press Emerges": 1–6. http://ourgame.mlbblogs.com/2011/10/20/the-baseball-press-emerges/ (Accessed 10/24/11).
_____. "Ya Gotta Believe": 1–4. http://ourgame.mlbblogs.com/2011/06/16/ya-gotta-believe (Accessed 6/24/11).
Trudeau, Christian. "Integration in Quebec: More Than Jackie," *Dominionball*, 23–24.
White, Richard. "Baseball's John Fowler: The 1887 Season in Binghamton, New York," *Afro-Americans in New York Life and History* (January 1992), 7–17.
Yu, Karlson. "John 'Bud' W. Fowler." *The Black Past*: 1–3. http://www.blackpast.org/?q=aah/fowler-john-bud-w-1858-1913 (Accessed 3/30/09).

Archival Material

Chronicling America http://www.chroniclingamerica.loc.gov/
  Belmont (St. Clairsville, Ohio) Chronicle
  Burlington (VT) Weekly Free Press
  Capital City (Lincoln, NB) Courier
  Carlsbad (NM) Current
  Deming Headlight (Deming, NM)
  Gallipolis (OH) Journal
  Honolulu (Oahu, Hawaii) Evening Bulletin
  Kansas City Journal
  Lancaster (Lancaster (PA) Daily Intelligencer
  Los Angeles Daily Herald
  Minneapolis Journal
  National (Washington D.C.) Republican
  New York Daily Tribune
  New York Spirit of the Times
  Omaha Daily Bee
  Pittsburgh Dispatch
  Richmond Daily Dispatcher
  St. Paul (MN) Globe
  Sacramento Daily Record-Union
  The (Lake Providence (LA) Banner-Democrat
  The Eddy (Carlsbad (NM) Current
  The Evening (Washington D.C.) Critic
  The Evening (New York) World
  The Kingston (NY)Daily Freeman
  The McCook (McCook, NB) Tribune
  The New York Clipper Annual
  The New York Sun
  The Philadelphia Evening Standard
  The Princeton (NJ) Union
  The Toronto World
  The Washington *(DC)Bee*
  The Weekly (Windsor, Ontario) Sentinel Review
  Wichita (KN) Daily Eagle
Fulton History Fultonhistory.com
  Albany Evening Standard
  Amsterdam (NY) Daily Democrat
  Amsterdam (NY) Evening Recorder
  Auburn (NY) Bulletin

Bibliography

Auburn (NY) Weekly News and Democrat
Binghamton (NY) Press
Brooklyn Daily Eagle
Buffalo Morning Express
New York Age
Niagara Falls (NY) Gazette
Syracuse (NY) Evening Telegram
The California Eagle
The Evening Telegram (NY)
The Hudson (NY) Evening Register
The New York Clipper
The New York Times
The Utica (NY) Observer
Utica (NY) Daily Press
Utica (NY) Herald Dispatch
Utica (NY) Sunday Observer Dispatch
Watertown (NY) Daily Times
Google News Archives http://www.news.google.com
The Freeman (Indianapolis, IN)
LA84 Foundation http://www.la84foundation.org
Sporting Life
Paper of Record http://www.paperofrecord.com
The Sporting News
Library of Congress http://www.loc.gov
"Adrian C. Anson" Baseball Cards from the Benjamin K. Edwards Collection (Lots 13163-05, no. 30 & 13163-01, no. 2). http://memory.loc.gov/cgi-bin/query/D/bbcards.2:/temp/-ammem_DQ3y:: (Accessed 3/29/11).
The Indianapolis (IN) Recorder
"Union Prisoners at Salisbury (NC)" (Lithograph). Copyright Otto Boetticher 1863. (Reproduction Number LC-USZC6-2-38)
New Mexico State Archives (Santa Fe, NM)
Albuquerque (NM) Daily Citizen
Albuquerque (NM) Morning Democrat
Las Vegas (NM) Optic
Lucien File Collection (Photographs)
Santa Fe New Mexican
NewspaperARCHIVE.com
Albany (NY) Evening Standard
Albany (NY) Journal
Albuquerque (NM) Citizen
Albuquerque (NM) Morning Democrat
Atchison (KN) Daily Globe
Boston (MA) Daily Globe
Brooklyn (NY) Eagle
Burlington (IA) Hawk-Eye
Cedar Rapids (IA) Evening Gazette
Delphos (OH) Daily Herald
Fitchburg (MA) Sentinel
Fort Wayne (IN) News
Galveston (TX) Daily News
Hutchison (KN) Daily News
Iowa State Review
Lima (OH) Times Democrat
Logansport (IN) Journal
Logansport (IN) Pharos
Lowell (MA) Sun
Mansfield (OH) News
New Castle (PA) News
Santa Fe (NM) Daily Herald
Santa Fe Daily New Mexican
Santa Fe New Mexican Review
Santa Fe Weekly New Mexican
Sterling (IL) Evening Gazette
The Cedar Rapids (IA) Evening Gazette
The Daily Herald (NM)
The Elyria (OH) Republican
The Fitchburg (MA) Sentinel
The Fort Wayne (IN) Weekly Gazette
The Fort Wayne (IN) News
The Herald (Syracuse, NY)
The New York Times
The New York World
The Sporting News
Waterloo (IA) Courier
Weekly New Mexican Review
New York Public Library (New York, NY)
"America's National Game." The Albert G. Spalding Collection of Early Baseball Photographs and Drawings"
Ohio Historical Society (Columbus, OH)
Cleveland (OH) Gazette
Palace of the Governors Photo Archives (Santa Fe, NM)
ATSF Train at Lamy Junction by J. R. Riddle (1884) (no. 076033).
Bisbee (Arizona) Baseball Association at Cloudcroft Lodge (NM) (no. 077564).
Buffalo Soldiers from the 10th Cavalry in camp, New Mexico by Henry R. Schmidt (no. 058556).
Las Vegas Baseball Team (1888) (no. 48385).
9th Cavalry Band at Santa Fe Plaza by Ben Wittick (1880) (no. 050887)

Railroad Engine circa 1895 (no. 101887).
St. Michael's College Junior Baseball Team (1888) (no. 50262).
Santa Fe Plaza Fourth of July circa 1890 (no. 011278).
Santa Fe Mechanics Baseball Team (1904) (no. 176972).
Santa Fe Stagecoach in the 1880s (no. 8290).
Silver City Stagecoach (no. 11193).
Students at Santa Fe Indian School by J. R. Riddle (no. 076039).
Troop L Fort Wingate Baseball Team (1888) (no. 98374).
Unidentified Gamblers by Jesus Cito Candelerio (Santa Fe 1886) (no. 099588).

Baseball Hall of Fame Library Photo Archives (Cooperstown, NY)
    Bud Fowler—1885 Keokuk Team Photo (194).
    Bud Fowler—1894 Findlay Team Photo (2623-97 PD).
    Moses Walker (825_71a_PD).
    Sol White (2776-73 crop PD).
    Frank Grant (5488-90 cropped).
    Charlie Grant (103.2008.4_HS_NBL_hogan).
    Jose Mendez (167-79 cropped).
    1888 Cuban Giants (249-97 PD).
    1895 Cuban X-Giants (35-73 PD).
    1897 Atlanta Baptist College (141_2008_2PD_hogan).
    US Military Civil War (125_84_PD)

Index

Numbers in ***bold italics*** indicate pages with photographs.

Adrian, Michigan 129, 131–132, 134–135
Adrian Cuban Giants 130
Adrian Reformers 134
All-American Black Tourists 133, 138–139, 173–176, 181, 183, 214n32
Albuquerque, New Mexico 104, 155, 204n59
Albuquerque Baseball Club 100, 103–112, 147, 149, 156
American Association 78–79, 93, 124, 149, 189
American League 182, 185–186, 188–189
Amsterdam, New York 186, 193
Anson, Adrian "Cap" 56, 93, 95, 99, 113, 128, 133, 173, 205n14, 208n13
Argyle Hotel (Babylon, Long Island) Baseball Club 170
Atchison Topeka and Santa Fe Railroad ***10***
Atlanta Association 124
Atlanta Baptist College ***174***
"Atlanta Compromise Speech" 55

Baltimore Orioles 146
Baltimore Peabodys 72, 206n40
Bancroft, Francis 69
Barnes, Ross 67, 205n14
Barnes American Colored Giants 176, 185
Baseball Hall of Fame 64–65, 199
Beadle's Dime Base Ballplayer 20
Beatrice (Nebraska) Indians 108
Beaumont (Texas) Baseball Club 116
Bellan, Esteban 51
Beyond a Boundary 9
Big New York Gorhams 170
Binghamton, New York 181, 183–184
Binghamton Bingos (Crickets) 63, 88, 89–93, 180, 201n3
Bisbee (Arizona) Baseball Association ***26***
"Black Codes" 41
Bond, Tommy 65, 205n5
Boston Americans 194

Boston Beaneaters 146
Boston Red Caps 65, 205n5
Bradbury (Missouri) Baseball Club 175
Bridgeport (Connecticut) Giants 176
Bridgewater, Henry 73–74
Brooklyn Athletics 168
Brooklyn Atlantics 31–34
Brooklyn Dodgers 196
Brooklyn Excelsiors 22–23
Brooklyn Royal Giants 181–182
Brooklyn Superbas 146
Buchanan, James 59
Bud Fowler's Black Wonders 175–176
Buffalo Bisons 93, 174
Buffalo Black Rocks 185
Buffalo Black Tourists 185
Buffalo Soldiers ***16***, 17–18, 154, 202n15
Burlington (Iowa) Baseball Club 123

California League 100
Carlsbad (New Mexico) Irrigators 176
"Casey at the Bat" 114, 196
Castone, Will 7, 127, 171, 201n10
Central Interstate League 98, 100, 105, 108, 114–115
Cerrillos (New Mexico) Baseball Club 149
Chadwick, Henry 20, 37, 192
Chelsea (Massachusetts) Baseball Club 65, 69
Chicago, Illinois 140–141
Chicago Kents 151
Chicago White Sox 194
Chicago White Stockings 93, 113–114
Chicago Unions 171, 178
Cincinnati, Ohio 135, 179, 181, 214n40
Cincinnati Browns 97
Cincinnati Red Stockings 34, 46
Cincinnati Shamrocks 151
Cleveland, Grover 59–61
Cleveland Spiders 146
The Color Line 58–59, 95, 166, 176

223

Colorado State League 85–86
Colored All-Americans 133
Colored All-Stars Baseball Team (Newark) 185–186
Colored Knights of Labor 62
Colored Texas League 179
Columbus (Ohio) Black Tourists 178
Comiskey, Charles 180, 189
Connecticut State League 128
Connolly, Tommy 214n4
Coolidge, Calvin 177
"Coon, Zip" 53
Cooperstown, New York 64–65, 183–184, 190, 205n4
Crawfordsville (Indiana) Hooisers 98–100, 180
Creighton, James 20
cricket 19–20, 143
Crosby, Ernest M. 39
Crystal Glen, Illinois 84
Cuban Fall League 181
Cuban Giants 52, 86, 92, 128, 130, 132–134, 137, 140, 167, **168**, 169–170, 173, 178–182, 195, 214n32
Cuban Stars 52
Cuban X-Giants 169, **171**, 173, 185
Cummings, William Arthur "Candy" 205n15
Curtis, R.W. "Nick" 83
Cushman, Charlie 93

Davids, L. Robert 199
Denver, Colorado 86
Denver Mountain Lions 87
District of Columbia League 179
Doubleday, Abner 64–65, 183, 190
Douglas (District of Columbia) Baseball Club 72
Drake, Dr. William H. 138–139, 173–175
Dubuque (Iowa) Baseball Club 99–100
Duncan, James 115

Eastern Interstate League 128
Eastern League 170
Eastern Massachusetts League 70
Eastern New England League 85–86
Evansville (Indiana) Hooisers 120, 210n1

Findlay, Ohio 128–129, 175
Findlay Colored Western Giants 128–129
Findlay Giants 174
Findlay Sluggers 126, **129**–130, 132, 136–137, 139, 174–175, 181, 184, 210n39
Fort Plain, New York 64, 193
Fort Wayne, Indiana 151
Fort Wayne Shamrocks 175

Foster, Rube 169
Fowler's Eastern Colored-Stars 178
Frankfort, New York 182–183, 185, 193, 199, 205n3
Freedman, Andrew 191
Freeman, Buck 116

Galesburg, Illinois 121–123, 128
Galesburg Baseball Club 120, 122–123, 214n33
Gallipolis (Ohio) Baseball Club 30
Galveston (Texas) Flyaways 135
Garvey, Marcus 177
Gilead 85
Goldsby, W.H. 88
Gordon (Chicago) Baseball Club 47
Grand Island (Nebraska) Sugar Citys 7
Grant, Charlie **57**–58, 180
Grant, Frank 7, 56, 93, **97**, 124, 138, 170, 180, 184
Great Bear Lake, Minnesota 82
Great Migration 55
Greater Boston Colored League 179
Greenville (Michigan) Baseball Club 116–117, 134
Grey, Zane 211n38
Griffith, Clark 189
Guelph (Ontario) Maple Leafs 70–71, 180
Guillot, Nemesio 51

Hanlon, Ned 146
Hapeman, A.G. 103–105, 108, 110, 209n51
Havana Red Sox (Watkins's Colored Giants) 181, 214n42
Hayes, Rutherford B. 40–41
Higgins, Robert 56, 91, 93
History of Colored Baseball 58
Hopper, DeWolf 114
Hoy, Dummy 174
Hulbert, William 161

Illinois-Iowa League 6, 121–122
Indian Schools **50**–51
Indianapolis Colored League 177
International Association 37, 56, 63, 65–66, 68, 89–90, 93
International League of Independent Professional Baseball Clubs 169
Iron and Oil League 169
Irvin, Monte 199

Jackson, John W. (Bud Fowler) 68, 182, 193, 205n4
Jackson, Randolph 90

Index

James, C.L.R. 9
Jim Crow Laws 40, 48, 63, 77
Joe Wall's All-Leaguers (New York City) 184
Johnson, Ban 188–189, 192–193, 214n2
Johnson, Dick (Dick Male) 58
Johnson, Grant "Home Run" 128, 181–182, 184–185, 211n38
Johnson, Jack 44

Kansas City Stars 173, 179
Keokuk (Iowa) Keokuks 82–85
Knickerbocker Club (Manhattan) 21

Laconia (New Hampshire) Baseball Club 95
Lafayette (Indiana) Baseball Club 98, 103–113
Lajoie, Napoleon 180, 189
Lancaster (Pennsylvania) Ironsides 206n47
Lansing, Carrie (Fowler's aunt) 193
Lansing (Michigan) Colored Capital All-Americans 133–134
Lansing (Michigan) Senators 134
Las Vegas, New Mexico 115
Las Vegas Baseball Club 100, 102–112, 148
Latham, Arlie 179
Lawson, Thomas 75
Leadville, Colorado 86, 126
Lima (Ohio) Baseball Club 136, 139
Lincoln, Abraham 25
Lincoln Giants/Kearney Cotton Pickers (Nebraska) 6, 8, 126–127, 171
Logan (Chillicothe, Ohio) Baseball Club 47
London (Ontario) Tecumsehs 66–67, 205n14
Lone Star Colored Baseball League of Texas 135–136
Louisville Grays 165
Lynch, Thomas 192–193
Lynn (Massachusetts) Live Oaks 66–69, 179, 205n15

Mack, Connie 189
Madrid (New Mexico) Baseball Club 149
Malden (Massachusetts) Baseball Club 70
Matthews, Bobby 68–69
Matthews, William Clarence 177
McCue, James 81
McGraw, John 180, 189, 192–193
McKenna, Brian 78
McNally, Dave 79

Memphis Eclipse 88
Mendez, Jose 52–*53*
Messersmith, Andy 79
Michigan State League 117, 133–134
Middle States League 128, 169–170
Missouri-Illinois League 179
Mobile, Alabama 71
Monitor (Brooklyn) Baseball Club 20
Monroe, Bill 182, 184–185
Monrovia (Indiana) Baseball Club 176–177
Montpelier (Vermont) Capital Citys 96, 201n3
Mullane, Tony 215n27
Muncie (Indiana) Londons 135
Murray Hill (New York City) Baseball Club 181
Mutrie, James 207n97

National Agreement 191
National Association of Base Ball Players 22
National Association of Colored Professional Clubs 182
National Colored Baseball League 97, 167
National Commission 64, 183, 189–190
National League 78–79, 93, 124–125, 149, 182, 185, 189
Nebraska State League 5, 7, 126–128, 171, 201n2
Negro National League 77, 169
New Bedford (Massachusetts) Whalers 68–69, 207n97
New England Colored League 179
New England League 95
New Hampshire League 95–96
New Mexico Baseball League 100, 105, 110, 112, 114–115
New Mexico Territory 101, 114–115, 123, 148–149, 151, 175, 194, 204n59
New Orleans City Colored Amateur Baseball League 72
New Orleans Cohens 88, 167
New Orleans Crescents 167
New Orleans Pickwicks 71
New Orleans Unions 88
"New York" Baseball 23–24
New York Giants 93, 114, 173
New York (Newburgh) Gorhams 63, 97, 128, 167–169, 170
New York Monarchs 170
New York Mutuals 51
New York State League 137
Newark (New Jersey) Eagles 56
Niles (Ohio) Grays 73, 206n42

9th Cavalry Military Band *154*
Northwestern League 69, 78, 82, 84–86, 180

Odom, Mrs. John (Harriet) (Fowler's sister) 193
Ohio League 175
Ohio State Colored League 178–179
Oil League 175
Omaha Omahogs 85
Oneida (New York) Ku Klux Klan 70–71
Onondaga Redskins (New York) Baseball Club 214n42
Ormsbee, Henry J. 89
O'Rourke, Jim 66
Oswego (New York) Starchboxes 91, 93
Ottumwa, Iowa 123
"Our Home Colony" 58

Page Fence Giants 46, 128, 130–132, 134–135, 139–140, 169, 171, 178–180
Pearshall, R.N. 133–134
pedestrianism 207n97
Pennsylvania League 169–170
Peoria (Illinois) Canaries 116, 121
Peters, Johnny 81–82
Petrolia (Ontario) Imperials 71
Philadelphia, Pennsylvania 74–75, 147
Philadelphia Athletics 23, 31–34
Philadelphia Giants 181
Philadelphia Keystones 168
Philadelphia Orions 72, 170
Philadelphia Pythians 24
Pittsfield, Massachusetts 70
Players League 79, 124, 189
Plessy v. Ferguson 44, 55
Portland (Maine) Baseball Club 85–86, 207n93
Presbyterian Base Ball League (Chicago) 179
Preston, George 102, 112, 115
Pueblo, Colorado 86, 178
Pueblo Blues 86
Pueblo Pastimes 85
Pulaski (Tennessee) Ku Klux Klan 75

Quincy (Illinois) Ravens 115–116

railroads and baseball *10*, 12–14, 22, 101
Reading (Pennsylvania) Actives 206n47
"Real 'White Man's Burden'" 39–40
Reconstruction 23, 41, 44, 48, 50
Remington Arms (Ilion, New York) 185
Renfroe, William 88–89, 91–92
Reserve Clause 35, 79, 125, 189, 212n35

Richmond (Virginia) Black Swans 72, 206n40
Robinson, Jackie 79
Robinson, Marilynne 85
Rock City (Tennessee) Baseball Club 135
Roosevelt, Theodore 12, 25, 40
Ross (Chester, Pennsylvania) Baseball Club 162–165
Roswell (New Mexico) Red Caps 176

St. Joseph (Missouri) Beauties 175
St. Joseph (Missouri) Reds 85
St. Louis, Missouri 86, 88
St. Louis Black Sox 73
St. Louis Browns 56
St. Louis Perfectos 146
San Bernardino (California) Baseball Club 115–116
San Francisco Pioneers 104
Santa Fe, New Mexico 101–102, 151, *152*–153, 156, *159*, 194–195, 209n42, 209n44, 212n23
Santa Fe Ancients 100, 103–113, 116, 148–149, 153
Santa Fe Baseball Association 102, 111
Santa Fe Mechanics 194
Schauffler, Robert Haven 38
"Scum o' the Earth" 38
Sebring, Francis 76
Shibe, Ben 189
Skinner, Mrs. Edward (Mary) (Fowler's sister) 193
Sleeman, George 71
Smoky City (Pittsburgh) Giants 173, 176, 213n25
Society of American Baseball Research 199
South Adams, Massachusetts 70
South California League 115
Southern League of Colored Base Ballists 88, 167
Spalding, Albert Goodwill 25, 35, 93, 113, 155, 189–191
Stars and Stripes AC (Niagara Falls) 185
State (New York) Colored League 168
Sterling (Illinois) Baseball Club 121–122
Stillwater (Minnesota) Baseball Club 69, 78–83
Stovey, George 56, 97, 170, 180
Strobel, Charles A. 132, 137
Syracuse (New York) Stars 6, 93–94

Taft, William Howard 190
"Take Me Out to the Ball Game" 190
Temple Cup 146
10th Cavalry Band 153

Terre Haute (Indiana) Hoosiers 99–100
Thayer, Ernest 114
Thorn, John 196–197
Thorpe, Jim 51
Tilden, Samuel J. 40
Tombstone (Arizona) Baseball Club 113
Topeka (Kansas) Capitals 87, 92, 179
Troop L Baseball Team (Fort Wingate, New Mexico) *18*
Troy (New York) Haymakers 51
Twain, Mark 190
Tweed, Boss 22

Union Association 124, 189
United States League of Professional Ball Clubs 16
United States military baseball 14–*15*, 16–18, 23, 25, 47, 50, 101, 202*n*17
Utica, New York 92, 98
Utica Pentups 137, 179

Virginia (Richmond) Baseball Club 162–165
von der Ahe, Chris 56
Von der Horst, Harry 146

Wade, Tom 115
Walker, Moses Fleetwood 54–55, 58–59, 93–94, 97, 204*n*54, 215*n*27
Warner, Pop 51
Washington, Booker T. 55, 182

Washington (District of Columbia) Manhattans 72
Washington (District of Columbia) Nationals 23
Washington (District of Columbia) Olympics 23
Watertown, New York 214*n*42
Watkins, John "Pop" 181, 214*n*43
Watkins All-Stars 181
Weeksville (New Bedford, New York) Unknowns 20
Western League 82, 84–86, 89, 92, 100, 105, 130, 133–134, 171, 174, 179
Wheeling (West Virginia) Ball Club 136
White, Sol 48, 56, 58, **60**, 64, 138, 184
Whitman, Walt 202*n*21
Wilson, George "Lefty" 130, 133–134, 138
Wilson, Woodrow 58
women and baseball 24–26, 36, 73–74, 186, 206*n*49, 212*n*44
Wood, George 66–67, 69
Worcester (Massachusetts) Reds 67–69
The World Series 189
Wright, George 66
Wright, Harry 65

Young, Cy 146

"Zip Coon" 53

www.ingramcontent.com/pod-product-compliance
Ingram Content Group UK Ltd.
Pitfield, Milton Keynes, MK11 3LW, UK
UKHW041948140426
5217IPUK00014B/694